DIANA VREELAND

THE EYE HAS TO TRAVEL

DIANA VREELAND
THE EYE HAS TO TRAVEL

LISA IMMORDINO VREELAND

WITH ESSAYS BY

JUDITH CLARK, JUDITH THURMAN,

AND LALLY WEYMOUTH

ABRAMS, NEW YORK

VREELAND, PHOTOGRAPHED HERE BY CLOSE FRIEND
DAVID BAILEY, ONCE SAID "'ALLURE' IS A WORD VERY
FEW PEOPLE USE NOWADAYS... BUT IT'S SOMETHING
THAT EXISTS. ALLURE HOLDS YOU, DOESN'T IT?"

INTRODUCTION

BY LISA IMMORDINO VREELAND

I wish I had met Diana Vreeland, as I have always marveled at her accomplishments. When I met her grandson, Alexander, and fell in love with him, I soon found myself a member of her family. It was at this time that I became fully immersed in her world and began to hear stories from her sons, Frecky and Tim, and the two grandchildren to whom I was closest: Nicky and Alexander. Their stories were peppered with hilarious accounts of their adventures with her, her illustrious career, and her attitude toward life and family. Her family was the most important thing to her. Her husband, Reed, was the only man she ever loved, besides her father, and her two sons were the "apples of her eye." Although she was considered the center of New York society, she was a private person who placed her family and friends above all else. People and relationships were integral to her identity, and she was genuinely interested in everyone. Her extroverted personality masked an important characteristic: She was a committed and loyal friend and a great listener. I admire these traits—they have always been important to me—and I found that her ability to live such a public life and maintain a private demeanor was something that is often overlooked today.

I got to know Diana Vreeland through her family's eyes, yet it was only when I began working on this book that I became truly aware of the scope, breadth, and richness of her career and became more familiar with that side of her. I began my research by meticulously combing the archives at *Harper's Bazaar*, *Vogue*, and the Costume Institute at the Metropolitan Museum of Art. Her archives illuminate her personality and passions, but more than that, they act as a time capsule. Her career spanned five decades and bore witness to major social upheavals and changes: the crash, World War II, and the sexual revolution. She made sure these

phenomena were reflected heavily in the pages of *Bazaar* and *Vogue*—in pieces that were considered shocking at times, but always innovative, vibrant, and unforgettable. "You don't learn fashion. It's got to be in your blood. I could have learned 10,000 things more than I know. Don't forget, I never see anything but a perfectly marvelous world of high fashion around me."[1]

Diana Vreeland believed her luck began the day she was born, in Paris. She spent her early childhood there, developing a strong affinity with all that was French. She always felt her birthplace played a pivotal role in molding her persona. It is evident that her parents, her American mother Emily Key Hoffman and

AN ORIENTALIST-STYLE PAINTING OF DIANA VREELAND BY EDWARD MURRAY, FROM THE LATE 1930s.

her English father Frederick Young Dalziel, immersed her in a lifestyle colored by extraordinary individuals and experiences that were influential in shaping the individual she would become. Her childhood was nontraditional, with social and cultural experiences largely supplanting a formal education: As a girl, Vreeland had the freedom to choose what she wanted to learn.

Although she had a privileged childhood, Diana's relationship with her mother was complicated and caused her much unhappiness during her youth. Ironically, and despite the troubled relationship, it can be said that her mother, a great adventurer and hunter, endowed Diana with one of her greatest assets: her daring to be different. She always looked to the unusual for inspiration, which would indeed be her greatest gift to us all.

After her marriage to T. Reed Vreeland and their move to London, she was still able to devote

Diana Vreeland has been described in multiple ways: birdlike, unusual, and, at times, ugly. At a young age, she realized she had to focus on more than just her appearance, and this insight gave her the determination to make something of herself very early on. Diana had a strong physical presence, an attitude, and a personality that could make people tremble. Her walk was that of a ballet dancer, as she glided into rooms with perfect posture. Cecil Beaton's description of Vreeland captured her flawlessly: "Mrs. Vreeland's head sits independently on top of a narrow neck and smiles at you. Everything about her features

HORST P. HORST BECAME AN IMPORTANT ASSET TO VREELAND DURING HER YEARS AT *VOGUE*— HERE, HE CAPTURES HER JOIE DE VIVRE.

her time to what she loved: books and travel. "I read everything. I would have read the phone book if you put it in front of me...."[2] As her son Tim Vreeland recalled, "We read everything: Balzac, Henry James, Truman Capote, Henri Fournier, Isak Dinesen, even *Les Liaisons Dangereuses*. Reading aloud had always been a tradition in our family. She and my father had read to each other from the time they were married. We read aloud at Brewster; reading was a form of communication between us, and at the end it brought us very close."[3]

is animated by amused interest: Her nose, as broad as an Indian's, is boldly assertive; her eyes twinkle; her mouth emits the most amazingly aggressive and masculine laugh, a red laugh that is taken up by her cheeks, expertly rouged with an art which has gone out of style and of which she is one of the few remaining masters. Surrounding these features like a metallic skullcap is her navy-blue hair, which she wears lacquered back from her face."[4]

I have often been told about the twinkle in her eyes, eyes which took in so much and gave us such remarkable gifts. It is said that she spoke in an affected manner, a mix of European royal and New York City taxi driver, with an odd inflection that accentuated certain words: "Mrs. Vreeland speaks one-third of the time like a gangster, one-third of the time like the head of a multinational corporation... and the rest of the time like an émigré from one of the French-speaking pixie kingdoms."[5] Her words were powerful and influential, and she used her hands in a theatrical manner to emphasize her points. Vreeland's physical appearance was certainly pivotal to her aura. She had the ability to engage people of all ages; she loved to ask questions and was eager to learn. She was a social success anywhere she went, a coveted dinner guest and hostess. Gatherings at her exotic red apartment at 550 Park Avenue were unforgettable experiences. The food was secondary to the drink, and laughter and conversation never ceased.

Vreeland's passion for life was her driving force. "Passion for passion, you can learn anything, you can do anything, you can go anywhere. Don't you think passion is very rare? And I think that it is getting rarer because there is so little around us."[6] The word *passion* is defined as a "very powerful feeling"; this was Diana Vreeland's *raison d'être*, and she applied it to all aspects of her personal and public lives. Her friends, enveloped by this energy, were taken under her wing and shown true friendship. This circle was not restricted to her social class and included diverse individuals who offered her an ongoing source of inspiration. She is also well known for loving the young people who played a pivotal role in her creative process during her years at *Vogue* and the Metropolitan Museum of Art. She reciprocated the energy she received from them by playing an important mentoring role in their life. Many influential designers and editors thank Vreeland for helping them decide on a direction for their careers.

One of Vreeland's most underrated qualities was her discipline. It was not just the discipline she applied to her work but the unrelenting rigor she applied to all aspects of her life. Those who worked alongside her and could not keep up with her pace and vigor were simply ignored. The fortunate coworkers who understood her were forever enriched by the experience of being at her side. She pushed them to test their creative limits, unleashing something in them even they didn't know they had. Her positive character, discipline, dynamic personality, and physical presence were integral aspects that led to her success in the world of fashion and in her life.

How did Diana Vreeland define fashion? She once said, "Like new architecture, it shocks, it breaks the rules. It is change, it gives a little air.... Fashion is for pruning... a woman's own form and circumstances. She should use it, not fight it, study it, observe it and then apply it, with discrimination, to herself, listen to the drum that beats for that and the lute that plays for this. She should hail the hero of the hour, the sport of the day, the place, the fun of fashion in all of its flavors—without prejudice, with humor and understanding. Fashion is made up of opportunity and change, and is therefore for the young, of every age."[7]

She felt that fashion played an important role in our world, and it was certainly her driving force and her addiction. Fashion was an integral element of her life from a young age, as she used it to create a world that embodied inspiration, joy, and adventure. Her years of wearing couture clothes gave her an innate knowledge and understanding of make, quality, and fit. Later, her career kept her in touch with her couturier and designer friends and encouraged her creativity in the world of dress and costume. Vreeland embraced fashion and shared her vision, representing not only the physicality of clothes but also another way of approaching life and the liberty to dream in another manner.

As Richard Avedon has noted, "Diana lived for imagination ruled by discipline, and created a totally new profession. Vreeland invented the fashion editor. Before her it was society ladies who put hats on other society ladies."[8] Her pages marked a revolution in editorial style and a revolution in the fashion industry itself, as her famed collaborations with photographers celebrated the luxurious wares from Paris to New York. As World War II began to unfold and the fashion world in Paris was silenced, American style began to gain momentum and notoriety within the pages of *Bazaar*. Although the war created an atmosphere of austerity and restraint, Vreeland's fashion pages continued to be rich while still conscious of the effects of the war. She respected the new roles women took on during this era, and reported on them in addition to the new fashions.

Glancing through the *Bazaar* issues from the forties through the early sixties, it is impossible to ignore the presence of the world's most important photographers. Lillian Bassman, originally hired by Alexey Brodovitch as an art director, soon began photographing the fashion pages of *Bazaar*. Bassman recalls: "I think Mrs.

DIANA VREELAND, FASHION EDITOR,
SANTA FE, NEW MEXICO, JUNE 1977.
PHOTOGRAPHED BY RICHARD AVEDON.

Vreeland was not only responsible for the fashion look of the magazine, but I think of fashion of the time. She was very influential with the designers, very important in the choice in color, of mood. I would say from a fashion point of view, *Harper's Bazaar* was a complete reflection of her taste and her input."[9]

Although Vreeland cannot be credited with the discovery of the photographers, she can be fully credited with the fashion stories on which they collaborated. Melvin Sokolsky remarks on her influence: "The only thing I could assume about Diana Vreeland is that she got up in the morning, she thrust forward with her imagination, she imported it to me, that whatever she imported triggered something in me, and a substrate was formed with an image on it that became something that people recognize. That's the only thing I know."[10]

She was rarely present at shoots, but for her, the photographer was the conduit which delivered her message. Brodovitch, on the other hand, was passionate about photographers and loved to interact with them and discuss their trade. They had mutual respect for one another, and their discussions on images often centered on the use of white space, which Brodovitch was obsessed with and wanted on every page. Today, the images so frequently referred to by stylists and photographers bear the fruit of this collaboration. Brodovitch inspired and liberated the photographers, and Vreeland's input gave them new ideas and approaches to their work.

When Carmel Snow's niece, Nancy White, succeeded her as the next editor in chief in 1958, it marked the end of an era. Four years later, Diana Vreeland left *Bazaar*.

Alexander Liberman, editorial director for Condé Nast Publications, and Diana Vreeland had known each other socially for years. Not surprisingly, he suggested Vreeland as a candidate for Jessica Daves's editor in chief position at *Vogue* to the magazine's publisher, Si Newhouse. In June 1962 Diana Vreeland became *Vogue*'s associate editor, and in January 1963 she took over as editor in chief. According to Susan Train in the Paris office of *Vogue*, who worked closely with Vreeland, "Diana differed from Jessica Daves in that she was a complete fashion person—she loved fashion passionately. Ms. Daves was more intellectual, and she had come from the business side of the magazine. She didn't get all excited about fashion... she didn't have the passion for fashion that Diana had, plus Diana was open to everything, open to change, she was curious about everything,

and she was much more European."[11] The move heralded the magazine's message to its competitors: *Vogue* was a serious fashion magazine that focused on more than just America. The convergence of the sixties and the beginning of Diana Vreeland's career at *Vogue* could not have been timed more perfectly.

Freedom was the essence of the sixties. The postwar baby boomers were desperate for change, and this need was reflected in lifestyles, education, fashion, laws, and value systems. Vreeland interpreted this zeitgeist throughout the magazine. For her, the sixties symbolized Courrèges, long hair, the Vietnam War, swinging London, blue jeans, the Pill, the jet set, the beautiful people, Plisetskaya, Mick Jagger, flower children, women's lib, and the youthquake. She made swift changes at *Vogue*, embracing the new energy. Manolo Blahnik, who credits Vreeland for encouraging him to become a shoe designer, said, "She had this incredible freedom that nobody ever, in magazines, dared to have.... She launched millions of people that you never expected she'd launch.... She made things happen through her pages."[12] While John Glenn was orbiting the moon for the first time, Diana Vreeland was busy turning *Vogue* upside down.

Within months of her arrival the magazine had evolved into the most successful publication on the newsstand. A grueling schedule was established: twenty issues a year, with two issues each month except in May, June, July, and December. It is hard to believe that such a frenetic pace was maintained and the quality and look of the magazine was never compromised. Although *Vogue* once conjured thoughts of exclusivity, wealth, and power, Vreeland's message was imminently closer to the word's actual meaning. She once said of *Vogue*, "*Vogue* always did stand for people's lives... a new dress doesn't get you anywhere, it is the life you are leading in the dress and the sort of life that you have lived before and what you do later."[13]

She opened the doors to all to appear on its pages, and the audience quickly evolved beyond the Park Avenue crowd. Her new readers were not only interested in fashion but in cultural happenings, and Vreeland's vision covered it all. Her openness to everything new is clearly expressed by writer Bob Colacello: "I think that Diana was really almost the epitome of what New York was about. This melding of Europe and America and this acceptance or openness to everything that was new and different and wild."[14]

Vreeland's approach to working at *Vogue* was unconventional. It has often been noted that she spent the early morning working at home, refining her ideas and culling her inspirations, writing her infamous memos and making phone calls. During these morning sessions she filled yellow legal pads with the famous single-word directives she used as the blueprint for the magazine. Her large pool of assistants knew to expect early phone calls during which they would transcribe her memos. When she arrived at her office late in the morning, the amount of work she had already accomplished was remarkable.

Vreeland left no part of the magazine untouched. As Alexander Liberman astutely remarked, "When the change came it was like

friend mentioning something at dinner, a literary influence, a painting, or the youthquake occurring in the streets. Remarking on the sixties, she notes, "But you see, in the sixties, there was something new all the time. You were on the air. You were running down the streets with flames in your nose."[17] It is important to realize that Vreeland's ability to be receptive to everyone and everything made her a perfect conduit for the magazine: She truly captured the times within its pages.

Today, the many innovative changes Vreeland made at *Vogue* make it difficult to pinpoint her greatest accomplishment. When looking at the fashion pages, we are struck by the strength of the images, the photogra-

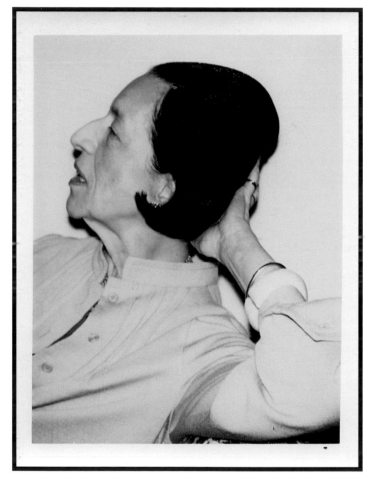

IN ANDY WARHOL'S INFAMOUS SERIES OF PORTRAITS OF HIS FRIENDS, VREELAND WAS CAPTURED AT HER BEST.

a knife cutting through butter."[15] She had a natural hand as an editor, understanding the rhythm a magazine required and when an editorial change would spark the reader's interest. She also believed that photographs were functional and were to be used for impact, not art. She noted: "I had no respect for photographers—only pictures.... A good photographer was never what I was looking for. I like to have a point. I had to have a point or I didn't have a picture."[16] In editing the magazine, she drew inspiration from a variety of sources: a

phers' style, the models—including actresses and society ladies—the hair, makeup, clothing, and location. The message was clear, and the clothes were always shown in a unique way. It is claimed that the photographers who graced these pages—Richard Avedon, Irving Penn, Bert Stern, David Bailey, Cecil Beaton, Franco Rubartelli, and William Klein, among others—did some of their best work during this time. Vreeland's choice of models redefined beauty to encompass the traditional aesthetic but also girls with exotic and "different" looks, who embodied a free spirit and had unexpected freshness. In a sense, she democratized the notion of fashion.

For Vreeland, the sixties also signified jet travel, and she opened the doors of the world to her readers through iconic fashion spreads by Henry Clarke. They visited luxurious homes in international locations with Horst P. Horst. He photographed Mona Bismarck's garden in Capri, the Grand Trianon in Versailles, enchanting rococo and baroque castles in Germany, Renaldo Herrera's home in Venezuela, and Truman Capote's weekend getaway. In the literary section of the magazine, readers were exposed to the musings of Violette Leduc on Balenciaga, Federico Fellini's thoughts on Marcello Mastroianni's love for women, and Cecil Beaton's profile on Jeanne Toussaint.

The famed "People Are Talking About" section piqued everyone's interest when the first photo of Mick Jagger by David Bailey was published, and the section went on to monitor new cultural trends in art, literature, and entertainment. Vreeland reserved the most extravagant and fantastic images for the December issue of *Vogue*. These issues included images of unthinkable journeys, unforgettable photgraphs of animals enveloped in white clouds by Lord Snowdon, and Irving Penn's elegant tulips and peonies brought to life on the page. These issues are collector's items today and are frequently referenced by art directors and photographers. It is clear that *Vogue* became an embodiment of Diana Vreeland's spirit. It captured her individuality, cosmopolitanism, and her priceless ability to look at other worlds and present them to her readers. On her watch *Vogue* changed forever, and she made *Vogue* what it is today. Her new audience became accustomed to innovative and sophisticated ideas and themes and to excitement, enthusiasm, and outstanding quality—difficult shoes to fill for any future editor in chief.

Vreeland's tenure at *Vogue* came to a deliberate, swift, and shocking end.

The fashion world was left speechless by upper management's decision to let her go. It seems that Alexander Liberman was the leading proponent for firing her, although Si Newhouse was the messenger. It is not officially documented, but hearsay confirms that their relationship had become difficult, and the cost of making her magazine had become exorbitant. It was also believed that she was out of touch with the new woman of the seventies. The "Me" decade, as Tom Wolfe called it, was a decade of self-awareness. Liberman and Newhouse must have

felt Vreeland's *Vogue* was too exotic, expensive, and adventurous to coexist with the new ideas of the times. Her assistant, Grace Mirabella, slipped into her red office and immediately painted it beige.

Nevertheless, a letter Vreeland wrote to Veruschka, a favorite model, points out that she understood quite clearly what the seventies were about: "I also think that we are going into a classical period and by that I do not mean we are going backwards, as that will not happen as that can never be called fashion. What I am talking about is a simplicity and subtlety in people's appearance that they have not had for a very long time, as the world is yearning for a certain simplification of all of the great charade that we have been living through."[18]

Coincidentally, when Diana Vreeland was let go, *Vogue* stopped publishing bimonthly issues, significantly and immediately increasing circulation.

For Vreeland, mourning was not appropriate behavior. She disappeared to Europe and sought refuge with close friends and by immersing herself in culture. She knew there had to be an *entr'acte* but was not sure what it would be. The transition was difficult, and although Condé Nast did give her financial compensation, Vreeland knew that she needed to work. When Ted Rousseau and Tom Hoving from the Metropolitan Museum of Art approached her, she welcomed them without realizing that this next step would become another important accomplishment. Hoving's plan for the Met was a massive expansion and commercialization that included the introduction of blockbuster shows. His vision included the Costume Institute, a sleepy department producing shows rarely visited by the public. Vreeland began her new job as special consultant to the Costume Institute at the Metropolitan Museum of Art in 1972. Since the Met was suffering financial stress at the time, faithful society friends banded together to pay her salary. The need for these contributions was short-lived—within a year the Met was fully covering her stipend, as she had quickly proven her worth.

Her tenure at the Costume Institute represents the last act of an extraordinary career. Vreeland designed and mounted fifteen unforgettable and extremely successful exhibitions. She challenged the old canons of museum practices and created original displays teeming with innovative ideas, applying sound, scent, and the essence of the theater of life and forever changing the role of dress and costume in museums worldwide.

Although Vreeland was a prominent figure in society and in the world of fashion, it was during her tenure at *Vogue* and later at the Costume Institute that she achieved permanent recognition in what might be termed the annals of popular culture and consciousness. Vreeland first entered public awareness with her legendary "Why Don't You?" column. During her years at the Costume Institute she published two very successful books: *Allure*, and her autobiography, *D.V. Allure*, published in 1980, was cowritten by Christopher Hemphill and is a collection of her favorite photographs: those which influenced her and those which she helped to create. This charming, anecdotal book brims with the ideas and things Vreeland loved and found inspirational. Jacqueline Kennedy Onassis, who edited the book, said, "These are all the pictures that have intrigued her the most…. They go from the most beautiful pictures of vintage quality to a paparazzi shot she tore out of a newspaper."[19] Today, *Allure* is a collector's item and is currently in its third printing.

D.V., her autobiography, edited by George Plimpton and Christopher Hemphill, is greatly enriched by colorful stories of her life. As she navigates the annals of her personal history, she entertains us and allows us to enter her extraordinary world. This book has been printed twice and was on the *New York Times* bestseller list for at least eleven consecutive weeks. Vreeland was immortalized on the big screen in *Funny Face*, in which actress Kay Thompson played her as the editor in chief of *Quality* magazine. Fred Astaire's character was based on her favorite photographer, Richard Avedon. She did not love this interpretation of herself, but it remains one of Audrey Hepburn's most iconic films. William Klein's film *Who Are You, Polly Maggoo?* captured Vreeland as the editor in chief of a famous fashion magazine, where her role is centered in a fantasy-like world of fashion.

Vreeland has been written about, photographed, and copied by endless people in the fashion industry, yet she stands above all others. Diana Vreeland is simply unique. She has left us with the gift of her accomplishments, which continue to reverberate and impact contemporary culture.

VREELAND WAS KNOWN FOR HER FAMOUS ARTICULATION AND GESTICULATION, CAPTURED BEAUTIFULLY HERE BY PRISCILLA RATTAZZI.

DIANA VREELAND'S FAMED SILK-STRIPED
DINING ROOM WAS A GATHERING PLACE
FOR THE INTERNATIONAL ELITE.

VREELANDMANIA

BY LALLY WEYMOUTH

Diana Vreeland was more than the most famous fashion editor of *Harper's Bazaar* and then *Vogue*, a woman who had enormous influence over fashion from 1936, when she started at *Bazaar*, to 1971, when her tenure ended at *Vogue*. When I set out to interview her for *Rolling Stone* back in 1977, I asked the author Truman Capote why he believed Vreeland would be remembered and indeed one day might be worthy of a collection of essays such as the compelling ones that follow.

> One can think of only seven or eight truly original women," Capote told me. "In America, we've had very few great original women. Emily Dickinson was one. But Mrs. Vreeland, or Madame Vreeland as I will always think of her, is an extraordinarily original woman— she's one of the great Americans. She has contributed more than anyone I can think of to the level of taste of American women in the sense of the way they move, what they wear, and how they think. She's a genius, but she's the kind of genius that very few people will ever recognize....

Born in Paris—in a year she refused to disclose—to a father who was a stockbroker and a mother she recalled as stylish but bored, Vreeland described a happy and interesting, if somewhat original, childhood. Her parents' home, she said, was filled with life and fun: The famous dancers Irene and Vernon Castle did the then-fashionable "Castle walk" dance, and music played all the time. But, Vreeland told me, she received no formal education. Thus, she explained, "everything visual has always remained very important to me because that's how I was brought up—with the visual."

Whatever formal education her parents failed to give her, they made up for by immersing her in various aspects of cultural life. She

was exposed to playwrights, musicians, and literary people. She particularly remembered the famed choreographer Sergei Diaghilev, whom she said changed ballet, as well as Vaslav Nijinsky, a star of the Russian Ballet. Both men came to her childhood home, and both impressed young Diana.

"Diaghilev and his Ballets Russes had an enormous impact on fashion," she told me. "The first great twentieth-century couturier, Paul Poiret, got many of his ideas from Diaghilev." What did Poiret do that was so special? Vreeland was ready to explain: "The naturalness of the body,

that's the most important thing he did.... Hard corsets disappeared overnight, and everyone was in a practically transparent chemise."

The biggest event of her childhood, she explained, was witnessing firsthand the coronation of King George V. Vreeland and her sister were sent to London to see the event, and, as she recalled it in a typical fanciful description, the celebration went on for four days. "We saw these beautiful prancing animals that were bred

VREELAND'S SOULFUL EYES AND TRADEMARK CIGARETTE IN HAND, CAPTURED HERE BY HOYNINGEN-HUENE.

(OPPOSITE PAGE) DIANA VREELAND, IN HER HOME IN LONDON, SITS IN FRONT OF THIS FAMOUS PORTRAIT PAINTED BY WILLIAM ACTON.

for carriages and liveries.... How can a child forget seeing screwball tigers, fantastic horses and elephants and maharajahs, kaisers and kaiserinas.... We saw kings like you see cigarettes around the house."

In 1914, the Vreelands moved to New York City, where Diana went to school for a few months. Handicapped by not knowing the English language, she dropped out and went to a ballet school instead. "The only thing I ever learned was how to dance," she told me. She added that Michel Fokine (head of the ballet school) "was the only imperial ballet master who ever left Russia. He was a remarkable man—frightfully strict. He taught me total discipline."

Vreeland told me that during her childhood, there was an outbreak of infantile paralysis in New York, so she and her sister and a nurse were sent out West to spend time with Buffalo Bill Cody. He gave the girls ponies, and as she recalled it, "We had a great life." She had a dramatic recollection of her time with Buffalo Bill: "Beautiful to look at. He wore the Edwardian clothes of the late sixties with the fringes."

Then it was back to New York. At the age of eighteen, she met and married Reed Vreeland. The young couple lived in Albany, where he trained at a bank, and she practiced domestic skills. In 1929, the Vreelands moved to London, where they lived for seven happy years.

It was the Roaring Twenties—"a youthquake just like the sixties. Everything changed: the paintings, the music, the way of life." And Chanel became Vreeland's favorite designer. "I met her [Chanel] in 1926, which was really the moment that the world's clothes totally changed: the clean shirt, the little jackets and skirts." But Vreeland was not working at this point; she was bringing up her two children and leading a fun life while her husband worked at a bank.

Vreeland said she loved clothes from the moment she was born, and so, living in London, she took trips to Paris and bought Chanel's clothes. "I learned everything from Chanel as far as the way I like clothes."

Vreeland claimed the stock market crash of 1929 brought bad times but did not kill fashion: "Fashion always takes place. Fashion is

VREELAND SHOWS US HOW AT-
TITUDE WORKS WELL IN PICTURE
POSING IN THESE STUDIES FOR
WILLIAM ACTON'S PAINTING.

always there. [P]estilence, death, economic crises—nothing affects fashion. Fashion goes right on. Women will always ornament themselves."

During the Depression, hems dropped and, Vreeland said, "the waist came back." But clothes, she noted, were not her only interest. She loved films and was friendly with Greta Garbo: "Garbo, Joan Crawford, marvelous. Pay your money and you were transported. I saw them all."

In her drawing room in London, she entertained a wide variety of friends, such as Evelyn Waugh and the set designer Christian Bérard—

WITH HER BELOVED REED AND SONS TIM AND FREDERICK IN THE BACKGROUND, AT THEIR COUNTRY HOUSE IN BREWSTER, NEW YORK.

whom she says was her best friend. Of Bérard, she remembered, "He had, without question, the greatest talent of anyone I've ever known." She went on to recall, "I was surrounded with so many people of such great taste." Cole Porter was also another close friend, of whom she said, "He was life itself.... He had real style."

When Diana Vreeland was thirty years old, her husband decided to move back to New York, and she needed to get a job if the Vreelands were to maintain the standard of life they had enjoyed in London. With typical exaggeration, she said, "I had to go to work [or] I was going to starve to death." She managed to get hired at *Bazaar* and after six months became the fashion editor.

As such, she was the judge, the arbiter of everything that went into the magazine—"whether it was a buckle or a girdle or a piece of fabric or a length of a sweater." Vreeland recalled that Andrew Goodman, then owner of Bergdorf Goodman, summoned her to his store one day to her immense surprise. He was worried that she was going to hurt the fur industry by promoting black mink. Astonished that she had the power to cause him to worry, Vreeland explained to Goodman that his fears were

groundless—she (in the pages of *Harper's*) was only talking about "your third-rate minks—dye 'em black. Black is very becoming to women at night."

During her stint as fashion editor of *Bazaar*, Vreeland actually discovered Lauren Bacall, who would go from model to movie star. Vreeland recalled that one of her assistants came into her office with Bacall and said she thought she would make a good model: "Betty [Bacall] sits down. She had literally nothing to offer except her existence. I believe she and her mother and her aunt lived in two rooms—no money, nothing." Vreeland would put her on the cover of *Bazaar*.

Soon, Hollywood producers wanted to meet the beautiful Bacall: "So Betty gets to Hollywood, appears in *To Have and Have Not*, and marries Humphrey Bogart. She really adored him," said Vreeland, recalling her first trip to the Bacall-Bogart home in Los Angeles.

According to Vreeland, the biggest change in fashion after the war was Dior's new look—long hems and tight waists. "He gave back the great name of haute couture to France through his fantastically beautiful clothes that the world came to see, to buy, and to wear. He was it in 1947."

After twenty-eight successful years at *Bazaar*, Vreeland felt the time had come for her to leave. In fact, she had failed to get the job of editor in chief when Carmel Snow retired, and so four years later, she quit. She was subsequently hired by *Vogue*, which she said was not as good-looking a magazine as *Bazaar* in those days. But, she observed dryly, it had one advantage—it came out twice a month, so it seemed to her as if it was always on the newsstands, whereas *Bazaar* only came out monthly.

Then-popular gossip columnist Eugenia Sheppard wrote that Vreeland's change from *Bazaar* to *Vogue* "is as startling as if Governor Rockefeller had moved over to the Democratic Party." Vreeland argued that *Vogue* needed what she termed "a new deal," and she gave it to the magazine.

How did she change *Vogue*? "You get into a desk and you start cooking," she explained in Vreelandesque fashion. It was the sixties, a "wonderful time to be a fashion journalist... everything was new. Don't forget the new music, the new paintings, the rebellion.... There were the flower children—most of them are either stockbrokers or dealmakers now.... They were the avant-garde of the revolution. It was a revolution, and, for the first time, youth went out to life instead of waiting for life to come to them. You read revolution in clothes—you read everything in clothes—that's why clothes are interesting."

Oscar de la Renta recalls that "Diana was the first person to pay attention to the youth revolution in the sixties. She was the first to use pictures in *Vogue* to make it younger and more happening. She took the young photographers of the time like David Bailey and turned the magazine around—obeying what was happening." De la Renta added, "It was the first time that fashion catered to and was influenced by the very young."

Vreeland said she loved the Beatles and put them in *Vogue* in 1963, followed by Mick Jagger the following year. She actually attended a Stones concert at the Garden: "There's never been anything like it at the Garden. Mick's such an actor. He's so intelligent to talk to.... Remember the night he was here and broke the chandelier?" she asked.

Under Vreeland, *Vogue* documented the beautiful people—including Carter and Amanda Burden: "They were beautiful; they were extraordinary, charming, lots of parties."

Asked to compare the beautiful Burdens and others to Jagger, she said sharply, "But he's a worker. You don't make a million dollars a concert because you are playing around."

But the epitome of style in the sixties was Jacqueline Kennedy: "She released style in this country. When she went into the White House and put a little style into the White House and into being the First Lady of the land, suddenly good taste was accepted as good taste. She got the best people—the best historians, the best horticulturalists, the best of everything for the White House."

It was Vreeland who suggested that the young and beautiful First Lady carry a fur muff on Inauguration Day in 1960—"I thought she was going to freeze to death and that it would be very pretty."

Vreeland agreed that what made her a great fashion editor was that she knew what she liked—as the designer Oleg Cassini said to me, she had "a determined point of view." Vreeland remarked, "I was definitely sure of what I was doing." She felt that the sixties afforded her the most interesting moment to preside over the leading fashion magazine in America.

But in May 1971, Vreeland was fired by *Vogue* and its parent company, Condé Nast. She said candidly, "They wanted a different magazine." And they did. The Condé Nast group wanted something aimed more at working women and less at the fashion-forward women leading a glamorous life.

But Vreeland—then more than sixty years old—managed to start a new career after *Vogue* as a "creative consultant" to the moribund Costume Institute of the Metropolitan Museum of Art in New York. Hired by the museum's then-president Tom Hoving, she set out to breathe life into the institute, and she did.

In 1976, she would cohost her third show with Jackie Kennedy: *The Glory of Russian Costume*. She had re-created herself—*Women's Wear Daily* covered the show; fashion designers and international socialites attended. Harold Koda, now head of the institute but a young man then, recalls that "her rolodex was fascinating—she knew everyone and brought that network of relationships to the museum."

Vreeland turned what had been a boring party into a yearly event that could not be missed. "You had Halston and the Halstonettes, you had fashion and Hollywood, and then international society," said Koda, who attended as a dazzled graduate student.

Vreeland enjoyed many years at the Costume Institute and put on shows that were very well attended. She caused controversy by painting the museum walls wild colors, having music piped in, treating the models in unconventional ways to make them look more abstract. Koda says Vreeland's approach—while popular with the public—was poorly received by many costume historians. She brought the same fantasy to the museum as she had brought to *Vogue*. Vreeland, Koda explained, came from an era before the career woman had emerged: "It was a fantasy of how one's life could be. She saw her magazine as something to inspire you to become a fashion consumer."

"I consider her a kind of genius," the author Bob Colacello told me recently. "She had a great influence going back to the fifties and sixties. She promoted individualism and creativity. She was the perfect editor. She discovered Veruschka, Marisa Berenson, and put Cher on the cover of *Vogue*. She was one of the first to mix high style with popular culture. She was very much behind the rise of Richard Avedon and Irving Penn—fashion photography had been staid until she came along. She was an inspiration."

I ADORE ARTIFICE, BUT I ALSO ADORE PERFECTION.

THE MAGAZINE YEARS 1936–1971

MARTIN MUNKÁCSI'S PORTRAIT OF VREELAND
PORTRAYS THE ENERGY SHE HAD DURING HER
DAYS WALKING TO 7TH AVENUE DURING WORLD
WAR II—"IT WAS ALL PART OF MY GREAT ADVENTURE,
MY MÉTIER."

WHY DON'T YOU?

BY JUDITH THURMAN

Few women have been better endowed for an accidental vocation than Diana Vreeland. "If I hadn't done what I did," she once remarked of her legendary career in fashion journalism, "I'd have done nothing." Nothing, one presumes from her biography, but revel in the well-ordered life of luxury and pleasure that she had enjoyed as a young matron. Her leisure wasn't wasted, though, not least because it freed her to devote "hours and hours of very detailed attention," she said, to her clothes. And of all the gifts that Vreeland brought to her twenty-six years at *Harper's Bazaar* (twenty-three as the fashion editor) and nine years as the editor in chief of *Vogue*, the rarest, perhaps, was a genius for play.

"To play" means to "exercise a craft; to move about with a lively or capricious motion; to change rapidly, as colors in iridescence; to wield something lightly or freely; to engage in a game; to exhibit to brilliant effect; to disport or frolic; to perform dramatically; to act the part of." Those definitions are a catalogue of the qualities reflected in the pages of Vreeland's magazines and embodied in her persona. Beneath their high finish, though, her eye for perfection was never at ease. Virtuosity is the art of making an arduous, artificial, endlessly rehearsed feat seem joyful and spontaneous. "Without exception," Richard Avedon said of Vreeland, "she was the hardest-working person I have ever known."

The advent of fashion magazines, in the mid-nineteenth century, coincided with the rise of a prosperous middle class hungry for the accoutrements of upper-class life. American fashion magazines, in particular, have always been an aspirational phenomenon. When Vreeland started out in the business, editors were still selling their readers the illusion of entrée to a restricted club: the *Almanach de Gotha*, *le Tout-Paris*, the *Social Register*, *Burke's Peerage*, the *Four Hundred*. Thoroughbred women of style had more

cachet as models than anonymous professionals, and having been such a *mannequin mondain*, Vreeland would always have a penchant for the type. C. Z. Guest, Gloria Vanderbilt, Jacqueline de Ribes, and Marella Agnelli were among the patricians whom she recruited for *Bazaar*. As times changed, and Vreeland discerned the kinkier charm of a new generation, she introduced Penelope Tree, Marisa Berenson, Loulou de la Falaise, and Veruschka at *Vogue*.

"Mrs. T. Reed Vreeland" had a public profile in the fashion world as a top-seeded amateur long before she went pro, and in January 1936, *Bazaar* published a full-length portrait of her in its fashion pages. The photographer was Martin Munkácsi, a Hungarian Jew and a refugee from the Nazis who is widely credited with inventing modern photojournalism and reinventing fashion photography in the same dynamic mold. Carmel Snow, *Bazaar*'s astute editor in

VREELAND WORE CLOTHES LIKE NO ONE ELSE—HERE, IN A SCHIAPARELLI JACKET, WITH HUSBAND REED.

chief, and Alexey Brodovitch, her visionary art director, were among the first to grasp Munkácsi's importance. His revolutionary pictures, shot on location in natural light, would make the studio portraiture of the old guard (photographers like George Hoyningen-Huene, Adolph de Meyer, and Cecil Beaton, who belonged to the same *gratin* as their subjects—aristocrats modeling their own clothes) seem static and quaint.

Munkácsi was fascinated by bodies in motion, and he captured his subject's distinctive sashay, in mid-stride, on a Manhattan sidewalk. She is wearing a smartly tailored, calf-length couture suit, with a nutria cape billowing from her shoulders, and a cocky, feather-trimmed fedora. Every detail of the ensemble has been minutely calibrated to produce the impression of sovereign nonchalance. A reader of the magazine might have been forgiven for presuming that this enviable, thirty-three-year-old socialite had not a care in the world. Six years into the Depression, however, financial necessity had driven Vreeland to an unusual resort for a woman of her class: She had been looking for paid work.

The Vreelands and their two sons had recently returned from a sojourn in England, where Reed Vreeland had been genteelly employed at an American bank, and the family had lived in a historic town house near Regent's Park, opulently decorated by Diana. They owned a Bugatti, and a liveried driver chauffered them to shooting weekends in Scotland, *villégiature* in Tunis or Biarritz, balls in Paris, and other such glamorous engagements. *Vogue* illustrated an article that lauded Mrs. Vreeland as a trendsetter for "the international set living in Europe" with a page of sketches in which she models two gowns and a greatcoat by Mainbocher. "She knows what she wants at a glance," the writer effused. Chanel was among the couturiers who, recognizing the value of Vreeland's imprimatur, dressed her for next to nothing. Those discounts had helped to subsidize the couple's lavish *train de vie*, and so did a strong dollar. But back in New York, they were running through her inheritance, Vreeland would say, "the way one goes through a bottle of Scotch, I suppose, if you're an alcoholic."

"*Le luxe*," Voltaire sighed in exile, as a permanent houseguest, "*chose si nécessaire*." Frugality was not in the character of either spouse (they defined an austerity measure as firing one's butler). On the fateful evening that Diana, in a white lace gown and bolero by Chanel, and white roses in her onyx hair, had inadvertently auditioned for a job at *Bazaar* by dazzling Carmel Snow with her chic, her charisma, and her joie de vivre, she and her dashing husband had gone dancing at the St. Regis.

The steely, decisive Snow had none of Vreeland's flamboyance. She was a proper-looking, devout Catholic, sixteen years Vreeland's senior who had been born into the minor Irish gentry. Her widowed mother had emigrat-

ed to Chicago and opened a shop that sold Irish handicrafts. It was a great success, and she branched out into custom dressmaking, taking her daughters to the Paris shows, where they were assigned to memorize every detail of the designs (Carmel focused on the bodices, her sister on the skirts), so that they could be copied. In 1903, the year that Vreeland was born, Snow's mother moved to New York and took over a well-established fashion house. Carmel supervised its workrooms—a job she hated, although it taught her, she said, "the architecture of clothes." In 1921, she was hired as an assistant fashion editor at *Vogue*, under Edna Chase. Condé Nast, *Vogue*'s proprietor, adopted her as a protégé and invited her to his famous parties. She mastered both the business and the social side of her métier, and married late (one well-born fiancé had ditched her because her mother was in trade). When she jumped ship to *Bazaar*, in 1933, both Nast and Chase considered it an act of treachery. The two magazines were, as they remain, archrivals, and still Vreeland would commit the same act of *lèse-majesté* by defecting in the opposite direction.

Once installed in the Hearst building, then on Madison Avenue, Snow wasted no time in surrounding herself with edgy and talented collaborators—photographers like Munkácsi; illustrators like Marcel Vertès and Christian Bérard (who had recently sketched the figure of Diana Vreeland—a calligrapher's brushstroke); the great Brodovitch—a melancholy White Russian and a pioneer of modernism in the graphic arts. She would succeed in her ambition to make *Bazaar* the most popular, but also the most stimulating, magazine of its kind. Not only the fashion, but also the art, fiction, and culture tingled with the shock of the new.

Frivolity always had its place, however. One of Snow's more sensational headhunting trophies was Daisy Fellowes. Fellowes, the daughter of a duke, the ex-wife of a prince of the blood, and an heiress to the Singer sewing machine fortune, was considered the best-dressed woman on both continents, and her every caprice was slavishly copied. "She wasn't nice," writes Penelope Rowlands, Snow's biographer—"few of those ultrachic Parisiennes, who lived to upstage one another, were—and she was beyond dramatic." Fellowes was supposed to write a fashion column and, between her tantrums and fittings, occasionally did.

Snow had been looking for a replacement

of the same ilk—someone, she wrote, who would "make news" for the magazine, albeit without making such a nuisance (or as much of one) with her histrionics, and on the morning after her glimpse of Vreeland at the St. Regis, Snow telephoned her to propose a job. Rather than jump at it, Vreeland displayed, or feigned, an atypical self-doubt. "Except for my little lingerie shop in London, I've never worked," she protested. (That shop was an ephemeral venture in Mayfair where Vreeland had sold—mostly to friends—boudoir and trousseau items fabricated in a Spanish convent.) "I've never been in an office in my life. I'm never dressed until lunch." Perhaps Snow rolled her eyes. "But," she replied, "you seem to know a lot about clothes."

Vreeland's column, "Why Don't You?" made its debut in the August 1936 issue and has since achieved a minor measure of immortality. "Why don't you rinse your blonde child's hair in dead champagne, as they do in France?" is the most often cited—reproached, laughed at, relished, admired for its gall—of her lifestyle advice items in an era of breadlines and Hoovervilles. "Why don't you carry on a long diamond stick a diamond rose with a sponge in the heart of the petals to waft your scent as you go?" "Remember, nothing is smarter with your shooting tweeds than linen

gaiters." She also approved the look of "bare knees and long white knitted socks," noting that Unity Mitford was thus attired "when she takes tea with Hitler at the Carlton in Munich."

Was it Munkácsi who pointed out that the vile Führer and the mad Mitford sister made dubious fashion icons? Their fleeting cameo in Vreeland's column only serves as a reminder that perfect taste is not always insurance against moral vulgarity. But to the degree that Vreeland had any allegiance that might be called political, it was hardly to brownshirts or jackboots. What stirred her imagination was an ancien régime notion of sumptuary grandeur and *savoir-vivre* wherever it has existed in time or geography: Tsarist Russia, Mughal India, imperial China, Cleopatra's Egypt, the Persia of Scheherazade, or Versailles. And while many readers, including S. J. Perelman, who parodied Vreeland's style in *The New Yorker*, perceived her as a modern-day Marie Antoinette (she framed the parody and was proud of it), her delirious advice of a piece with the shimmery mirages of the same period—escapist comedies set in art deco penthouses and shown in art deco movie theaters—distracted America from its privations.

Cecil Beaton once observed of his friend Diana that her speech had "a poetical quality"—an intoxicated freedom of association—that gave "color and life to the most commonplace event." The source of that poetry was an exaggerated horror of the prosaic which is often the hallmark of a fashion priestess. The Marchesa Casati comes to mind, but so does a great fabulist like Isak Dinesen, a woman whom Vreeland revered not only for her tales of a lost world, but also, as she once put it to me, as "the greatest aristocrat I have ever known." (I would not have dared to contradict her, yet Dinesen's nobility was mostly a state of mind. She was a rich, middle-class Danish art student who had made a marriage of convenience with a poor and rather boorish but titled cousin in order to escape her family.) Perhaps, like both of them, Vreeland reinvented her image and history to erase the memory of a glum, unlovely little girl in whose body and existence she had once been trapped. A primal yearning for singularity often gives one an unerring instinct for it.

In Vreeland's early years at *Bazaar*, she worked mostly from her red-lacquered apartment in the East Nineties. "She used to come in once a week to talk," an assistant recalled,

"I WAS ONLY ROMANTIC, IMAGINATIVE, AND MY MIND WAS ALWAYS FAR AWAY."

VREELAND ON SET AT AN AVEDON
SITTING FOR *HARPER'S BAZAAR* IN 1946.
PHOTOGRAPH BY RICHARD AVEDON

and "she just gave Mrs. Snow a stream of consciousness. Mrs. Snow would edit all the material for use in the magazine. Diana was so full of ideas," she continued, "but she needed an editor and Mrs. Snow was that." One of her brainstorms was inspired by a favorite Chanel ensemble, daring for its time, of trousers and a tailored shirt with inside pockets. With even bigger pockets, Vreeland argued, a woman could carry all of her necessities—lipstick, comb, rouge, powder, cigarettes, and money (hers was ironed by the French maid) but not keys (a *Bazaar* reader was presumed to have a servant who opened the door)—without the burden of a "bloodly old handbag that one leaves in a taxi." "Listen, Diana," Snow retorted. "I think you've lost your mind. Do you realize that our income from handbag advertising is God knows how many millions a year?"

Fashion has an evolutionary logic that isn't always apparent until one imagines that each new fad, innovation, or shift in erotic focus conveys a Darwinian advantage upon those who adapt to it before their rivals. Vreeland, in that respect, was the fittest of her species. She was alert to beauty and novelty the way a hunter's senses are attuned to the subtlest smell, shadow, or rustle in a landscape, and whatever one thinks of fashion's importance or lack of it in a universal scheme, that keenness is a form of superior intelligence.

By 1939, it was obvious to Snow that Vreeland's divining powers for the next object of desire were invaluable to the magazine, and she made her the fashion editor, with an office and a staff. She now had to get dressed sometime before lunch (a peanut butter sandwich and a jigger of Scotch, consumed at her desk, between cigarettes). The timing of this promotion, however, was opportune, for when World War II started in Europe, couture clients in North America were housebound by German U-boats, and American designers were able to come into their own. Seventh Avenue was Vreeland's beat—mostly by default, as covering the biannual shows in Paris had always been, and would remain after the war, Snow's prerogative.

"I tramped the streets," Vreeland wrote in *D.V.*, "I covered the waterfront.... I'd walk home those sixty blocks alone all those years. I loved the fur district, and that's where I'd walk when I finished working.... I was so happy when I was down on Seventh Avenue. I was always going up rusty staircases with old newspapers lying all over the place and the most ghastly-looking characters hanging around... but it was all part of the great adventure, my *métier*, the scene."

VREELAND, WORKING WITH MARISA BERENSON,
ONE OF THE MOST IMPORTANT MODELS OF THE
SIXTIES, AT *VOGUE*.

CECIL BEATON, A CLOSE FRIEND OF VREELAND'S, TOOK THIS PORTRAIT.
DESCRIBING HER, HE SAID: "THERE IS NOTHING ARTIFICIAL ABOUT
HER; SHE WILL NEVER LEAD YOU OFF THE SCENT AND HAS NO DESIRE
FOR PRETENSE. SHE HAS WISDOM AND A HARD PHILOSOPHICAL
CORE, HAS BECOME CULTIVATED THROUGH HER ENTHUSIASMS,
ACQUIRING THE EXACT POETIC APPROACH. BUT FOR ALL HER RE-
MARKABLE HUMAN TALENT, DIANA VREELAND IS NO EGOIST."

Vreeland did more than go to the New York collections and the showrooms to choose clothes for her features. She played an instrumental role in helping designers to refine their ideas and, as Bettina Ballard, her counterpart at *Vogue*, recalled, "to create and to motivate fashion," rather than simply report it. (Not everyone was thrilled by her refinements. She once asked Baron Nicolas de Gunzburg, the only male in her department, "What is the name of that Seventh Avenue designer who hates me so?" "Legion," he replied.)

"A fashion editor in those days," writes Amy Fine Collins, "had to be a resourceful combination of movie director, propman, seamstress, and beautician." Vreeland was, in particular, peerless as a sittings editor, which is to say as a stylist, and when a model or an outfit looked insipid, she always managed to spike their voltage for a photograph with a tuck or a flourish. Not only had this high school dropout miraculously acquired a vast knowledge of art history; she had a painter's eye for light and color. (The gray of Pauline de Rothschild's drawing room was like "the inside of a pearl.") And for all her affectation of speech and manner, Vreeland's love of fashion was an authentically devout, sacred ecstasy—a rite of Dionysus. In that respect, it is not impossible that she consciously modeled herself on those female oracles of the classical world who, by speaking in riddles, foretold what was to come.

Vreeland's own sibylline pronouncements ("Pink is the navy blue of India"; "Elegance is refusal") were part of her mystique. They annoyed or amused linear thinkers, but they would, I suspect, have beguiled the nineteenth-century French symbolist Stéphane Mallarmé—and not only because he wrote, edited, and published every word of a fanciful fashion journal, *La Dernière Mode*. His cryptic life's work as a poet demonstrates that it is possible to fabricate an experience of revelation from which the conventional meaning has evaporated like a volatile spirit, leaving an essence only the senses can grasp. And as he and Vreeland both understood, that is what great clothes do.

Vreeland, Brodovitch, and Snow have often been described as a "triumvirate." *Bazaar*, however, functioned as a hierarchy, with Snow at the top. The art director's purism was a foil for the fashion editor's exuberance, but the editor in chief controlled the look and tone of her magazine. Vreeland's biographer, Eleanor Dwight, describes how she would "waltz in" to an ideas meeting wreathed in smoke and blithely decree that "the whole June issue should be magenta." Snow might indulge her with a two-page spread. Vreeland, in turn, was just as proprietary on her own turf. "The amazing gallery of her imagination," as Avedon put it, was a storehouse of exotic visions, "but she wasn't interested in photographers' imaginations," he said, "and certainly not in mine."

"Why Don't You?" petered out during the war, not only because Vreeland's other duties increased and the formula came to seem "a bit frivolous" to her, but because the ever-practical Snow was in the habit of hijacking the column for product placement. Its author had no objection to shameless name-dropping if the name in question belonged to a duchess. Hyping the manufacturers of a beauty cream, or collapsible lawn chairs, was less amusing.

Reed had moved to Montreal in the early forties to manage a bank for a friend in Paris. His wife eventually discovered that he was living with another woman there, though their marriage would survive. She would always dissemble her chagrins with a mask of insouciance—another aspect of her genius for play. From her British father she had inherited a reserve belied by her appetite for drama. From her adventurous mother, on the other hand—a white huntress (and notorious adulterer)—she had inherited an ethos of conquest. When she told a friend, "I am mad for armor—simply *mad* for it," it wasn't just a figure of speech. Consider her image as a grande dame: the samurai hairdo, the scarlet warpaint, her profile of a Sioux chieftain, the cigarette holder that she brandished like Don Quixote's lance, her fencer's posture, and, around her neck, the talisman of a huntress like her namesake—an ivory tusk on a golden chain. High style, as Vreeland understood it, derives from aristocratic, which is to say, from military, ideals of pride, stoicism, hardness, swagger, and snobbery—of trial by ordeal and tournament chic.

With her husband on sabbatical from their marriage and her sons at boarding school, Vreeland was free to travel. About the time that the Japanese were bombing Pearl Harbor, she was on a train, crossing the country with Louise Dahl-Wolfe and a large crew. Their destination was Arizona, where she would orchestrate the kind of spectacular location shoot that would become a hallmark of her *Vogue* years.

The theme of the spread was vaguely patriotic, and the can-do American spirit was represented by the cheeky and youthful

sportswear of Claire McCardell. It was photographed in a ghost town, an old mission, and
at Frank Lloyd Wright's Taliesin. When one
of the models fell ill, Vreeland volunteered
as a stand-in. No longer young, and never
beautiful, she was still supremely photogenic,
and her pre-Columbian features, lanky silhouette, and prickly energy seemed native to the
Western landscape.

In one picture, Vreeland sits in profile
hugging her knees. The cigarette between
her fingers—long and shapely, with a perfect
manicure—has burned to a stub. She is still
wearing the sombrero, with a white shirt,
a blown rose behind one ear, and smiling
enigmatically. It is the masterful study of a hy-
brid character in which intense femininity
vied with ruthless lordliness. The famous epithet
from a stele that refers to Cleopatra VII as
"the Queen Himself" would have made a
nice caption.

As Avedon once remarked, Vreeland invented "a totally new profession": the fashion editor
as a creature of myth—Pygmalion. Models,
assistants, designers, and photographers all
had stories of her sometimes inspired, sometimes
alarming efforts to meddle with their clothes,
images, posture, grooming, manners, and even
their sex lives. Lillian Bassman, whose career

matured at *Bazaar* partly under Vreeland's tutelage, and whose dreamy, high-contrast photographs have become part of the fashion canon,
liked to visit the editor in her office at the end
of a long day. She could always look forward
to an entertaining monologue, and it was, she
said, "like going to the theater." "Do you stand
on your head?" Vreeland asked her, out of the
blue. "No. Why?" Bassman replied. "Well, my
dear... you will never have an orgasm."

Funny Face, a film of 1957 directed by
Stanley Donen with a score by George
Gershwin, was a Pygmalion story in the form
of a parody about the fashion world. It starred
Fred Astaire as a photographer like Richard
Avedon, Kay Thompson as an editor like Diana
Vreeland, and that quintessential Galatea,
Audrey Hepburn. (Hepburn had made her acting debut as Gigi, on Broadway, then played
Sabrina, and, a decade later, Eliza Doolittle
in the film version of *My Fair Lady*.) Like *Gigi*
and *Sabrina*, *Funny Face* is set in an operetta
City of Light, and its heroine is a ravishing inge-
nue who captures the heart of a jaded prince,
receiving, in the process, both a glamorous
makeover and an old-world education in sexual
wisdom and feminine cunning. Thompson's
imperious and campy "Maggie" gestures with a
cigarette holder as she intones her motto for the

season: "Think Pink!" When Hepburn's bookish Jo rebels at being treated like a doll with no free will whatsoever, we see the fashion editor in her true light: as a bully. It ends happily, though, which is to say with a runway show, and with Jo modeling the last number: a bridal gown by Givenchy.

Carmel Snow was thrilled with the publicity that *Funny Face* generated for *Bazaar*, but Vreeland was not. She attended a preview with her staff, and "when the show was over," Penelope Rowlands writes, "the editor got up with great dignity; as she left the screening room she uttered one brief sentence to the young editor at her side... 'Never to be discussed.'"

The show was almost over for the old regime at *Bazaar*: first for Brodovitch, who descended into alcoholism; then for Snow, who took the same path to oblivion; and finally for Vreeland, who would rise like a phoenix. The Hearst management had begun the search for a new editor in chief well before Snow was forced into retirement, and Vreeland presumed that she was, at the very least, on their short list. They had, however, settled on another candidate—Snow's niece, Nancy White. Despite appearances, no nepotism was involved, because Snow was outraged at the thought of her timid niece (the fashion editor of *Good Housekeeping*, who specialized in cozy features on wash-and-wear for the American housewife) trying to fill her shoes.

But did Hearst expect White to fill them? In fact, she was hired because the industry was changing, and she represented what, in principle, is most refreshingly egalitarian about American style, and much of American fashion journalism, but also what is most pedestrian: It is too remedial.

Snow learned that she had been deposed early in 1957, and Vreeland heard the news shortly thereafter. When she asked Snow if her name had been mentioned as a successor, the reply was brutal: It had not come up. According to Rowlands, Snow was incensed at the very idea that Vreeland would have considered herself worthy of the mantle, and it was rumored that she had "urged the men running Hearst Magazines to pass [her] over for the job, arguing that she lacked the discipline and judgment to head a magazine." Whatever jealousy or bitterness was involved, Snow's assessment of Vreeland was widely shared: "She was always late with her pages." "Her business plan wasn't obvious." "She snubbed the advertising department." "She was much too eccentric."

"She was this wonderful prima donna... but you can't really run a railroad like that." And Vreeland's assessment of White? "We needed an artist and they sent us a house-painter."

Vreeland soldiered on at *Bazaar* for another five years. In 1961, a young Catholic president and his wife—a dark beauty, ardent Francophile, and former deb of the year—moved into the White House. Vreeland, who knew Jacqueline Bouvier Kennedy socially and had snared her coming-out pictures (taken by Beaton) for *Bazaar*, became her *éminence grise* in matters of style. They conspired to reconcile Jackie's passion for French couture with the political necessity of patronizing American designers (a quandary that Vreeland shared). It was Vreeland who suggested that a sable muff would add a regal, romantic touch to the cloth coat that Jackie wore to her husband's inauguration, and she had consulted on the ballgown: a columnar sheath.

The First Lady expressed her gratitude by giving *Bazaar* the privilege of publishing the first pictures of the Kennedys in their new home.

DIANA VREELAND WITH CLOSE FRIEND C. Z. GUEST AT A FASHION SHOW.

That plum fell to Avedon. When he asked Vreeland what she wanted, she told him, typically, "Just get that voice."

Kennedy had been in office for about eighteen months when Vreeland left *Bazaar* for *Vogue*. That magazine had a new owner, Samuel Newhouse, and his wife, Mitzi, was said to be a great Vreeland fan. "They offered me a large salary, an endless expense account... and Europe whenever I wanted to go. That's what hooked me," Vreeland said. Jessica Daves, the outgoing editor in chief, stayed on for a tense transition period of a few months. But in

January of 1963, Vreeland's name, for the first time in her life, topped a masthead.

When Vreeland arrived at *Vogue*, Alexander Liberman had been its art director since 1943. He, like Brodovitch, was a soulful, Russian-born artist, photographer, and graphic designer with a strong modernist sensibility tempered by hardship. Born in 1912 into a rich family of Jewish timber merchants, Liberman had survived the Soviet revolution and escaped to Paris, where he met the artists whose work would define the new century. When the Germans invaded France, he escaped a second time—to New York. One of his first hires at *Vogue*—a young painter named Irving Penn—had briefly held the same assistant's job under Brodovitch at *Bazaar*. When the *Vogue* staff photographers couldn't execute a picture that Penn had designed for a 1943 cover, Liberman said, "Try it yourself." And a master was born.

The president of Condé Nast, Iva Patcevitch, had wanted Liberman, not Vreeland, to succeed Daves, but Liberman had demurred. "I'm a man," he said. "I have no intention of becoming that involved with fashion." He also had no intention of reporting to Vreeland, so the management created a new position for him: "editorial director." A memo circulated in the company

VREELAND WITH GEORGE HOYNINGEN-HUENE.

announced that "'Diana Vreeland will work closely with Alexander Liberman.' They wanted me controlling her," he told Amy Fine Collins. "But Vreeland was uncontrollable."

Liberman was a passionate advocate of modernity who never had any patience for the gauzy "visions of loveliness" that had prevailed at women's magazines before he arrived

to dispel them. *Vogue*, he believed, according to his biographers Dodie Kazanjian and Calvin Tomkins, "was not really about fashion... it was about women"—individuals of the female gender who were neither chimeras nor objects of fantasy. Vreeland, a fantast and a chimera herself, would nevertheless set about transforming *Vogue* for a new era by adapting Liberman's insight to her own purposes. "Society is démodé," she told Cecil Beaton early in her tenure. "Today," she explained, "only personality counts... ravishing personalities are the most riveting things in the world—conversation, people's interests, the atmosphere that they create around them."

Vreeland's *Vogue* chronicled a boom period of radical upheaval in the arts and social experiment—the "youthquake," the counterculture, the Pill (and pill-popping), Warhol, Courrèges, the Beatles, and the Jet Age. Commercial plane travel dealt one of the death blows to couture (it made steamer trunks obsolete), but it also transformed fashion coverage, which became, under Vreeland's regime, gorgeously global and exotic. For the first time, women of color modeled high fashion. (In 1959, on assignment for *Bazaar*, Avedon had photographed the half-Asian China Machado in *maja* dress by Dior. But, he said, "she wasn't considered 'white' enough, and I had to threaten that I'd leave for *Vogue* if they didn't use her pictures.") Balenciaga retired in May 1968, as the barricades were going up in the streets of Paris, sighing bitterly, "There is no one left for me to dress." That festive insurrection attracted its share of chic walk-ons in Saint Laurent, the bad boy wonder from Oran. Saint Laurent didn't invent ready-to-wear (Pierre Cardin did), but he was the first couturier to make a cult of it, and the opening of the Rive Gauche boutique in Saint-Germain heralded a retail revolution.

The fashion establishment on the Right Bank, in the meantime, was eclipsed by London, and by an upstart, mod generation who spoke the English of Eliza Doolittle. The old class prejudices that Vreeland had once cherished were being subverted—with her blessing and connivance. (The process, however, had actually begun, virtually unnoticed, about the time she was born; in Paris—her birthplace—and in the couture salons that were her place of worship, where the courtesans of the era began, heretically, to rub elbows with Proust's duchesses. Once the moral boundaries between castes of women had been blurred, it was only a matter of time before the distinction between *racé* and racy—between social celebrity and sexual notoriety—would likewise be confused.)

Not long ago, on the hottest day of a record summer, I took refuge from the torrid sun in the library at the Condé Nast building, which is now in Times Square. It holds every issue of Vreeland's *Vogue* (and every other *Vogue*, since 1893). The light is dim, and the air is kept at the temperature of a meat locker—or of a time capsule. I went through her issues, each one a madeleine. In a spirit of Vreelandish free association, here is what struck me:

leggier than ever, scamper over the sacred statuary in the Hall of Heroes at Jaipur.

Not all is fast-forward. Mrs. Vanderbilt in Mainbocher, as if two decades had not elapsed. What, exactly, is a fabric called "wuthering grey bouclé"? But how lovely Candice Bergen and Kitty Hawk are at eighteen. And elfin Mary Quant.

Fashion is cruel. Fashion of the sixties is a frenzy of sartorial matricide. Wear if you can the micromini and the monokini. Yet Vreeland has a heart: There are caftans and more caftans.

African savannahs. The splendors of Leningrad. Frosted pink lipstick and mahogany tans. Babe Paley in her "secret garden."

A white ostrich coat by Georges Kaplan worn with Halston's white "space hennin" (a steeple-shaped headdress of the Middle Ages) photographed in the Arctic Circle. Geisha makeup. Ermine dresses. Violet mink. Fitted chinchilla. Maya Plisetskaya in Russian sable. How Vreeland loved fur!

People Are Talking About: whatever "riveting personality" (Zero Mostel) or "new beauty" (Baby Jane Holzer) excited Diana. Truman Capote's "Party of the Century"—his Black and White Ball of 1966—reported by a young journalist named... Gloria Steinem.

Is cool the new hot, or is hot the new cool? 1967: hideous Peter Pan collars (but only in an ad). Endless splashes: Jean Shrimpton, photographed by David Bailey, on Stavros Niarchos's yacht in the Aegean. A blaze of "exotic radiance": twenty-six pages on India, photographed by Henry Clarke. His models,

(The Duchess of Windsor is wearing a rather loud one as she cuddles her pug.)

Vreeland's love affair with Morocco: "Stretching from the Atlantic Ocean to the Sahara, [it] contains glories as large as the Atlas Mountains under pearl skies, as immediate as sable-brown camels, black sheep, nonesuch roses, and as remote as the horizon eternally traced with still another crenellated city."

Big and ever bigger hair (referred to as "manes") is "tawny and marvelous." Mick Jagger is sullen and marvelous. Less marvelous are fuchsia eyelids, nose jobs, and crazy psychedelic Dynel hairpieces (two hundred pounds of gold and silver Dynel for a shoot in Tahiti. "Leave it behind," Vreeland told the crew).

The harem of Topkapi Palace is no match for the Vogue harem. "Beauty as Personality: the Born Free Look." Vreeland's prime directive: Discover your inner lioness.

An attempt at outreach to the masses: Fashions with "more dash than cash" (but not many). Twenty-six pages of Veruschka, in furs, with a sumo wrestler, on the north coast of Japan. Veruschka modeling the "Queen Cristina look" (chartreuse fox, black velvet, embroidered collars) at a desolate Swedish chateau. Amazonian Veruschka, who grew up like a poor gypsy after her father, Baron von Lehndorff, was executed for plotting to assassinate Hitler. (Whatever happened to the Carlton in Munich? Was it bombed?)

Lesley Blanch reports from the Valley of the Kings and Syria and Jordan: "A Rhapsody on Middle Eastern Themes." (My local librarian refused to let me, at twelve, check out her bestseller, The Wilder Shores of Love, but I got hold of it. Abductions to a seraglio! Mad love by moonlight with a sheik of Araby! All very Vogue.)

Frances FitzGerald reports from Vietnam. (FitzGerald? Is she related to the Knight of Glin? No, but her half-sister is Penelope Tree.)

Lauren Hutton dressed like a genie, for some reason, in diaphanous lime green, integrates a male initiation rite in Bali.

The seasons turn: "Fab Boots" come in, and so does "Drug Abuse." Allene Talmey writes an admonitory feature. (Meanwhile, though, wan, ethereal Edie Sedgwick and languorous Talitha Getty, both Vogue It girls, are shooting heroin.)

Titled beauties and their fairy-tale weddings are still in vogue, but the professionals are no longer anonymous. (Twiggy and more Twiggy.) The Queen of Thailand wears Balmain, but shy Hope Cooke—recently a Sarah Lawrence coed, now the Queen of Sikkim—opts for a sari. Who knew so many queens still existed?

Jackie Kennedy told Oleg Cassini (it wasn't reported at the time) that she didn't want to be perceived as the Marie Antoinette of the sixties, but of course, she was. Why not, instead, dress like her lover, the Swedish Count Axel Fersen, in a pair of court breeches with a jaguar "fencer's blouse" by Emeric Partos? But the real endangered species was Vreeland.

She cavalierly spent way too much money, sometimes on spreads that would never run, or on three-hour phone calls to London, but that wasn't it. She could be an appalling tyrant, but her tough love had its charm. She kept her limousine waiting for hours, but grandiosity was part of her job description. She offended the designers whose shows she skipped, and they pulled their ads. As her book got thinner, she clashed with Liberman, who admitted his impotence to rein her in: "Things," he said later, "were getting out of hand."

But what, perhaps, was most out of hand, and not only at *Vogue*, was the indocility of girls and women. They weren't burning their bras (bra-burning is a myth), but they were burning with ambition. They wanted to reinvent themselves, though not every month or necessarily with the help of false eyelashes and Dynel. They didn't disdain seduction or hate fashion, but Vreeland's *Vogue* began to seem frankly reactionary, and when the recession, like an eclipse, dimmed the wattage of the go-go years, it even seemed garish.

The day that she was blindsided by the news that she had been fired was a winter morning in 1971. Colleagues had tried to warn her, they said, but she hadn't listened. The decision had been made by Si Newhouse, and by the president of Condé Nast, Perry Ruston, but she blamed Liberman, and she told him that she had known Red Russians and White Russians, but until then, she had "never known a yellow Russian." He later said simply, though not to her, *"Mea culpa."*

At sixty-eight, a recent widow, she should have been broken, but she freshened her makeup and moved on. And so shall I, but with a final reflection.

Talleyrand, a maker of kings, was a man after Vreeland's heart. He was a great voluptuary, ordained as a priest, who served Louis XVI but miraculously kept his head, then advised Napoleon (not shrewdly enough), and, after him, used his consummate powers of intrigue to help restore a Bourbon to power, dying at eighty-three. "Those," he said, "who have not known life before the Revolution can never know the sweetness of living."

DAVID BAILEY'S PHOTOGRAPH OF VREELAND WITH
ALEXANDER LIBERMAN IS ALL TELLING—HER ABRUPT
FIRING FROM *VOGUE* SENT SHOCK WAVES THROUGH-
OUT THE WORLD OF FASHION. SHE RECALLED, "I WAS
FIRED... THEY WANTED A DIFFERENT SORT OF MAGA-
ZINE, BUT THEY NEVER TOLD ME WHAT."

REVIEWING LAYOUT WITH CARMEL SNOW AND
ALEXEY BRODOVITCH WAS PART OF VREELAND'S
DAILY ROUTINE AT *BAZAAR*.

HARPER'S BAZAAR

1936-1962

THOSE WERE THE DAYS WHEN PEOPLE DRESSED FOR DINNER,
AND I MEAN DRESSED—NOT JUST CHANGED THEIR
CLOTHES. IF A WOMAN CAME IN IN A BALENCIAGA DRESS,
NO OTHER WOMAN IN THE ROOM EXISTED.

BALENCIAGA'S BLACK VELVET DRESS WITH BOLERO AND APRON OF WHITE EYELETTED PIQUÉ

BALENCIAGA'S BUSTLE DRESS OF BLACK AND WHITE CHECKED SILK TAFFETA. HATTIE CARNEGIE

50

51

JULY 1939
PHOTOGRAPHED BY GEORGE HOYNINGEN-HUENE

Like the rest of the fashion world, Vreeland was enchanted
by the designs of Cristobal Balenciaga.

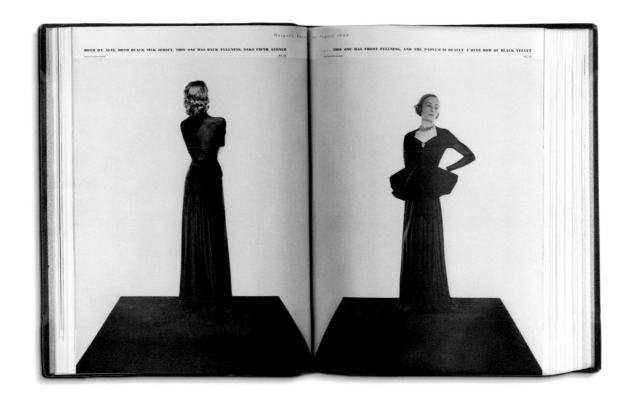

AUGUST 1939
PHOTOGRAPHED BY GEORGE HOYNINGEN-HUENE

Vreeland was a fan of Alix Grès's sumptuous draped dresses—she was an admirer of the way in which they were created directly on a woman's form.

SEPTEMBER 15, 1939
PHOTOGRAPHED BY GEORGE HOYNINGEN-HUENE

"WHY DON'T YOU... As Schiaparelli. Why don't you realize that this wonderfully creative woman is expressing our life and times in her little suits and dresses and in her unique materials... and realize that it is up to you to match her genius by adding perfect details to make them part of you?"

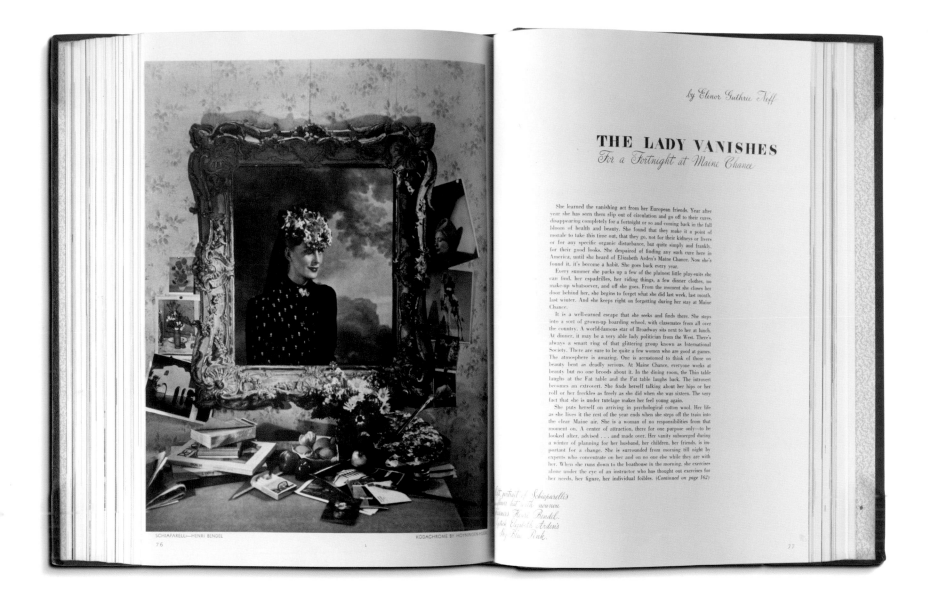

by Elinor Guthrie Neff

THE LADY VANISHES
For a Fortnight at Maine Chance

She learned the vanishing act from her European friends. Year after year she has seen them slip out of circulation and go off to their cures, disappearing completely for a fortnight or so and coming back in the full bloom of health and beauty. She found that they make it a point of morale to take this time out, that they go, not for their kidneys or livers or for any specific organic disturbance, but quite simply and frankly, for their good looks. She despaired of finding any such cure here in America, until she heard of Elizabeth Arden's Maine Chance. Now she's found it, it's become a habit. She goes back every year.

Every summer she packs up a few of the plainest little play-suits she can find, her espadrilles, her riding things, a few dinner clothes, no make-up whatsoever, and off she goes. From the moment she closes her door behind her, she begins to forget what she did last week, last month, last winter. And she keeps right on forgetting during her stay at Maine Chance.

It is a well-earned escape that she seeks and finds there. She steps into a sort of grown-up boarding school, with classmates from all over the country. A world-famous star of Broadway sits next to her at lunch. At dinner, it may be a very able lady politician from the West. There's always a smart ring of that glittering group known as International Society. There are sure to be quite a few women who are good at games. The atmosphere is amazing. One is accustomed to think of those on beauty bent as deadly serious. At Maine Chance, everyone works at beauty but no one broods about it. In the dining room, the Thin table laughs at the Fat table and the Fat table laughs back. The introvert becomes an extrovert. She finds herself talking about her hips or her roll or her freckles as freely as she did when she was sixteen. The very fact that she is under tutelage makes her feel young again.

She puts herself on arriving in psychological cotton wool. Her life as she lives it the rest of the year ends when she steps off the train into the clear Maine air. She is a woman of no responsibilities from that moment on. A center of attraction, there for one purpose only—to be looked after, advised . . . and made over. Her vanity submerged during a winter of planning for her husband, her children, her friends, is important for a change. She is surrounded from morning till night by experts who concentrate on her and on no one else while they are with her. When she runs down to the boathouse in the morning, she exercises alone under the eye of an instructor who has thought out exercises for her needs, her figure, her individual foibles. *(Continued on page 162)*

SCHIAPARELLI—HENRI BENDEL
76

KODACHROME BY HOYNINGEN-HUENE
77

FIRST CONFESSION
by Frank O'Connor

MAY 1939
PHOTOGRAPHED BY GEORGE HOYNINGEN-HUENE

"UNDERLINE WHY DON'T YOU... Photograph her sitting at the mirror? The full reflection is adorable."

MARCH 1, 1939
PHOTOGRAPHED BY GEORGE HOYNINGEN-HUENE

Among her many gifts as a fashion editor, Vreeland's greatest talent was allowing a woman to dream.

OPPOSITE PAGE
JULY 1941
PHOTOGRAPHED BY LOUISE DAHL-WOLFE

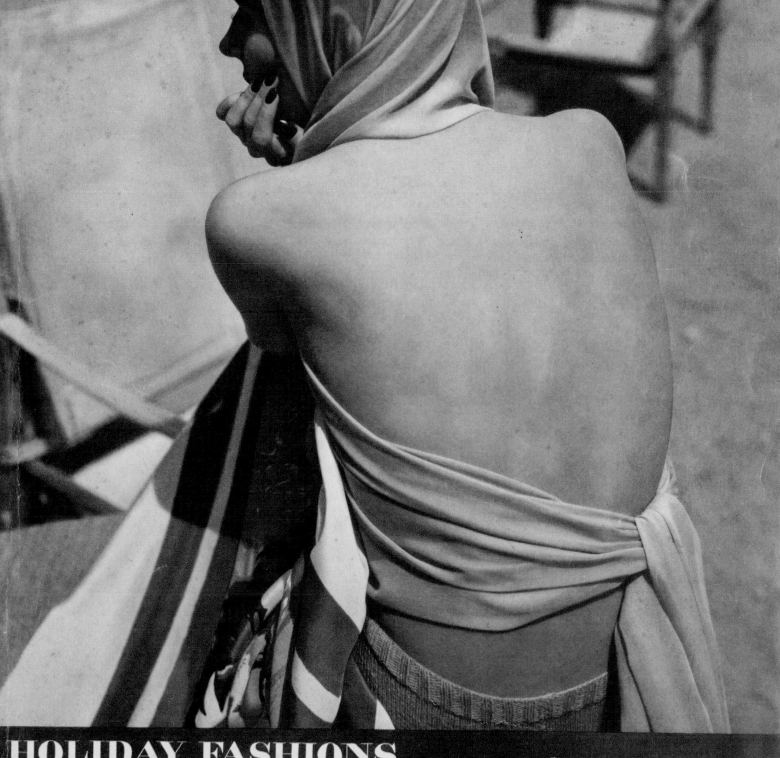

Harper's BAZAAR

July 1941

HOLIDAY FASHIONS

50 cents · 60 cents in Canada · 2/6 in London

RED IS THE GREAT CLARIFIER—BRIGHT, CLEANSING,

AND REVEALING. IT MAKES ALL COLORS BEAUTIFUL.

I CAN'T IMAGINE BECOMING BORED

WITH RED—IT WOULD BE LIKE BECOMING BORED

WITH THE PERSON YOU LOVE.

**OPPOSITE PAGE
SEPTEMBER 15, 1940
PHOTOGRAPHED BY GEORGE HOYNINGEN-HUENE**

Although she loved all colors, Vreeland is most associated with the color red.

**NOVEMBER 1939
PHOTOGRAPHED BY GEORGE HOYNINGEN-HUENE**

"WHY DON'T YOU... Someone once said, 'Genius is the capacity for taking infinite pains.' Therefore, when dressing, be absorbed completely and utterly in yourself, letting no detail escape you. However, once dressed, be interested only in those about you."

"ALLURE" IS A WORD VERY FEW PEOPLE USE

NOWADAYS, BUT IT'S SOMETHING THAT EXISTS. ALLURE

HOLDS YOU, DOESN'T IT? WHETHER IT'S A GAZE OR A

GLANCE IN THE STREET OR A FACE IN THE CROWD, SOMEONE

SITTING OPPOSITE YOU AT LUNCH... YOU ARE HELD.

SEPTEMBER 15, 1940
PHOTOGRAPHED BY LOUISE DAHL-WOLFE

OPPOSITE PAGE
NOVEMBER 1941
PHOTOGRAPHED BY GEORGE HOYNINGEN-HUENE

"Fashion must be the most intoxicating release from the
banality of the world."

Harper's

BAZAAR

November 1941

WINTER FASHIONS

50 cents · 60 cents in Canada · 2/6 in London

MARCH 1, 1941
PHOTOGRAPHED BY LOUISE DAHL-WOLFE

Estrella Boissevain, a bullfighter and flamenco dancer, wears Balenciaga. Vreeland said of Balenciaga, "His inspiration came from the bullrings, the flamenco dancers, the loose blouses the fishermen wear, the cool of the cloisters... and he took these moods and colors and, adapting them to his own tastes, literally dressed those who cared about such things for thirty years."

Harper's Bazaar for December 1940

• The one-piece idea hits everything from slacks to ski suits. Below, the perfect slacks of the year, made like an aviation mechanic's suit—slim and easy, zipped up the front. In stark white sharkskin, with a tan leather belt. Bergdorf Goodman.

• Knee-length, side-wrapped, the newest shorts in town—in natural linen with a wrapped top of red and natural rayon hand blocked with bamboo palms. Underneath, a two-part bathing suit. By Brigance, at Lord and Taylor. Torben Müller designed the stairway.

DECEMBER 1940
PHOTOGRAPHED BY LOUISE DAHL-WOLFE

Vreeland created the fashion editor: "The fashion editor really was quite important. That is to say I wasn't a fashion editor—I was the one-and-only fashion editor. I judged everything that went into the magazine whether it was a buckle or a girdle or a piece of fabric or a length of a sweater or anything..."

Harper's Bazaar for January, 19

• Cut by the inventive scissors of Charlie James . . . Left: Shorts that must be seen to be believed. On the surface, they're shorts in back only—the front is a skirt, buttoned across in gold. Underneath they're shorts all the way round. • Right: The chic of these shorts is their length—they nearly graze the kneecap.

80

**JANUARY 1941
PHOTOGRAPHED BY
GEORGE HOYNINGEN-HUENE**

... I **BELIEVE** TOTALLY IN ROMANCE, LOVE, PLEASURE, AND BEAUTY.

Harper's Bazaar for January, 1941

HOYNINGEN-HUENE

• Above: The skirt-in-front, pants-in-back principle in a Southern dinner suit, with an Indian-dancer top and pearl buttons. • All three white rayon Ripcord outfits, and the U. S. Rubber Company locker sandals, at Altman; Carson Pirie Scott, Chicago; Burdine's, Miami. • Archery tackle, Abercrombie and Fitch.

81

MARCH 15, 1942
ILLUSTRATION BY MARCEL VERTÈS

Marcel Vertès's whimsical drawings were a delightful contribution to *Bazaar*. Although it was Carmel Snow who introduced Vertès to *Bazaar*, he quickly forged a friendship with Vreeland.

MARCH 15, 1942
PHOTOGRAPHED BY
GEORGE HOYNINGEN-HUENE

Carmel Snow was never seen without a hat during her days as editor in chief at *Bazaar*, while Vreeland famously wore a snood.

**NOVEMBER 1942
PHOTOGRAPHED BY
GEORGE HOYNINGEN-HUENE**

By 1942 Vreeland's reputation as the fashion editor of her time was established. Bettina Ballard, who worked in Paris for *Vogue*, said of her, "Her strength has always been in her unavailability and in her oracular approach to fashion. Her concept of being a fashion editor is to create fashion for *Harper's Bazaar*, to motivate it, not simply to report on what Seventh Avenue has to offer."

**FOLLOWING SPREAD
MARCH 1942
PHOTOGRAPHED BY LOUISE DAHL-WOLFE**

BLACK WITH BROWN . . . A SHAWL WITH SLACKS. CIGAR-BROWN SLACKS IN CROWN TESTED RAYON AND COTTON. A BRASSIERE COVERED BY A FRINGED BLACK SHAWL IN RAYON JERSEY. JAY THORPE, I. MAGNIN, CALIFORNIA.

40

Harper's Bazaar, January 1942

ONE OF FRANK LLOYD WRIGHT'S FAMOUS HOUSES, CLINGING LIKE AN EAGLE'S NEST TO A MOUNTAINSIDE. THE MID-CALF SKIRT IN BLACK LINEN, BELTED OVER A HALTER-NECK CHALLIS SCARF. JAY THORPE, I. MAGNIN, CALIFORNIA.

KODACHROME BY LOUISE DAHL-WOLFE

JANUARY 1942
PHOTOGRAPHED BY LOUISE DAHL-WOLFE

Vreeland and Louise Dahl-Wolfe spent many years creating fantasy within the pages of the magazines. Here they traveled to Scottsdale, Arizona, to shoot at Frank Lloyd Wright's winter home, Taliesin West. This home was used as a studio and architectural laboratory and continues to be active today. Vreeland stepped in for a model after she became ill, creating these infamous but iconic images.

Flight to the Valley of the Sun

Harper's **BAZAAR**

January 1942

**TRAVEL
FASHIONS**

50 cents · 60 cents in Canada · 2/6 in London

BLONDE PUTS PALE AMBER OVER GRAY AND AMBER WOOL

A shaggy camel's hair coat
in a new pale yellow
over a strictly tailored
suit, both Stroock wool
Lord and Taylor;
Neiman-Marcus, Dallas;
Thalhimer, Richmond
Lilly Daché's large gray
fur felt. Kislav gloves.

Ruth Ford poses
and jacke
Marshall Fiel
The John Freder
is sweepin
Hansen glove
Revlon
nail polish
Van Clee

KODACHROME BY LOUISE DAHL-WOLFE

KODACHROME BY LOUISE

RUNETTE WEARS BRILLIANT GREEN

OVER SHEER PLAID WOOL

na-Norell dress
3onwit Teller;
Magnin, California.
eret that
country.
ed in the belt.
. Miniver Rose
pstick.
Arpels jewels.

WOLFE

MARCH 1943
PHOTOGRAPHED BY
LOUISE DAHL-WOLFE

During the war, Louise Dahl-Wolfe and Vreeland spent endless hours on shoots. Said Dahl-Wolfe: "She was tops. No one knew color or could pull a sitting together like Diana.... We had to photograph clothes we laughingly called 'pearls of little price'; that meant they came from manufacturers that advertised, so the more they spent, the bigger the picture. Sometimes you would get them and just not know what to do, but Diana always managed to make it work and Carmel would just say 'Hide as much of it as you can.'"

OPPOSITE, CLOCKWISE FROM TOP LEFT:
JUNE 1940–PHOTOGRAPHED BY HERBERT MATTER,
NOVEMBER 1942–PHOTOGRAPHED BY ERWIN
BLUMENFELD, APRIL 1945–PHOTOGRAPHED BY
LOUISE DAHL-WOLFE, APRIL 1946–PHOTOGRAPHED
BY ERNST BEADLE, MAY 1944–PHOTOGRAPHED BY
LOUISE DAHL-WOLFE

AUGUST 1941
PHOTOGRAPHED BY LOUISE DAHL-WOLFE

Vreeland's role as a sittings editor is perhaps her most memorable. Below, in action with Louise Dahl-Wolfe, she puts the finishing touches on a cover shoot. Her keen editor's eye never forgot the last detail, whether it had to do with an accessory that was not right or a shade of color that did not tie the outfit together.

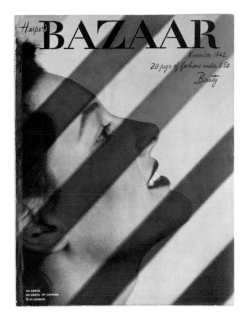

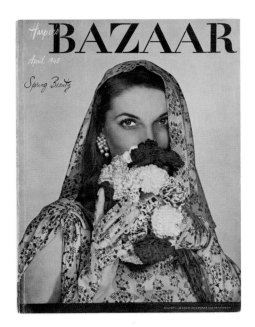

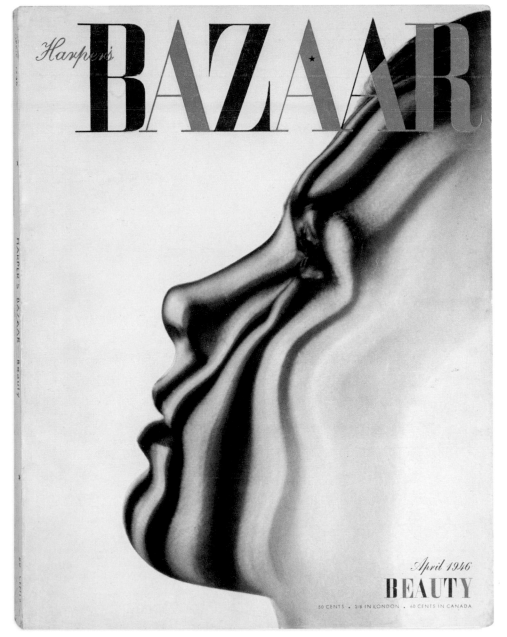

DORA

by Saul Bellow

I'm so far behind in my work I couldn't be further if I was sick in bed. When a thing gets hold of me, it really does. And what else makes my work worth while, when all is said and done? But that's all right as long as I know where I'm at and what I'm doing. Otherwise it may not be so good. I think, though, when you are *in* a thing you don't know how wrong it may be. You see the right and it is familiar but it may be in reverse, like a thread that is winding one way instead of another. And you recognize the thread so you assume it is right until you catch on how it is running—feeling a little anxious but going on when out of the blue you see how the bobbin is turning. Without realizing how and where, you are doing something very unusual all of a sudden. As in my case, never using make-up, I find myself in the middle of the afternoon in the sunshine by my dresser (so it can't be imagination) putting lipstick on my lips. Bam! Each time there is lightning it divides the sky up in a new way. I suppose it is never the same way twice.

I'm so restless and uneasy. Nothing is being accomplished. I ought to send for Mrs. Spiesman to come and take over the house and everything herself. It usually isn't much of a hardship to be in charge of it. The hot water pressure has two needles on the gauge which have to be together and also in the attic there's a glass tube—the water has to be about in the middle, and there's nothing to worry about. Once a day is all I have to look after it. It's set up so that it runs by itself, practically. But you do have to know. Mrs. Spiesman wouldn't feel safe, even if it is almost foolproof, going away with no one to rely on in case of an emergency. But as long as I'm here she can go with a free mind. I can start the furnace if it goes out and even fix the stoker if the screw breaks down, though now in the spring is not the time something like that would come up. However, I can do it and I have. I'm strong for a person of my size and in good condition from being active. Many women far from old give in, cry and worry. That's especially with married women who begin to see their youth behind them. But I, as long as death doesn't collect me, I'll be and act the same regardless—lucky I'm free from that.

Another advantage for Mrs. Spiesman is that I'm around the house in the morning nearly every day, and if there is some business—as there is in any ordinary house, let alone a rooming house—like the gas or laundry or the collector for the pay phone, it's mostly in the morning. And usually, not as this time, not only do I not mind, I even like it. For when she's at home, I've lived here long enough to go where I want to go in the house, but I don't often do it, walking straight up to my room from the street when I come in. It is different when I am left the keys and have to go down in the basement. It makes all the difference in the world, although I don't have to ask permission, I could do it any time, practically one of the family after eleven years. That's just an expression. There is no family. Mrs. Spiesman has a son in Wilmington, Delaware, who's a chemist in the dye industry with a family of his own, and she has a sister in Dover Plains and likes to go to one place or the other. The sister is a twin, and it's interesting, on pictures through the years and even now you can hardly tell them apart but when you see them together you realize how many differences there are and how, toward the end of their lives, a person takes all that has happened to him or her into the face, and how important it is. I am interested in how it works out because I myself haven't got anybody. I grew up in an orphanage and don't have much of an idea about my own people, except my mother's father, and I like to study how people resemble each other and how it *(Continued on page 188)*

(Continued on page 188)

We Believe in Make-Believe—and in fantasies like these of colored stones and mock pearls and sparkles tossed together with imagination and chic. Note particularly the tiara, the dangle earrings and the giant pearl choker. Jewels, by Arpad, Saks Fifth Avenue.

KODACHROME BY ERNST BEADLE

HARPER'S BAZAAR

**NOVEMBER 1949
PHOTOGRAPHED BY
ERNST BEADLE**

"WHY DON'T YOU...
Wear an extremely low
black evening dress with
a Madame X décolletage
edged in gold... then around
your neck lay a superb Indian necklace of gold inlaid
with pearls?... and earrings
and a bracelet and ring of
the same Hindu splendor?"

Harper's BAZAAR
March 1943
AMERICAN RED CROSS
BLOOD DONOR SERVI
50 CENTS • 60 CENTS IN CANADA • 2/6 IN LONDON
SPRING FASHIONS

OPPOSITE PAGE
MARCH 1943
PHOTOGRAPHED BY LOUISE DAHL-WOLFE

Lauren Bacall's stage career changed after she met Diana Vreeland. Hollywood heavyweights finally noticed her after she was seen on this cover.

Remembering the first time she met Vreeland, Bacall said, "The fashion editor's name was Diana Vreeland... we could go in to where an extraordinary-looking woman sat at a desk covered with papers, photographs, boxes with bits and pieces of jewelry, scarves. She was very thin. Black hair combed straight back, turned under and held in place by a black net snood with a flat band on top. She was wearing a black skirt, a black sweater, and black ankle boots. She had white skin, brown eyes, red mouth, long nose, pink cheeks, lovely teeth, long fingernails painted dark red. Definitely an original."

MARCH 1944
PHOTOGRAPHED BY MAN RAY

"WHY DON'T YOU... Realize that you are infinitely smarter this year if you dine out with tiny sleeves in your evening dress, no matter how naked your back or under arms, than in a sleeveless dress?"

SEPTEMBER 1944
PHOTOGRAPHED BY GEORGE HOYNINGEN-HUENE

"WHY DON'T YOU... Remember that the smaller your head, the more extreme shoulders you can wear on your coats and the more extraordinary your accessories, furs and all your effect may be?"

OCTOBER 1944
PHOTOGRAPHED BY MARTIN MUNKÁCSI

When Vreeland joined *Vogue* in 1962, she became fascinated by the jet plane. Here, the significant role women played to keep the American economy running during the war and the realities of the war's end are depicted.

STYLE WAS A STANDARD. DIDN'T HURT ANYONE...

BUT YOU GOTTA HAVE STYLE. IT <u>HELPS YOU</u> GET DOWN

THE STAIRS. IT HELPS YOU GET UP <u>IN THE MORNING</u>.

IT'S A WAY OF LIFE. WITHOUT IT YOU'RE NOBODY. I'M NOT

TALKING ABOUT <u>LOTS OF CLOTHES</u>.

PREVIOUS SPREAD
FEBRUARY 1945
PHOTOGRAPHED BY LOUISE DAHL-WOLFE

Here, Vreeland's love of color is matched by Louise Dahl-Wolfe's magical ability to capture it. Of her collaborator, Vreeland said, "Louise was passionate, more ignited by her métier than anyone I have ever known. She was a great experimenter—but once her decision was made she was very positive. She was one of the first to use daylight lighting for fashion photography, a pioneer in color and daylight. She was great to work with—she always had a contagious spirit."

OPPOSITE PAGE
JUNE 1946
PHOTOGRAPHED BY LOUISE DAHL-WOLFE

ABOVE
MARCH 1945
PHOTOGRAPHED BY LOUISE DAHL-WOLFE

RICHARD AVEDON SPOKE AT DIANA VREELAND'S MEMORIAL SERVICE

AT THE METROPOLITAN MUSEUM OF ART IN 1989.

We met at *Harper's Bazaar* in 1945. Diana Vreeland was the fashion editor. Carmel Snow, the editor in chief, had sent me to meet her for my first assignment. I was twenty-two. My time at the merchant marine was over. The goal of my life had been to photograph for *Harper's Bazaar*.

Mrs. Vreeland had a long narrow office—at the far end was a gothic-looking model in a gothic, stiff wedding dress. I was standing in the doorway. Mrs. Vreeland never looked at me. She cried, "Baron!" Beside her stood Baron de Gunzburg, the only male fashion editor in the world—a pincushion hanging like a *Croix de guerre* from his throat, from a ribbon at his throat—and she cried, "Baron," and she stared straight at the gothic girl and the gothic wedding gown, and she cried, "Baron, the pins!" She took one pin and walked, swinging her hips, down the narrow office to the end. She stuck the pin not only into the dress but into the girl, who let out a little scream. Diana returned to her desk and looked up at me for the first time and said "Aberdeen, Aberdeen, doesn't it make you want to cry?" Well, it did. I went back to Carmel Snow and said, "I can't work with that woman. She calls me Aberdeen," and Carmel Snow said to me, "You are going to work with her," and I did, to my enormous benefit, for almost forty years.

It soon became clear to me that the photographers were there for her, as everyone else was, only to put into action the amazing gallop of her imagination. She didn't like being inspired by anyone alive; her references were always to the past, to the sphinxes of the early nineteenth century, to the intonation of Utomara's throats. She was not interested in photographers' imaginations, not Louise Dahl-Wolfe's, not Huene's—certainly not mine.

She didn't report on fashion. Designers had to follow her, the fashionable world had to follow her. I once heard her say in a moment of frustration, "I know what they are going to wear before they wear it, what they are going to eat before they eat it, and I know where they are going before it is even there."

She willed us to see her as she wanted to be seen, but what she presented was not who she was. Diana preferred to be perceived as frivolous: Lillian Hellman once said to me, "I met your friend Diana Vreeland last night. I think she was wearing two dresses." Well, of course she was! In fact, Diana had a sense of humor so large, so generous, she was ever ready to make a joke of herself, and if she could have, that night, she would have worn three dresses at the same time.

Diana worked like a dog; she did not want to be perceived that way, but she was, without exception, the hardest working person I've ever known. She worked harder and in more detail and more precisely than she would ever want anyone to ever know. But I worked with her from 1945 into the 1980s, all the years of her strength, and unrelenting rigor—combined with those unexpected Vreeland eyes that gave the lie to her baritone falsetto. I am here as witness. Diana lived for imagination ruled by discipline, and created a totally new profession. Vreeland invented the fashion editor. Before her, it was society ladies who put hats on other society ladies! Now it is promotion ladies who compete with other promotion ladies. No one has equaled her—not nearly. And the form has died with her.

It is just staggering how lost her standards are to the fashion world. She has shown us the perfect surface of things as an adventure and made us know the full impact of what is lost.

Farewell, dear Vreeland, from your Aberdeen.

Richard Avedon, speech at Diana Vreeland's memorial at the Metropolitan Museum of Art, November 6, 1989

OPPOSITE PAGE
**DIANA VREELAND, DOVIMA, AND RICHARD AVEDON,
HAIR BY ENRICO CARUSO, NEW YORK, JULY 1955**

FOLLOWING SPREAD
JANUARY 1947, JUNE 1951
PHOTOGRAPHED BY RICHARD AVEDON

Harper's **BAZAAR**

January 1947

Harper's

BAZAAR

Incorporating Junior Bazaar

Summer Travel
Summer Fashions

June 1951

60 cents
65 cents in Canada

A NEW PERSPECTIVE FOR FALL

• In the foreground, a two-piece
flannel suit in classical gray,
which we back as one of the three big young
colors of the year. The silvery-buttoned
jacket is belted in the back,
the eight-gored skirt is flared out to take
the miles in its stride. In Winthrop flannel,
about $30. Ciro, at Saks Fifth Avenue;
Julius Garfinckel, Washington.
Sally Victor hat of glass green felt.
Shoes by Sandler of Boston.
• In the background, a blacky-gray herringbone
tweed dress-and-topper to carry you right through the fall.
The dress has a red jersey turtle-neck top
for a surprise. Dress, about $40;
topper, about $55. Izod of London, at Jay Thorpe;
Hudson's, Detroit; The Blum Store, Philadelphia.
Bags by Leather Masters, Daniel Hays gloves.

AUGUST 1946
PHOTOGRAPHED BY RONNY JAQUES

OPPOSITE PAGE
SEPTEMBER 1945
PHOTOGRAPHED BY GEORGE HOYNINGEN-HUENE

VREELAND'S <u>LOOK AND STYLE</u> DICTATED THE LOOK OF THE MAGAZINE.

TO HER, STYLE MEANT "THERE'S GOT TO BE A MIND AND <u>A DREAM</u> BEHIND IT.

PEOPLE NEVER GIVE UP STYLE—IT'S FROM THE CRADLE TO THE GRAVE—IT'S <u>INNATE</u>."

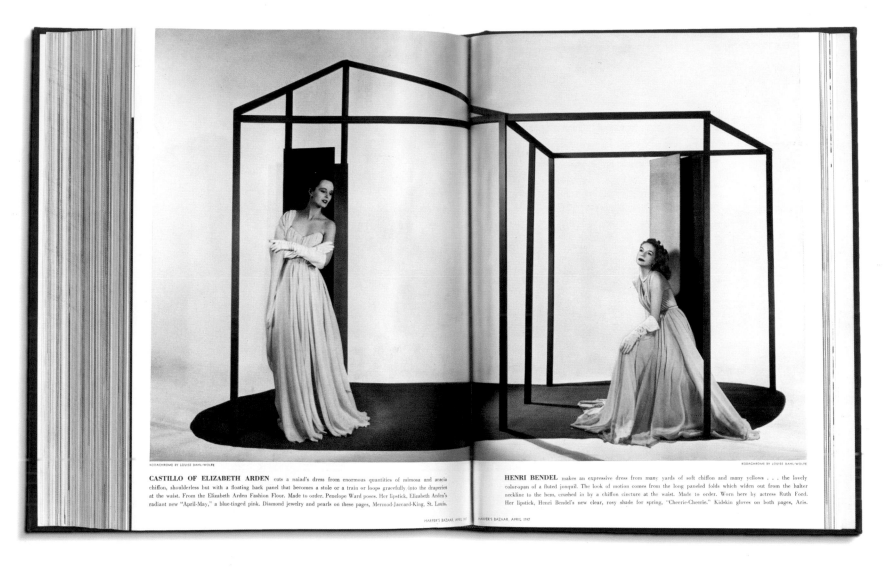

CASTILLO OF ELIZABETH ARDEN cuts a naiad's dress from enormous quantities of mimosa and acacia chiffon, shoulderless but with a floating back panel that becomes a stole or a train or loops gracefully into the draperies at the waist. From the Elizabeth Arden Fashion Floor. Made to order. Penelope Ward poses. Her lipstick, Elizabeth Arden's radiant new "April-May," a blue-tinged pink. Diamond jewelry and pearls on these pages, Mermod-Jaccard-King, St. Louis.

HENRI BENDEL makes an expressive dress from many yards of soft chiffon and many yellows . . . the lovely color-span of a fluted jonquil. The look of motion comes from the long paneled folds which widen out from the halter neckline to the hem, crushed in by a chiffon cincture at the waist. Made to order. Worn here by actress Ruth Ford. Her lipstick, Henri Bendel's new clear, rosy shade for spring, "Cheerie-Cheerie." Kidskin gloves on both pages, Aris.

ABOVE
APRIL 1947
PHOTOGRAPHED BY LOUISE DAHL-WOLFE

"There's nothing more boring than narcissism—the tragedy of being totally... me. We're all capable of it. And we all know examples of it—these beautiful tragedies. Many of them, of course, are mannequins. Mannequins are either divine—or they're the most boring girls in the world."

MARCH 1947
PHOTOGRAPHED BY LOUISE DAHL-WOLFE

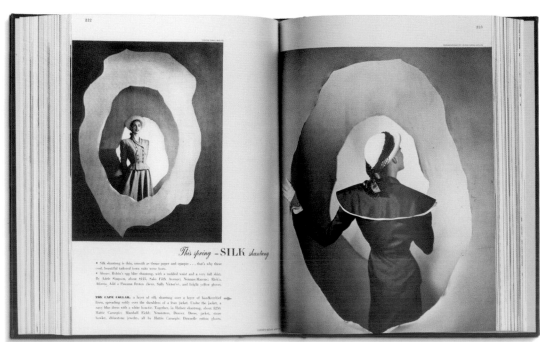

WE'D NEVER SEEN SUCH <u>EXPOSURE</u> OF SKIN,

AND SHE SAID, "WITH AN <u>ATTITUDE</u> LIKE THAT, YOU KEEP

<u>CIVILIZATION</u> BACK [A] THOUSAND YEARS."

MAY 1947
PHOTOGRAPHED BY TONI FRISSELL

After spotting this bikini on a trip to the French Riviera, Vreeland commissioned a copy of the suit for *Bazaar*—the first bikini to be shown in a magazine. Barbara Slifka, an assistant to Vreeland and later a fashion editor at *Bazaar*, remembered the arrival of the suit: "Well, there was a moment when she had the first bikini, and she put it on [the] model and we were all in her office and we were all dazed, you know, we'd never seen such exposure of skin, and she said 'With an attitude like that, you keep civilization back [a] thousand years.' And you know, that's making you open your eyes a little more."

NOW BRODOVITCH WAS THE TUTOR OF THE ALL

THESE PEOPLE OF *HARPER'S BAZAAR* OF LAYOUT, AND MANY

OF THEM HAD GONE TO HIS CLASSES AT NIGHT. HE

WAS A VERY REMARKABLE MAN, HE LOVED HIS WHITE SPACE,

HE LOVED EMPTY PAGES—OH, HE COULDN'T STAND ME.

I MEAN, I WANTED, OF COURSE, TO PUT IN AS MUCH AS

POSSIBLE. I ONLY WANTED FASHION.

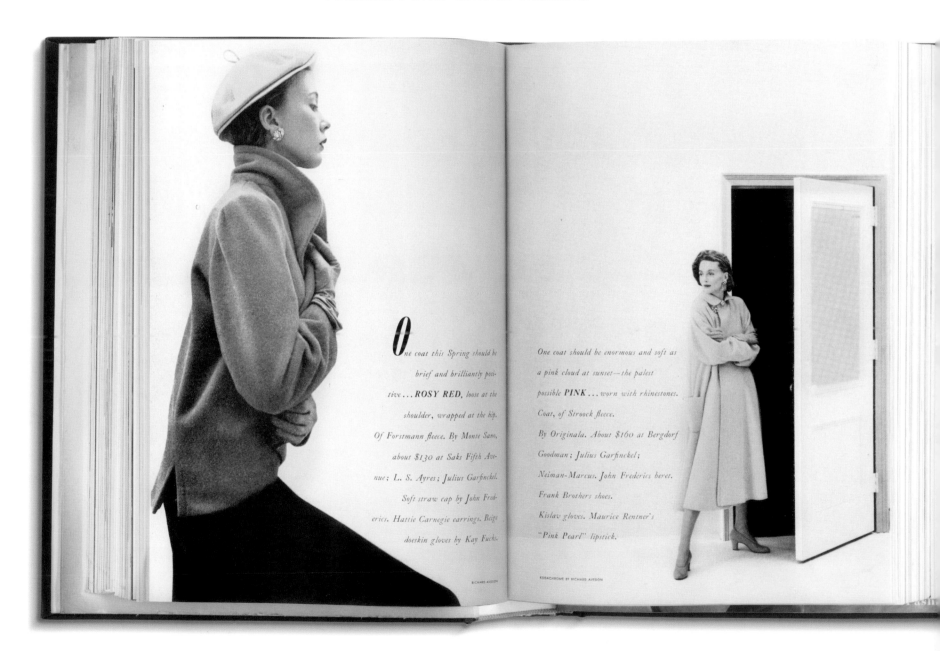

FEBRUARY 1948
PHOTOGRAPHED BY RICHARD AVEDON

Avedon began attending Alexey Brodovitch's design classes soon after he began working for the influential designer at *Bazaar*. From the outset, Avedon's artistic evolution was indebted to Brodovitch's spare, minimalist designs. Vreeland admired Brodovitch but was determined to have her way.

PAS DE TROIS

Butterfly dresses of imported Swiss organdie, strewn with appliquéd broderots and embroidered folds of flowers. Faithfully following their lines—silk taffeta underpowers of buttercup yellow and cotton-candy pink that echo tightly bound sashes with flyaway bows, gold-piped taffeta slippers: Traina-Norell, Yellow dress, Lord and Taylor; I. Magnin. Pink dress, Benoit Tuliet; Julius Garfinckel; Woolf Brothers, Kansas City. All shoes, Van Acker.

• Embroidered coin dots scattered on a blue butterfly dress. The white Swiss organdie is cut away low at the neck, showing a straight band of taffeta. Dress, Traina-Norell; At Lord and Taylor; L. S. Ayres; Frost Brothers, San Antonio. All the roomy kid gloves, flowers in the hair, pearl and rhinestone chokers, dewdrop rhinestone earrings: Traina-Norell. The romantic coiffure, by Charles Bock. Glowing "Pretty Pink" lipstick, by Marchabelli.

ACHROME AND PHOTOGRAPHY BY RICHARD AVEDON

CHEESE DREAMS

• Sampled on these pages—the delicious new cheese colors. Two pale cheese-tinted wool dinner dresses. Against their mat surface . . . the furry depth of an ocelot bag (note: bright fur bags for spring) . . . the polished sheen of blond satin slippers . . . a big evening coat of deep cheddar-cheese faille.
• Specifically—Eyelet dress of Forstmann wool by Jo Copeland. About $155. Saks Fifth Avenue; Harzfeld's. Ocelot bag, $35.* At Thea. Cheese-colored beads, by Marvella, $10.* Lord and Taylor. Coat by Ceil Chapman, about $85. Bergdorf Goodman; I. Magnin.

← Opposite: Pale cheese-colored Miron worsted flannel dress, the Bazaar's choice for the March of Dimes Fashion Show. By Claire McCardell. About $60. Lord and Taylor; L. S. Ayres; Seidenbach's, Tulsa. Ankle-strap pumps by Julianelli. Amber-colored beads, Castlecliff. Nylon stockings by Mary Gray. Pale Polara gloves, Frances Denney's warm "Coral" lipstick.

ANYONE WHO'S AFRAID AND DOES NOT <u>SEARCH AND</u>
<u>GIVE</u> AS MUCH AS POSSIBLE TO <u>THE WORLD</u> OF <u>PLEASURE</u> IS A
TOTALLY IGNORANT PERSON. WE WERE PUT HERE FOR THE
JOY OF IT, <u>FOR THE HELL OF IT</u>, AND IT'S ALL HERE NOW; NOTH-
ING HAS BEEN TAKEN AWAY. IT'S A QUESTION OF CREATING IT.

The two-tone dinner dress, in shades of mauve anemones—a pale silk faille bodice, a floor-length skirt of Bianchini's deep purple silk chiffon. An Henri Bendel original. Jewels, by Verdura. Anita Colby poses.

The two-color party dress, in bands of white organdie and electric blue lace, lit from top to toe by sprinkles and embroidered sprays of bright blue paillettes. It is worn by Mary Martin, star of the new Rodgers and Hammerstein musical, *South Pacific*. The dress, from the Salon Moderne at Saks Fifth Avenue. Jewels, by Van Cleef and Arpels. Miss Martin's "Fledgling" coiffure, by Antoine of Saks Fifth Avenue.

APRIL 1949
PHOTOGRAPHED BY RICHARD AVEDON

Molded silk chiffon, mounted on heavy net—
a chiffon drapery across the bosom,
and several hooped, looped
panels giving sway to the skirt.
The color, purest orchid.
From the Bonwit Teller Custom-Made Salon, in Bianchini chiffon.

MADE TO ORDER IN AMERICA

Beginning six pages on the American dressmakers:

Polished tailoring, in navy blue Rodier wool jersey with white
pin dots and white point-ups—buttons, boutonniere, revers and gloves of heavy
chalky piqué. Suit, designed by Leslie Morris, made
to order at Bergdorf Goodman, meant to be worn with Bergdorf Goodman's
neat cap and crisp "Number Nine" perfume. The steel and canvas
chair used throughout these pages, by Ferrari Hardoy, at Knoll Associates.

The tailored décolletage, opposite, a new note in a suit of sharp-woven gray wool. The jacket is
double-breasted, with big news in the low round neckline filled in with a Regency
beau's silk stock stuck with two fresh flowers. The scarf is red and white
surah, the bag black calf. The face is held in a mesh veil under a small
dark blue Milan straw hat. All, custom-made by Hattie Carnegie.

Infanta hips, below, in a beautiful floor-length evening dress of pure silk taffeta,
in changing shades of faded rose. It has horizontal tucks across
the bodice, and a skirt flat in front and back, with big
fullness at the sides. A Jay Thorpe original. Jewels, by Van Cleef and Arpels.

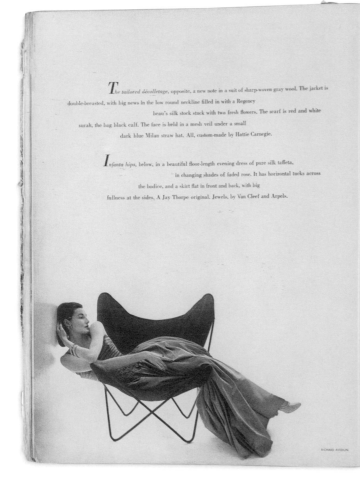

"DIANA LIVED FOR IMAGINATION RULED BY
DISCIPLINE, AND CREATED A TOTALLY NEW PROFESSION.
VREELAND INVENTED THE FASHION EDITOR."

—RICHARD AVEDON,
FROM HIS SPEECH AT DIANA VREELAND'S MEMORIAL SERVICE

ABOVE
MAY 1949

LEFT
FEBRUARY 1948

OPPOSITE PAGE
APRIL 1950
ALL PHOTOGRAPHED BY
RICHARD AVEDON

Harper's

BAZAAR

Incorporating Junior Bazaar

April 1950

BEAUTY

60 cents

65 cents in Canada

116

Take an Idea from Africa

● Take a little beach shirt with a herd of embroidered elephants. Take a jungle-colored bathing suit, a straw bathing suit, swimming trunks pied all over with African daisies, swimming bloomers with a thicket of strange leaves, Zulu necklaces—black, white and thick all over—souvenirs of American designer Carolyn Schnurer's flying (B.O.A.C.) trip to the Gold Coast of Africa. A newly discovered gold mine for the beach, these bathing suits are the easiest way to get in and out of the water, these playing clothes are extremely simple in design, both made more fun with zip imported from another continent.

HARPER'S BAZAAR, DECEMBER 1952

117

LOUISE DAHL-WOLFE

DECEMBER 1952
PHOTOGRAPHED BY
LOUISE DAHL-WOLFE

Louise Dahl-Wolfe said of Vreeland, "Fashion editors are of great importance before the photographing begins. If they have an eye for color, style, form, taste and individuality, they can pull together a ready-made dress in no time at all. Very few of them have the outstanding creativity of Diana Vreeland. She was tops on a sitting. You would be given a dress to do and you had to make a picture. Diana helped brighten up the dress, and her eye would come to the rescue. She'd always produce something, like the addition of a scarf, to help liven up your photograph.

• Opposite: Those elephants, on a shiny white cotton shirt that bulks and juts out over black embroidered black cotton shorts that couldn't be much shorter. In Ameritex Everglaze fabric, about $28. Those heavy Zulu necklaces and bracelets by Accessocraft.
• Above: That green—a bathing suit of stinging green from the jungle, the color of an African pear. On the elastic waistband, a parade of beaded elephants. In J. P. Stevens Everglaze, about $28. Both suits at Peck and Peck; Joseph Magnin. The leather sandals on both pages, Bernardo, $14.95 at Peck and Peck. The rug, from the Afro-Arts Bazaar.

174

175

LILLIAN BASSMAN

A Gallery of Contemporaries—Suits and Small Coats

• The straight, close suit, this spring's most
engaging newcomer, in Cobb and Jenkins
sand-grained English tweed.
By Rothmoor. $79.95.
Frederick and Nelson. Ronay calf portfolio.

• The straight suit in grained gray British
tweed, with an even countenance for
in town or afield. By Rosenblum
of California. About $60. Altman;
May Company, Los Angeles. Bucket bag, Josef.

• The small coat, good in city reference or
country frame. By Baitch and Castaldi,
in Einiger beige fleece. About $65.
Russeks; Strawbridge and Clothier.
Lean brown wool skirt, by Evan-Picone.

• The short coat to wrap or button, in Stroock
yellow fleece—wonderful with a beige skirt.
By Harry Williams. About $70. Lord
and Taylor; L. S. Ayres. All shoes, by I. Miller.
Stockings on both pages, Shaleen.

HARPER'S BAZAAR, FEBRUARY 1953   HARPER'S BAZAAR, FEBRUARY 1953

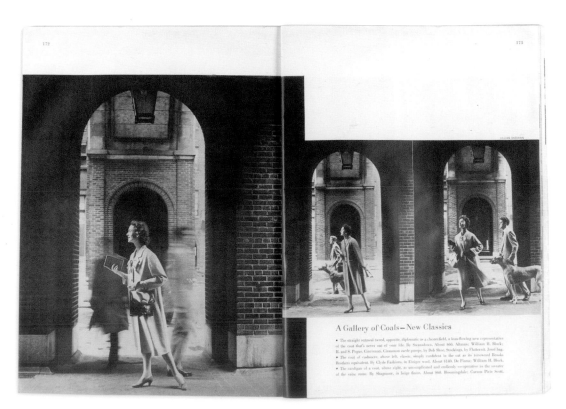

A Gallery of Coats—New Classics

FEBRUARY 1953
PHOTOGRAPHED BY LILLIAN BASSMAN

Lillian Bassman's fashion photography was by no means
traditional; she benefited from her classes with Brodovitch
at the New School: "Brodovitch's whole theory and the
way he taught, was… 'Why have bacon and eggs everyday for breakfast?' He really believed that one should experiment, try, work for something that didn't exist, that you
could find in yourself, and push for it. It's how he taught the
class—'Don't be satisfied with your first answer, work on it
and find something, some new way to say something that
had been said a thousand times.'"

STYLE: ALL WHO HAVE IT SHARE ONE THING—ORIGINALITY.

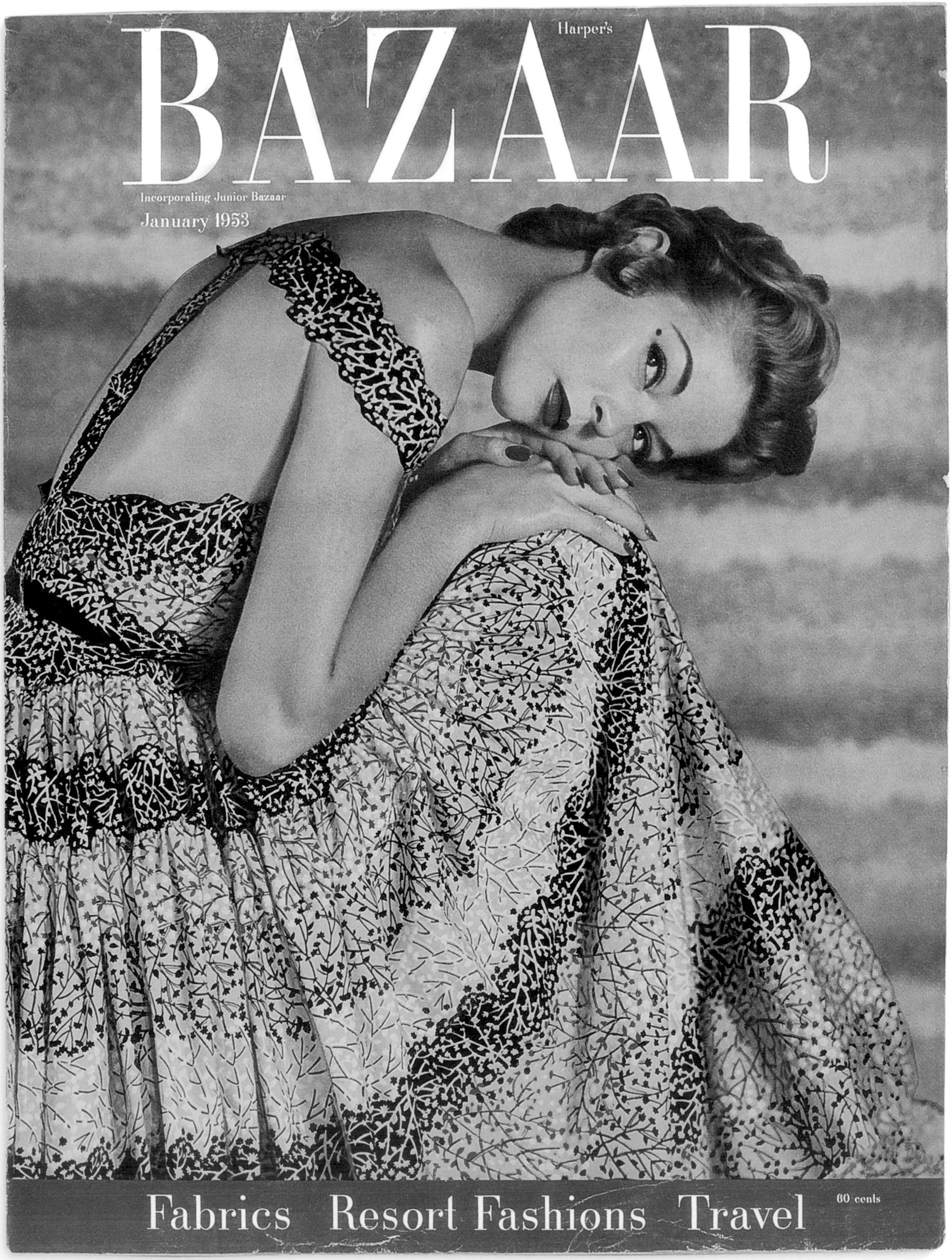

Harper's

BAZAAR

Incorporating Junior Bazaar

January 1953

Fabrics Resort Fashions Travel

60 cents

**OPPOSITE PAGE
JANUARY 1953
PHOTOGRAPHED BY LOUISE DAHL-WOLFE**

**MARCH 1953
PHOTOGRAPHED BY LOUISE DAHL-WOLFE**

Bettina Ballard, like many fashion editors and aficionados, felt that, "Fashion is something that Diana Vreeland believes enters into everything in life: the way one walks, talks, lives, breathes, eats and thinks—and certainly the way one loves as well as what one wears. She carries this belief into her editing. She had created a fashion look, a fashion identity of her own, long ago, emulated by many young neophytes in the business, a look colored by imagination and eccentricity."

Pongee, the Original Natural.

Rough Silk in Cocoa Colors.

Mink Fold-Ons— The Pale, the Deep

• Mink that slips over or folds around the shoulders . . . and makes just the right depth of "coat" for spring evenings; mink in a pale, shadowed beige or a deep dark luster, the choice to be cast by your own skin and hair colorings.
• Opposite: Great Lakes dark mink in a narrowing stole to fold around you and loop like a fichu, in front or in back. At Revillon Frères. Scent it with "4 Vents." Revillon's warm, spring-smelling perfume. Pale suede gloves, by Kislav.
• Above: A bolero stole in Umpa Starlight mink, with little sleeves to push your arms through as you wrap in its tawny paleness. By Maximilian, at Holt Renfrew of Canada. Long, pale beige doeskin gloves, by Viola Weinberger.

212

213

DERUJINSKY

Black and White
In New Laminations

• Bared-shoulder diabolo (opposite, far left). Heavy,
shining white satin, spiraled with a tasseled
mesh of glittery jet beads. The line and the lights
of it benefiting from the new longer-
than-daytime grace. By Jo Copeland, in Bianchini satin.
About $395. Saks Fifth Avenue; Harzfeld's.
Rhinestone freshet earrings, Castlecliff.
White satin sandal-pumps by Evins.
• White lace over laminations of black net and taffeta
(left). A dress cascading all the way,
to the lengths of dressing-for-an-evening that occur more
and more often in American lives. Black velvet
crosses the bodice, rushes down toward the hem.
By Will Steinman, in Stern and Stern lace. About $100.
Best's; Joseph Magnin. Earrings by Vogue.
• Black cashmere sweater, lace skirt (right).
A soft, clinging blackness, now incorporated into
an evening look. Slashed with lace;
the skirt, a diabolo cone of corded French lace
over beige chiffon. Sophie Originals, ready to wear.
Saks Fifth Avenue. $395. La Tausca earrings.

BAZAAR SEPTEMBER 1953

SEPTEMBER 1953
PHOTOGRAPHED BY GLEB DERUJINSKY

SHE MADE <u>THE LOOK</u>, BRODOVITCH MADE THOSE
PORTRAITS OF LOOK <u>FLOW THROUGH</u> THE BOOK, SNOW TOOK
CARE OF UPSTAIRS AND <u>SEVENTH AVENUE</u>.

210

211

DERUJINSKY

Black, Lustered and Longer

• The blown-back line (left), dominating evening movement
of this year, in the midnight sheen of black
silk barathea. A diamond neckline; a skirt straight as
a column when you walk into a room—wings of flying
fullness to follow you. There's a little jacket
that covers to the waist. By Branell. About $135.
Bloomingdale; Strawbridge and Clothier; Woolf Brothers,
Kansas City. Pearly suspension earrings by Coro.
• The diabolo line (opposite). A cone, wide at the
shoulders, spun fine and taut through the
waist, spreading out again into the
new proportions of lengthened evening skirts.
• Right, the carbon smoothness of black gros de Londres
cut with an unseamed princesse smoothness.
By Adele Simpson, in William Rose silk. About $125.
Saks Fifth Avenue; Julius Garfinckel. Mosell earrings.
• Far right, black satin, pulled widely across
from the back, plastered with a bow.
By Larry Aldrich, in William Rose silk satin. About $95.
De Pinna; The Blum Store, Philadelphia.
Kramer earrings. Sandals on both pages by Julianelli.
All stockings by Holeproof. Essence of flowers to
color all shades of black. Le Galion's "Sortilège" perfume.

HARPER'S BAZAAR, SEPTEMBER P

Beautie

Photograp

> • *That whic*
> *as transitor*
> *difficult, dis*
> *On these pa*
> *feeling we h*
> *This is not*
> *within the*
> *some artific*
> *contemplatio*
> *paragraph j*

"Woman is absolutely right, and eve
and supernatural; it is her duty to
herself to be worshiped. She must th
nature in order the better to subjuga
the ruse and the artifice are known to
The use of powder, which has been so
only this object and result: to remov
by nature, and to create an abstract
which, like that produced by the chis
that is to say, to a divine and superio
and the rouge which marks the upper
the same principle, from the desire to
opposite desire. The rouge and black
the black frame makes the eye look do
window opened upon the infinite; the
still further increases the light of the
mysterious passion of a priestess. Thu
be used for the vulgar unacknowledge
rivaling youth. Besides, observation
service to beauty. Who would dare to
Make-up has no need to hide itself:
at least with a kind of frankness. Thos
searching for the Beautiful even in its
reflections; I shall content myself wit
who were given at birth a spark of the h

Signora Gianni Agnelli, the former Marella
of a tightly drawn out, linear classicism; her extraordinary
colorless looks borne out on the intensely personal atmos

PER'S BAZAAR, APRIL 1954

**APRIL 1954
PHOTOGRAPHED BY RICHARD AVEDON**

The elegance of these images—captured by Richard
Avedon—embodied the classic swanlike beauty of the
fifties. Marella Agnelli, a close friend of Vreeland's, has
always considered this one of her favorite portraits.

105

# of Our Time

Richard Avedon

ften call Beauty is a variable standard, dictated by ideas
hort-lived as today. Beauty is more than this: it is an ideal—
nfathomable—and we would not have it otherwise.
six very dissimilar beauties, who illuminate the
ut this eternal riddle. Here is Beauty as an achievement.
rily something one is born with; it is something created
d for most women, there is a mystical privilege to employ
d this achievement, to be worthy of another's
rivilege championed, with poetic logic, in the following
rles Baudelaire's essay "In Praise of Paint and Powder."

rms a kind of duty, if she applies herself to appearing magical
nd cause wonder. Being an idol, she should gild
w from all the arts the means to raise herself above
art and strike the spirit. It matters very little that
heir success is sure and their effect always irresistible....
nly anathematized by the candid philosophers, has
the complexion all the blemishes outrageously cast over it
n the texture and color of the skin, a unity
nediately approaches the human being to the statue,
g. As regards the artificial black which borders the eye,
f the cheek, although their use is derived from
s nature, the result is of a kind to satisfy an altogether
ent life—a supernatural and excessive life;
d stranger, and gives it a more decided appearance of a
, which sets the cheekbone on fire,
and adds to a beautiful feminine face the
u understand me properly, the painting of the face should not
ject of imitating beautiful nature or of
that artifice does not beautify ugliness and can only be of
to art the sterile function of imitating nature?
on the contrary, expose itself, if not with affectation,
are prevented by their heavy seriousness from
est manifestations have my ready permission to laugh at my
aling to real artists, as well as to those women
with which they would like to be altogether illuminated."

   —from *Constantin Guys, the Painter of Victorian Life*, trans-
   lated by P. G. Konody, published by The Studio Ltd., London.

rciolo; hers, a dark Italian beauty

vagantly

she creates for herself.

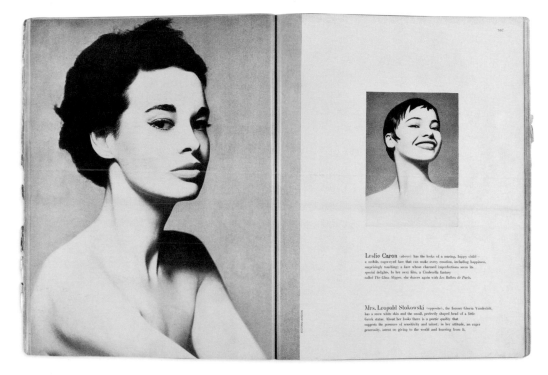

Leslie Caron (above) has the looks of a musing, happy child—
a mobile, expressive face that can make every emotion, including happiness,
surprisingly touching; a face whose charmed imperfections seem its
special delights. In her next film, a Cinderella fantasy
called *The Glass Slipper*, she dances again with *Les Ballets de Paris*.

Mrs. Leopold Stokowski (opposite), the former Gloria Vanderbilt,
has a more white skin and the small, perfectly shaped head of a little
Greek statue. About her looks there is a poetic quality that
suggests the presence of sensitivity and talent; in her attitude, an eager
generosity, intent in giving to the world and learning from it.

Contessa Madina Arrivabene (above) moves
in an aura of the complete romantic, has the romantic looks of the
fair Venetian. Her blond and silver hair floats carelessly about
an oval face poised on a long white neck; she is living
proof of Sir Francis Bacon's famous observation, "There is no
beauty which hath not some strangeness in its proportions."

Miss Dolores von Fürstenberg (opposite)
has already, at seventeen, the long bones, the assured look of a
great beauty; and in her manner a certain youthful
stillness, a look of inquiry, tentative, waiting. She is the
daughter of Mrs. Loel Guinness, herself a classic, dark-eyed
Latin beauty, and Count Franz Egon von Fürstenberg.

HARPER'S BAZAAR, APRIL 1955

$160

Foxy Black
Cashmere Cardigan

$99

Lean Black
Cardigan Suit

$40

Blue-Flowered
Shirtwaist Dress

$25

Dotted Tangerine
Shirtwaist Dress

FEBRUARY 1955
PHOTOGRAPHED BY RICHARD AVEDON

*"What the magazines gave was a point of view. Most
people haven't got a point of view; they need to have it
given to them—and what's more, they expect it from you."*

$70

$55

Print Dress,
Print-Lined Coat

Golden Mesh
Sweater Dress

$55

$125

Cardigan Suit,
Minimized Tailoring

Short-Sleeved Jacket
and Dress

The Vicomtesse de Ribes,
whose almond-eyed Renaissance
beauty conquered New York this winter,
lives with her husband and two
little children in Paris, where she
devotes herself to a major
charity event, Le Bénéfice de l'Essor.

APRIL 1956
PHOTOGRAPHED BY RICHARD AVEDON

Jacqueline de Ribes and Diana Vreeland shared a passion for couture. After they met, Jacqueline was asked to pose for this photograph for Richard Avedon. She recalled working with Vreeland that day: "She taught me that day to be very self-confident, and she told me something very important: 'Whatever you are going to decide for yourself is going to be the right thing. Don't get influenced.'"

Mrs. E. Haring Chandor

has the clear-featured handsomeness
of the ideal American beauty.
She lives in New York, where, this
spring, she is serving on the committee
for the Heart Fund's "Heart of
America" ball at the Ambassador Hotel.

RICHARD AVEDON

SHE LOVED THE AVANT-GARDE, BUT BENEATH IT
ALL SHE WAS VERY OLD-FASHIONED IN THE BEST SENSE.
SHE HAD THE GRAND MANNER AND ALL THE MARVELOUS
MANNERS. SHE LOVED FUN AND SHE LOVED YOUNG PEOPLE
BUT PROBABLY NOT AS MUCH AS THEY LOVED HER.

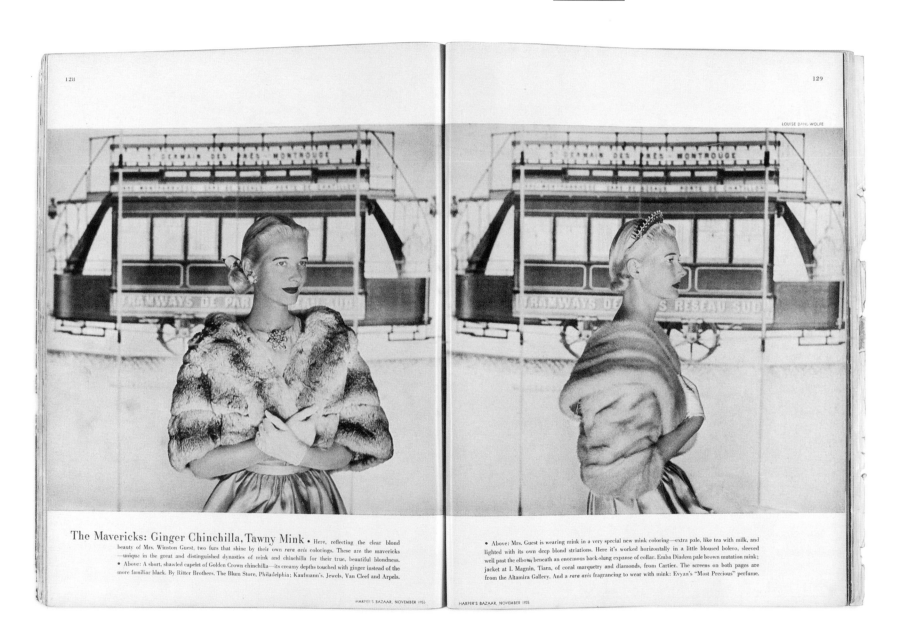

128

129

LOUISE DAHL-WOLFE

The Mavericks: Ginger Chinchilla, Tawny Mink • Here, reflecting the clear blond beauty of Mrs. Winston Guest, two furs that shine by their own *rara avis* colorings. These are the mavericks—unique in the great and distinguished dynasties of mink and chinchilla for their true, beautiful blondness.
• Above: A short, shawled capelet of Golden Crown chinchilla—its creamy depths touched with ginger instead of the more familiar black. By Ritter Brothers. The Blum Store, Philadelphia; Kaufmann's. Jewels, Van Cleef and Arpels.

HARPER'S BAZAAR, NOVEMBER 1955

• Above: Mrs. Guest is wearing mink in a very special new mink coloring—extra pale, like tea with milk, and lighted with its own deep blond striations. Here it's worked horizontally in a little bloused bolero, sleeved well past the elbow, beneath an enormous back-slung expanse of collar. Emba Diadem pale brown mutation mink; jacket at I. Magnin. Tiara, of coral marquetry and diamonds, from Cartier. The screens on both pages are from the Altamira Gallery. And a *rara avis* fragrancing to wear with mink: Evyan's "Most Precious" perfume.

HARPER'S BAZAAR, NOVEMBER 1955

NOVEMBER 1955
PHOTOGRAPHED BY LOUISE DAHL-WOLFE

Vreeland's friends were an extraordinary mix of family and society. She was always able to put them in the pages of her magazines. C. Z. Guest was no exception.

**RIGHT
OCTOBER 1956
PHOTOGRAPHED BY LILLIAN BASSMAN**

**BELOW
JANUARY 1956
PHOTOGRAPHED BY LILLIAN BASSMAN**

Lillian Bassman recalls: "Mrs. Vreeland was not only responsible for the fashion look of the magazine but, I think, for fashion of the time. She was very influential with the designers, very important in their choice of color, of mood. I would say, from a fashion point of view, *Bazaar* was a complete reflection of her taste."

Cosmetic Color: Vibrant Violet

• Opposite: Vibrant violet, new radiant-complexion lighting, applied here to a wand-slim chemise dress that descends in a narrowing line from a cowl collar and a back-plunging décolletage. By Grenelle-Estevez, in Oriental Textiles raw silk. About $70. Miss Bergdorf of Bergdorf Goodman; Dayton's, Minneapolis; Joseph Magnin. Hat by Lilly Daché; Kayser's "Plaza Pink" stockings.
• Above: The irradiating glow of a violet linen suit, cut along straight lines, is heightened by a white silk damask shirt. Suit (by Harry Frechtel, in Moygashel Irish linen, about $90) and shirt (by Mayehoff) at Lord and Taylor. Suit, also at Montaldo's; I. Magnin. Mr. John hat. Extra lighting effects, both pages: Tiffany jewels; Charles of the Ritz "Moss Rose" lipstick.

HARPER'S BAZAAR, APRIL 1958

Cosmetic Color: Mimosa Yellow

• Opposite: Mimosa yellow is a melange with tender porcelain—an effective beauty potion for the woman who combines her fashion with a sprinkling of pure perfection. A double measure, here: one part overblouse, elasticized at the waist; one part easy skirt. By Nelly de Grab, in cotton by Fuller Fabrics. About $23. Miss Bergdorf of Bergdorf Goodman; Burdine's, Miami; Frederick and Nelson, Seattle. Mr. John's mimosa straw hat.
• Right: Mimosa yellow, cap-a-pie—a sleeveless shift in linen; silk drops plumb to a "drawstring" flounce. It's hatted (by Mr. John) in yellow blossoms. Dress by Larry Aldrich. About $95. Bonwit Teller; Harzfeld's, Kansas City; Sakowitz, Houston. "Buttercup" stockings, by Christian Dior; mimosa shoes; Amalfi. "Saucy Red" lipstick by Beauty Counselor, both pages.

HARPER'S BAZAAR, APRIL 1958

**APRIL 1958
PHOTOGRAPHED BY LOUISE DAHL-WOLFE**

Vreeland always loved color: "Violet is a color I really like. But then I like almost every color. I have an eye for color, perhaps the most exceptional gift I have. Color depends entirely on the tonality."

**OPPOSITE PAGE
APRIL 1958
PHOTOGRAPHED BY LOUISE DAHL-WOLFE**

Harper's

BAZAAR

April 1958

Incorporating Junior Bazaar

The Most
Beautiful Time
of Your Life

In This Issue:

Mary McCarthy

E. M. Forster

Joyce Cary

Chef's Salad Diet

60 cents

LIGHTING IS EVERYTHING IN A COLOR. IT'S AFFECTED BY THE WAY THE SUN SHINES IN CERTAIN COUNTRIES, AND THE FARTHER NORTH YOU GO, THE MORE SENSE OF COLOR YOU GET.

THE ULTRA VIOLETS

• Above: Nelly de Grab's wide swath of flecked Strong Honett wool (a mix of violet with green, red, white) may be taken in part (the jacket, about $23, the skirt, about $25, and the beige wool overblouse for about $35), but we prefer the look of the whole, which is about **$63.**
At Bloomingdale's; R. H. Stearns, Boston; Stix, Baer and Fuller, St. Louis.
• Opposite: Townclife fur-shaped magenta travel suit a particularly able exposition of the blouson jacket suit, holds the waistline with elastic.
At Bloomingdale's; Kaufmann's, Pittsburgh; Dayton's, Minneapolis; I. Magnin. About **$80.**
Stockings, Van Raalte. Shoes, I. Miller. Madcaps hats, opposite and above, at Bloomingdale's.

AUGUST 1958
PHOTOGRAPHED BY RICHARD AVEDON

the H B look

• This issue is addressed to the pretty girl, the busy girl, the one who writes her own. She has a *joie-de-vivre* about about the new and untried. We love her because hers to new fashions—she's the of the audacious, imagina

• "Can't" isn't in her brig to wear violets—mauve . . . ravishing colors that haven (Her unerring timing conc that's sweeping the country four-cent stamp replacing gas stations sprouting purp of the *Purple Pe*

• Last spring, sh and stopped traffi she'll look for *sh* changing face of fuzz and fluff an heavenly tweeds, and those fashion amusements, masquerade furs. will have a *dégagé* blown ease, hanging from the or deep yokes, or the rib cage. She's thrown the to the winds. Her violet coat will be collarless (sh a big fringed scarf with the bravado of Zorro), it at the hem. She'll own a leather bucket cap and k sometimes knitted ones, like nannies wear. She'll a violet-checked overblouse and skirt and she'll c a matching lift-boy's cap. She'll have a dress of m its high waistline loosely marked by a drawstring

• Like her coat, everything about her suit will be neckline, shoulders, even the edge of the jacket r never pressed flat. As on the cover, she'll add a h of stiffened fabric like a child's paper cap and a c She'll definitely have some new sweaters: a violet to wear with a lilac mohair skirt, or a wild violet that falls well past her hips and is matched to a l She'll pick her make-up from a field of violets, dip her dark hair in a violet rinse.

• Opposite: Mauve-flecked violet wool, its neckli at the throat, shoulders curved into raglan sleeve a flare to the hem. By Brittany, in Stroock wool. Coat and ponyskin domed cap (a Dachette) at Bl Coat also at Harzfeld's, Kansas City; Dayton's, M I. Magnin. Suede and lizard pumps: Millerkins.

young American woman:
girl on-the-go,
ion rules.
es, a sense of adventure
make her a marvel.
key that opens doors
g
igner.
con. She'll be first
pea . . . wisteria . . . pansy—
seen since the Mauve Decade.
ith the violet wave
ess the ultra-violet
nestic three-center;
ol pumps; the invasion
ers.)
tened her skirts
s fall
nd for the
e
giness,
ed wools
thing she wears
ers,
ained waistline
d
den
gloves,

mohair,
ide belt.
ded:
nder,

se.
ed one
ere
rdigan.

nded

$119.
gdale's.
polis;

RICHARD AVEDON

Leather News: Color, Color, Color

everywhere—starting right this minute, exit the all-black shoe. And enter a whirl of lively leathers ready to start off with this fall's all-clear for bright color in fashion. More to look for: long-haired leathers, touches of patent leather, extension soles, and heels that are not so high and often made of stacked leather. 1. Ruby red—a pump scrolled in black patent leather. By Millerkins, in Davis calfskin. About $22. I. Miller. 2. Bright blue—clear-as-daylight view of the shoe on a black patent leather heel. By De Liso Debs, in Donovan suede. About $20. Bloomingdale's. 3. Autumn leaf gold—warm new coloring for the belted pump. By Degas, in Haus of Krause suede. About $16. Saks Fifth Avenue. 4. Shamrock green—a calfskin pump instep-braceleted and extension-soled. By Fortunet. About $12. Arnold Constable. 5. Sea blue, in a very new, long-brushed suede, makes a stacked-heeled pump. By Customcraft, in Fleming-Joffe suede. About $23. Lord and Taylor. 6. Smoky brown suede—the slender pump bow-tied and heeled in glistening black patent leather. By Gamins. About $20. Andrew Geller. 7. Carmine suede—a pump with a squared-off toe. Heel build-up: stacked leather. By Amalfi. About $17. Lord and Taylor.

HARPER'S BAZAAR, JULY 1958

JULY 1958
ILLUSTRATION BY ANDY WARHOL

Though Vreeland and Andy Warhol became close friends in the 1970s, they had known each other since her days at *Bazaar*, when Warhol would do fashion illustrations for the magazine. Bob Colacello said, "She had, and what Andy also had, if you want to make that comparison, this great sense of curiosity and this great fascination with youth and beauty and beautiful youth. They both really wanted everything to be new, they wanted to be first, they wanted to shock but not in an offensive way."

11 12 13 14 15

16 17 18 19 20

8. Pine green—fresh fashion for the slim pump slicked with black patent leather. By Martinique, in Hubschmann calfskin. About $25. Bloomingdale's. 9. Deep-grape purple calfskin widow-peaked at the instep. By Fiancées. About $13. Arnold Constable. 10. Orange marmalade—that's exactly the color of this pump in wide-grained lizard. By Troylings. About $22. Hudson's, Detroit. 11. Lava brown kidskin and paler suede paired in an open pump, double-buttoned in coral red. By Capezio. About $17. Bonwit Teller. 12. Woodsmoke brown suede with a slim toe dipped in lizard. By Valley. About $21. Best's. 13. Deep crimson suede crisscrossed in lizard. By Mademoiselle, in Harvey suede. About $19. Lord and Taylor. 14. Mossy green—suede bow-collared and piped in calfskin. About $19. From Florsheim. 15. Cognac brown—a smooth calfskin shoe shows its reverse plushy side in back. By Quat- tro. About $15. Stern's. 16. Brown-green suede—a square-toed pump stroked with matching lizard. By Delman- ette. About $23. Miss Bergdorf of Bergdorf Goodman. 17. Rope tan—a buckled Loewenstein calf shoe on a layered heel. By Caprini. About $27. Jay Thorpe. 18. Indigo blue—a suede pump rainbowed in front. By Valentine. About $13. Rich's, Atlanta. 19. Vapor brown calfskin, punched out. By Cellini. About $19. Bonwit Teller. 20. Sharp blue—a squared-off suede pump, cross-strapped and heeled in black patent leather. By Deb. About $13. Altman's.

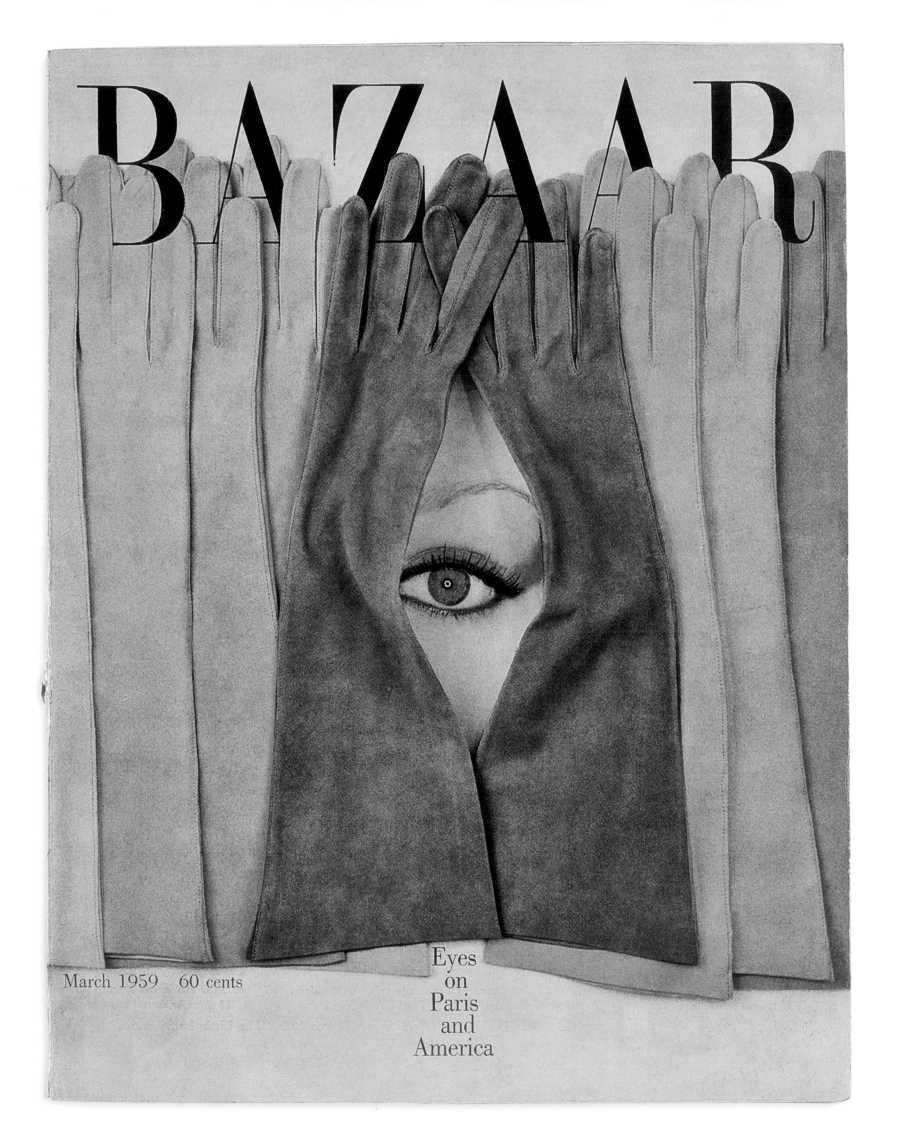

BAZAAR

March 1959   60 cents

Eyes
on
Paris
and
America

THE TINY CANOTIER A boater done on the smallest possible scale with a black silk mesh over-veil that falls to the shoulders. It is blonde Venetian straw bound in red grosgrain. By Chanda. At Lord and Taylor; Hudson's, Detroit; Joseph Magnin. Notice the new point to poise a jewel—on the grosgrain binding. The pin shown is by Schlumberger for Tiffany.

THE DOUBLOON DOTS A large black straw, slip-covered in wonderfully outsize black and white polka dots of polished cotton. There is a high, turret crown bound in black silk grosgrain which makes for arresting balance. From Sally Victor. Also at Marshall Field, Chicago; Famous-Barr, St. Louis. The diamond and pearl ear clips by Schlumberger for Tiffany.

ABOVE
MARCH 1959
PHOTOGRAPHED BY LOUIS FAURER
John Fairchild, the influential owner and editor in chief of Fairchild Publications who transformed *Women's Wear Daily*, remembers Vreeland's significant role at *Bazaar*: "I think her legacy, important legacy, was that she gave some pep and energy and fantasy to fashion. She made it interesting—fashion is a very boring subject."

JUNE 1959
PHOTOGRAPHED BY HIRO

OPPOSITE PAGE
MARCH 1959
PHOTOGRAPHED BY BEN ROSE

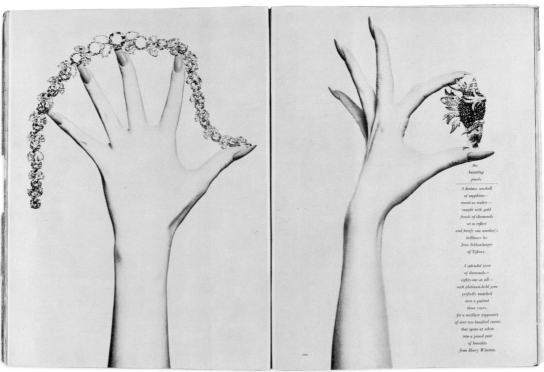

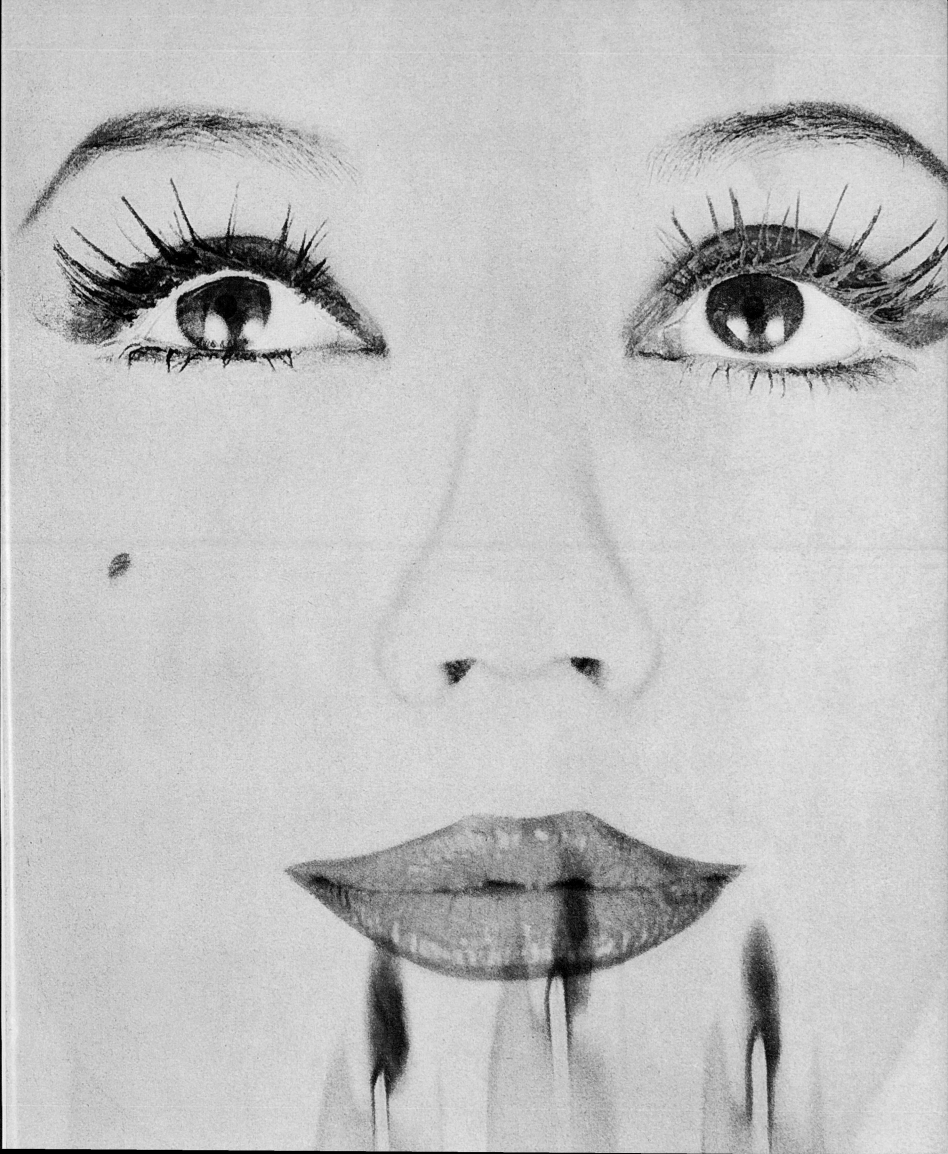

FASHION EVERY DAY OF THE WEEK IS DIFFERENT.

YESTERDAY IS HARDLY TODAY. FASHION IS IN THE DAILY AIR.

THAT MUST BE RECOGNIZED. IT ISN'T A

THING THAT'S CONSTRUCTED AND PROJECTED—IT COMES,

IT KEEPS COMING, IT KEEPS COMING.

PREVIOUS SPREAD
MAY 1959
PHOTOGRAPHED BY BEN ROSE
*"My immediate instinct is to want to blow it up—make it
big! It can't look as if it's been taken out of a silver frame!
You've got to make something out of it!"*

FEBRUARY 1960
PHOTOGRAPHED BY RICHARD AVEDON

OPPOSITE PAGE
FEBRUARY 1960
PHOTOGRAPHED BY RICHARD AVEDON

HARPER'S
BAZAAR

FEBRUARY 1960
60 CENTS

WIDE-EYED
VIEW
OF
FASHIONS
FOR
THE WORLD
OF NOW

ECCENTRICITY:
A MASK
FOR MISERY
BY ANTHONY WEST

Anyway, Bless You *by Sylvia Ashton-Warner*

Alongside this hall I've not asked about I notice a mighty stone church; forbidding gray stone all the way to the highest tip of her spire; rearing above the low earthquake-fearing buildings about her, the only edifice with the faith to grow tall again. I notice the trees about her too, even gardens for some reason, and at her holy feet facing upon the main thoroughfare some picturesque stone seats to match. What a place to build a church—bang in the middle of an idolatrous city with the fumes of industry about her spire, shops, bars and traffic lights about her feet, jukeboxes contesting her bells. Are God and Baal pals in these parts? But don't let me wander; where was I. . . .

It is while I am resting on one of these stone seats this spring evening after hours of music in the hall nearby that I unexpectedly see you.

It must be you, *mon cher*.

For one thing you come out of this church and for another you are dressed as a minister. You come out from the back through some private holy door that people like me never darken. You emerge as casually as anything as though the black of the Cloth and the white clerical collar were the most common of clothes; as though life were the most usual affair.

It's not easy to see you at first what with the lights of the street and the shadows of the trees arguing for possession of you. But I can make out your head set forward, your shoulders broad and your arms and legs too long. Not handsome, not young and no doubt married. What makes the inner music I constantly hear lurch to a halt? There's nothing to my taste about you.

Now is the time to ask you for permission to practice in your hall that I've already been practicing in and get it over and done with. There are you, here am I and beyond the church the hall. What am I wearing for this? The cream coat with the sputnik line and the blue stars at the throat. Will these aid the asking or are ministers immune to Style?

Now why don't I get up and do it? Why don't I stand up right here and now and introduce myself and ask for the use of the hall? I can't go on using a church hall without asking permission. But no, all I do is sit with the inner music profoundly silent. Come on, Germaine, be yourself! Yet here

I remain gazing up from one of your stone seats, not unlike the drunk on the next, as if ministers' were immune to staring also.

Here I pause, though I never pause, while you stroll along the pavement toward me; your eyes brown, I notice, your brow low, your jaw sure and a look of serenity about you; all quite mere and usual. Here I wait on this seat set between God and Mammon, undecided whether to get up or not, until by the time you are abreast of me I am looking up at you so widely that you glance down in my eyes as you pass. "Anyway," you say to me, "bless you."

The next time I run into you is one night, later in the week, when I'm still practicing in your hall; lingering, playing on in the darkness. The spring-afternoon sunlight shafting in has long since given way to the more passionate tones of a sunset. Absorbed in the argument and counter-argument of the concerto, I've forgotten I've arrived in New Zealand and am working in a hall unasked for. I am such oceans and continents distant I don't hear the sound of steps, so that the click of the switch is too sudden and the flash of the light too harsh. What a way to crash in on music! What murder of a master! Are ministers also immune to sound?

Your broad outline in the doorway with your head set forward and your arms and legs too long . . . but I don't hesitate this time, I abandon the keyboard and rise *con brio*. I lower the top of the grand, pull the cover over, swing on my coat, walk across the stage and make my way out the side door and down the steps into the street and along the sidewalk to my car. I should have retreated last time.

But glancing back as I pull out into the traffic I find I have not quite evaded you. I see you standing out on the pavement, feet astride, hands pocketed, head forward and looking after me in a way that makes me sure you are thinking. "Bless you."

People like me are just as likely as not to find themselves going to church on a spring evening, supported by a preliminary cocktail of course . . . actually entering this edifice of stone. It is hardly my natural habitat; it was the very last thing I had in mind when I began (Continued on page 142)

Two-piece dress of frosted brown calmly capsules all you need know about fashion perfection: soft drape of overblouse, its neckline wide and open; slight skirt, sharply pleated; throw of fringed scarf—all, making this *the* new street look. Dress, jewelry, hat, stockings: by Christian Dior-New York. Dress of Rodier wool and rayon. About $235. At Saks Fifth Avenue; Harzfeld's, Kansas City; Neiman-Marcus.

MELVIN SOKOLSKY

AUGUST 1960
PHOTOGRAPHED BY MELVIN SOKOLSKY

Melvin Sokolsky joined *Bazaar* during Henry Wolfe's tenure as art director. He worked with Vreeland for two years before she left for *Vogue*. "The only thing I could assume about Diana Vreeland is that she got up in the morning, she thrust forward with her imagination, she imported it to me, that whatever she imported triggered something in me and a substrate was formed with an image on it that became something that people recognize. That's the only thing I know."

OPPOSITE PAGE
APRIL 1961
PHOTOGRAPHED BY SAUL LEITER

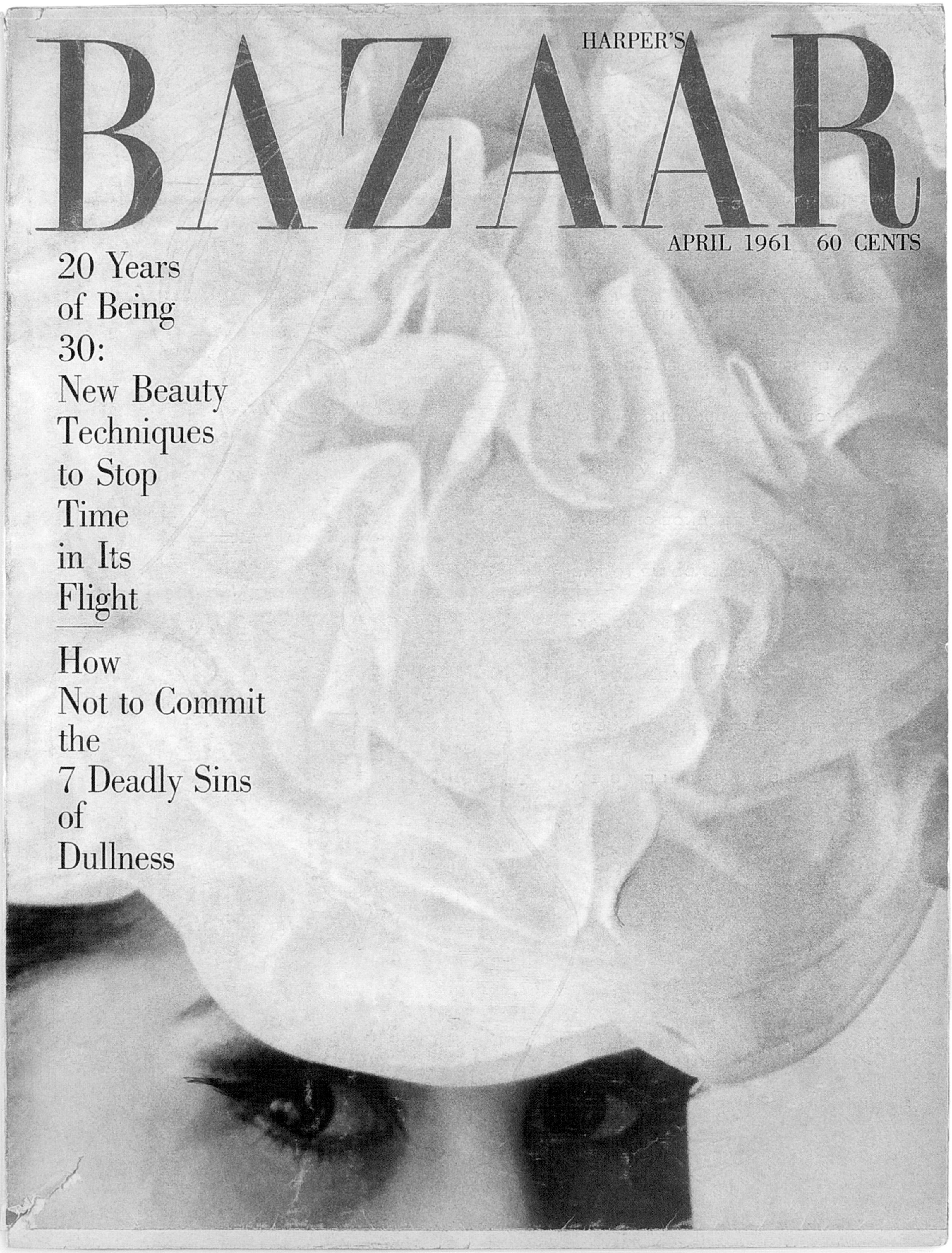

HARPER'S

BAZAAR

APRIL 1961   60 CENTS

20 Years
of Being
30:
New Beauty
Techniques
to Stop
Time
in Its
Flight

How
Not to Commit
the
7 Deadly Sins
of
Dullness

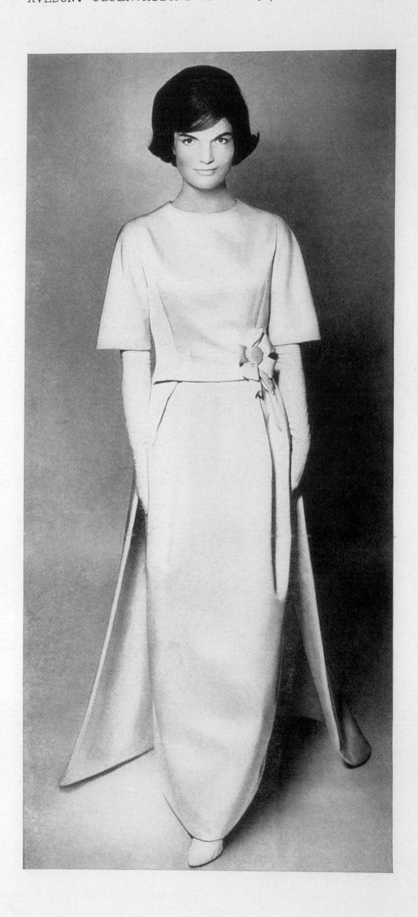

**FEBRUARY 1961
PHOTOGRAPHED BY
RICHARD AVEDON**

Mrs. Jacqueline Kennedy Onassis wrote in a letter to Diana Vreeland, "I was furious today when I read *Newsweek*—on how everyone is wondering why we chose *Harper's Bazaar* and they invent a million reasons and no one says the real one—which is you."

**FOLLOWING SPREAD
FEBRUARY 1961
PHOTOGRAPHED BY
RICHARD AVEDON**

AVEDON: OBSERVATIONS ON THE 34TH FIRST FAMILY

John Fitzgerald Kennedy

Jacqueline Bouvier Kennedy

Caroline Bouvier Kennedy

John Fitzgerald Kennedy, Jr.

The first in a monthly series of Observations by Richard Avedon on aspects of contemporary life

Opposite: An outgoing little suit kindled by a *fantaisie* tartan as brilliant as Sante Fé in spring. Thong-snugged waist, perch-away notched collar. By Pattullo-Jo Copeland, in Gerondeau wool tweed. About $300. At Bonwit Teller; Julius Garfinckel, Washington; Neiman-Marcus. The shoes by Herbert Levine. *Right*: A putty-pale wool sunbeam of a coat, given walking room by deep surprise side pleats. Discreet accents of inset belt, welted sides and collar. By Ben Zuckerman. About $265. At Lord and Taylor; Marshall Field, Chicago; Harzfeld's, Kansas City. Shoes by Christian Dior. Both pages: hats by Halston of Bergdorf Goodman. Bone colored kidskin gloves by Wear-Right. Stockings by Van Raalte.

SLIM
AND MOBILE

HARPER'S BAZAAR, FEBRUARY 1962

FEBRUARY 1962
PHOTOGRAPHED BY LOUIS FAURER

By 1962 Vreeland was ready to move on from *Bazaar*. She had a magical career but was overlooked when Carmel Snow's niece, Nancy White, was made editor in chief. Vreeland left an indelible mark on *Bazaar*'s pages. There was a spark in the air as the energy of the sixties hit the streets, and Vreeland left to capture this in the pages of *Vogue*.

Left: A suit of gingerbread silk deliciously set off by a milk white blouse, black polka-dot spiced. A no-strings jacket, slightly gathered straight skirt, sleeveless blouse cut-to-the-collarbone—chin-upped by a matching scarf. By Adele Simpson, in Chardon-Marché silk. About $200. At Henri Bendel; Julius Garfinckel, Washington; I. Magnin, Halston of Bergdorf Goodman hat. Marvella earrings. Phoenix stockings. Newton Elkin shoes. *Opposite:* A whipped-cream wool suit and cap-sleeved chocolate linen blouse garnished by a tangerine silk hat. Judicious welting extends into a midriff bow bridging the skirt's full front panel. By Jablow. About $215. At Bonwit Teller; Woodward and Lothrop, Washington; Joseph Magnin. Lilly Daché derby. Both pages: gloves by Lanolav.

SMALL SUITS,
SPRING CLEAN

LOUIS FAURER
HARPER'S BAZAAR, FEBRUARY 1962

VREELAND, PHOTOGRAPHED IN HER INFAMOUS OF-
FICE AT *VOGUE* WHERE HER BULLETIN BOARD WAS
FULL OF INSPIRATIONAL IMAGES. "I DON'T THINK
ANYONE HAS EVER BEEN IN A BETTER PLACE AT A
BETTER TIME THAN I WAS WHEN I WAS THE EDITOR
OF *VOGUE*."

VOGUE
1962–1971

NOVEMBER 1, 1962
PHOTOGRAPHED BY BERT STERN

Bert Stern never intended to be a photographer, but was struck at a young age by a cover that Irving Penn had photographed for *Vogue*. From that moment on photography became Stern's passion.

Stern's relationship with Vreeland was easy: "She had style, flair, and imagination, and she was willing to let people be creative—very creative." Stern's first choice was to photograph fashion on personalities: "Personalities were more interesting, because I had impressions of them from when I was younger, you know, like Gary Cooper, or Cary Grant, I'd seen in movies. So to me they were giant figures in my mind. And I was always very taken with shooting personalities."

ecco
SOPHIA LOREN

A great beauty, a fiery actress, a sort of natural marvel like Halley's Comet—and like it, trailing sparks: Sophia Loren is discussed on these pages by one of her discoverers and perhaps her greatest director, Vittorio de Sica. "Few people know it," he says, "but she is a great worrier...Again and again, she has to be reassured."

THE BLACK COQ FEATHER HAT
AND STOLE BY FORQUET OF ROME.

98

"IT WAS A REVOLUTION, AND FOR THE FIRST TIME YOUTH WENT OUT TO LIVE, INSTEAD OF WAITING FOR LIFE TO COME TO THEM, WHICH IS THE DIFFERENCE BETWEEN THE SIXTIES AND ANY OTHER DECADE I'VE LIVED IN." ALTHOUGH VOGUE WAS STILL CONSIDERED AN ELITIST MAGAZINE, VREELAND'S VERSION SHOWED A CROSS SECTION OF PERSONALITIES THROUGHOUT THE WORLD. HER PAGES WERE DIVERSE, AND SHE CELEBRATED THE FIRST CELEBRITIES WHO GRACED THE COVERS OF MAGAZINES.

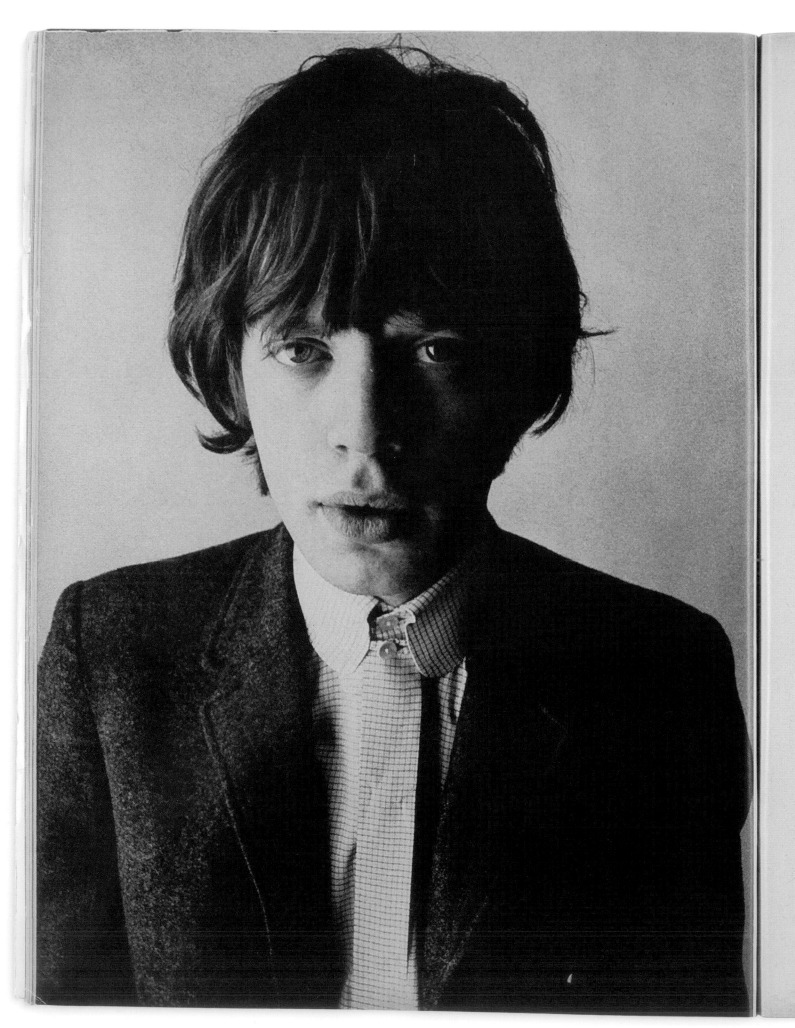

PEO
ARI
TAL

MICK JAGGE
To the inner group in Lo
Stones, those singers whe
perverse, unsettling sex
Pacemakers, The Searche
ing, to men, a scare. (Me
banged to the eyebrows.
perhaps because their me
and more terrifying. "T

DAVID BAILEY

JULY 1964
PHOTOGRAPHED BY DAVID BAILEY

Vreeland's "People Are Talking About" pages in *Vogue* were full of the most important cultural highlights of the 1960s. David Bailey, who photographed this famous picture of Mick Jagger, recalls that "*British Vogue* said 'No, who is this guy' when he offered them the picture and it went on to become the first American published picture on Mick Jagger because when Vreeland saw it, she said 'I don't care who it is, I'm going to publish it. It's such a great picture.'"

PLE

KING ABOUT...

PEOPLE ARE TALKING ABOUT . . . The swift burn of politics. . . . The fervour of the Young Republicans arriving already in San Francisco for the Republican Convention. . . . The statistics boys of both parties who were once described as people "who draw a straight line from an unwarranted assumption to an unsupported conclusion.". . . The beguiling Catherine Spaak, all eyes, legs, and lean brown midriff, in *Crazy Desire*, an Italian movie about a middle-ager trapped by teen-agers, that newly found European take-over generation who do all the things teen-agers have always done, but now in bikinis.

PEOPLE ARE TALKING ABOUT . . . The force of Sir Laurence Olivier who plays *Othello* in London with the desperation of Russian roulette. . . . Marlene Dietrich in Moscow where she sang "Falling in Love Again" to audiences that fell again. . . . The pleasure of the book, *The Earth Rests Lightly*, in which the Countess of Quintanilla has put some of the suspense of a thriller into the story of her rediscovery—and restoration—of her husband's mediaeval Spanish house and demesne.

PEOPLE ARE TALKING ABOUT . . . In England, the fun-house tour of Shakespeare's life put on at Stratford-on-Avon in a new pavilion that looks like a cluster of jousting tents, with the brilliant impresario, Richard Buckle, putting on this extraordinary exhibition which includes not only true Elizabethan portraits but Pop Art artifacts as well as an eerie semi-abstract view of London during the plague, a real lavender garden, and, on tape, the voices of such Shakespearean masters as Sir John Gielgud, Paul Scofield, and Sir Michael Redgrave; many of the painters and sculptors whom Buckle commissioned for special works found Shakespeare "a very square gentleman," which led them to jounce both him and history up.

PEOPLE ARE TALKING ABOUT . . . The Swiss architectural delights of the Lausanne Exposition where a flight of bright, plastic buildings has settled down on the edge of the lake. . . . Lausanne's separate but magnificent "Masterpieces from Swiss Collections," an exhibition that underlines the daring of the Swiss collectors who early bought Monet, Cézanne, Vuillard, Bonnard, Soutine, and, of course, Picasso. . . . In London, Moulton bicycles, low, collapsible, city-sized. . . . In Washington, the marvels of the show, "Seven Thousand Years of Iranian Art," at the National Gallery. . . . The quickie film (in the Johnson's Wax Pavilion at the World's Fair) in which any number of joyful, splintered images race over three screens, settling down into one wide view of a swooning ride down a hill in a kid's wagon, an experience like total immersion. . . . *A Letter to Myself*, the new book by Françoise Mallet-Joris, a fine French novelist who has noted down a salad of ideas, scathing, revealing, mocking; she throws out criticisms as though they were clay pigeons and she had an unerring eye. . . . The lilty, wistful tune, "Walk On By," sung by Dionne Warwick whose light voice sticks on the mind like honey on a finger.

A BRITISH "ROLLING STONE" ROCKER

, the new spectacular is a solemn young man, Mick Jagger, one of the five Rolling
out to cross America by bandwagon in June. For the British, the Stones have a
l with Jagger out in front of his teammates who in turn are out in front of The
he Breakaways, and Freddie and the Dreamers. To women, Jagger looks fascinat-
the groups look pretty much alike, dressed in their own costume way, their hair
h, especially, "Not Fade Away," The Rolling Stones pushed ahead of the Beatles,
and their music is a shade more gutsy. They are quite different from the Beatles,
ect is sex," wrote one observer, "that isn't sex, which is the end of the road."

PLISETSKAYA

"Tall, with astonishingly lovely arms...
Maya Plisetskaya is the greatest dramatic
dancer the world has known since Pavlova."
—Sol Hurok

166   Plisetskaya—
the splendour of
sable to the ground.
Coat by Maximilian.

APRIL 1, 1964
PHOTOGRAPHED BY CECIL BEATON

Vreeland wrote a memo to Cecil Beaton about this famous
shoot of Russian dancer Maya Plisetskaya.

"Please send me a wire after you finish photographing Maya Plisetskaya. That is the only thing on my mind.
Naturally, I see a long, exciting folio—and I feel sure she
will do anything for you, so long as you have a Russian interpreter in the studio, some music, (perhaps something that
she is dancing in...), and the air charged with excitement...
everything lovely, and making her feel like the enormous
star which she actually is.

"This would be our greatest coup, and I cannot help but
feel that you are as interested as I, in bringing it off.

"I only hope that all goes well, as she is rather mad
and wild, and can be sullen. On the other hand, when the
lights go on and when she knows that she has a full audience of everyone in the studio (and she knows audiences...),
then she has everyone rapt and spellbound, and she adores
every moment."

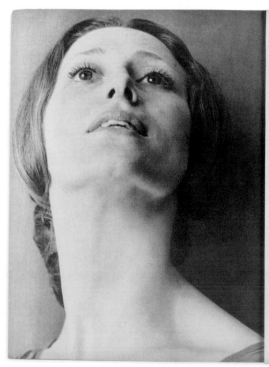

THE GREATEST
PRIMA BALLERINA
IN THE WORLD—THE MOST
DRAMATIC, THE STAR OF THE
BOLSHOI BALLET COMPANY.
A PHOTOGRAPHIC ESSAY
FOR VOGUE
BY CECIL BEATON

PLISETSKAYA

BY SOL HUROK

I ONLY HOPE THAT ALL GOES WELL, AS SHE IS RATHER

MAD AND WILD, AND CAN BE SULLEN.

PLISETSKAYA

"Her neck, with its swan-like thrust, and the head it held, a royal head . . . were perfectly suited to her wondrous purposes."
—Truman Capote
Opposite: Maya Plisetskaya wears a red crêpe chiffon dress from Grès that gives and takes a beauty of motion.

THE SIXTIES WERE ABOUT PERSONALITIES.
IT WAS THE FIRST TIME WHEN MANNEQUINS BECAME
PERSONALITIES. IT WAS A TIME OF GREAT GOALS, AN
INVENTIVE TIME... AND THESE GIRLS INVENTED
THEMSELVES. NATURALLY, AS AN EDITOR I WAS THERE
TO HELP THEM ALONG.

JEREMY STEIG, *above left,* flutist, jazz Pan, at twenty-one forming a new quartet. "I'm opening up a whole new thing. I can play three notes at once," said Steig, making his old Louis Lot instrument cry, groan, project. "It just comes and I let go. I usually write music about girl friends. One girl's last name is London, so I wrote 'London Broiling.'" Neck-deep in tub water, Jeremy Steig usually composes in the bathroom, awash with his murals of pipers, monkeys, and bugs peering from a wild green, blue, and yellow Chagallian jungle. He designed the cover and cartoons for the sleeve of his Columbia album, *Flute Fever.* "We're all artists in the family," said Jeremy Steig, whose mother is a painter, whose father is the famous Small Fry Steig man.

FRANK STELLA, *above right,* a painter who at twenty-nine has had eight one-man shows, thirty group shows, is one of six Americans chosen to exhibit at São Paulo's Bienal in September. Restless and inquiring, Stella guards the Trappist privacy of his New York studio. There he paints his precise Stripe Paintings, often in metallic colours, parallel to and framed in complex shapes: decagon, pentagon, trapezoid. His mechanical bite, lean and persistent invention led one critic to name Stella "among the handful of major artists working today."

JOAN RIVERS, *left,* twenty-odd, blond, with a pumpkin smile, pointed joints, and a voice like puréed pumice, who thinks of herself as a "funny Jean Shrimpton," but comes through on TV: clean, biting fizz. "I walk around with myself; I'm the first method comedian," said Joan Rivers, a talker-taper. She feeds the recorder, types the tape, spins out dialogue for Ed Sullivan's Topo the Mouse, for a new Peter Sellers movie, for herself. Her new recording for Warner Bros.: *Joan Rivers Presents "Mr. Phyllis" and Other Stories.* "I'm a piece of Pop Art," said Joan Rivers, who longs to be in a movie as "the funny friend giving advice to Tuesday Weld."

EDITH SEDGWICK, *right,* twenty-two, white-haired with anthracite-black eyes, and legs to swoon over, who stars in Andy Warhol's underground movies. "It's like watching Henry Moore sculpture out of focus," said Edith Sedgwick, who toyed with the movie name Mazda Isphahan for *Poor Little Rich Girl.* With the Pop artist Andy Warhol on camera, undergrounds roll out like crêpes: *Vinyl* is in the can: *Vacuum* about to turn "when we find a pure white kitchen." *Rich Girl* was made in Miss Sedgwick's apartment where she is shown here arabesquing on her leather rhino to a record of The Kinks. (In the background, her sketch of a stallion.) In Paris Warhol's gang startled the dancers at Chez Castel by appearing with fifteen rabbits and Edie Sedgwick in black leotard and a white mink coat. In her deep, campy voice, strained through smoke and Boston, she said: "It's all I have to wear."

PEOPLE ARE TALKING ABOUT...
YOUTHQUAKERS

AUGUST 1, 1965
PHOTOGRAPHED BY ENZO SELLERIO

Edie Sedgwick, Andy Warhol's It girl, was adored by
Vreeland. She symbolized the freedom of the 1960s.

BURTON WRITES OF TAYLOR

The house in California—it was in the Bel Air district of Los Angeles, I think—looked as if it had been flung by a giant hand against the side of a hill and had stuck.

From the main living room, master bedroom, guest bedrooms, dining room, kitchen level, the house jutted and dropped one floor to a "playroom."

The "playroom" was not for children.

It was complete with bar and barman, hot-dog simmerer, king-sized double-doored two-toned refrigerator, drugstore hotplates, big-game trophies on the walls (the host was a big-game hunter who acted in his spare time), and huge, deep, low divans and easy chairs—villainously uncomfortable for men, but marvellously made for cute little women who could tuck their cute little legs away and blazingly efface their cute little pretty little pouting little personalities in niches of the vast furniture and make like cute little pussycats.

Below the "playroom" the house again jutted and dropped to the swimming pool, the showers, and the changing rooms.

It was my first time in California and my first visit to a swank house. There were quite a lot of people in and around the pool, all suntanned and all drinking the Sunday morning liveners—Bloody Marys, boilermakers, highballs, iced beer. I knew some of the people and was introduced to the others. Wet brown arms reached out of the pool and shook my hand. The people were all friendly, and they called me Dick immediately. I asked if they would please call me Richard— Dick, I said, made me feel like a symbol of some kind. They laughed, some of them. It was, of course, Sunday morning and I was nervous. (Continued on page 131)

Richard Burton, who loves to write—and does it with vigour, excitement, and amazing descriptive powers—calls this article on Elizabeth Taylor, quite simply, "The Vogue Story," for he wrote it especially for Vogue. A careful man with an indiscreet typewriter, he dislikes any editing, can not bear to have his work touched. William Klein took the two colour photographs of Elizabeth Taylor on the sets in Paris of the newest Burton-Taylor movie, The Sandpiper. After Burton finishes his present filming of The Spy Who Came In From the Cold, the extraordinary Burtons will fight together in the acid movie, Who's Afraid of Virginia Woolf?

128

BURTON
WRITES
OF TAYLOR

"She was totally ignoring me."

I was enjoying this swell social triumph, but then a girl sitting on the other side of the pool lowered her book, took off her sunglasses and looked at me. She was so extraordinarily beautiful that I nearly laughed out loud. I didn't, of course, which was just as well. The girl was not, and, quite clearly, was not going to be laughing back. I had an idea that, finding nothing of interest, she was looking right through me and was examining the texture of the wall behind. If there was a flaw in the condition, I knew she'd find it and probe it right to the pith. I fancied that if she chose so, the house would eventually collapse.

I smiled at her and, after a long moment, just as I felt my own smile turning into a cross-eyed grimace, she started slightly and smiled back. There was little friendliness in the smile. A new ice cube formed of its own accord in my Scotch-on-the-rocks.

She sipped some beer and went back to her book. I affected to become social with the others but out of the corner of my mind—while I played for the others the part of a poor miner's son who was panicked, but delighted by the attention those lovely people paid to him—I had her under close observation. She was, I decided, the most astonishingly self-contained, pulchritudinous, remote, removed, inaccessible woman I had ever seen. She spoke to no one. She looked at no one. She steadily kept on reading her book. Was she merely sullen, I wondered? I thought not. There was no trace of sulkiness in the divine face. She was a Mona Lisa type, I thought. In my business everyone is a type. She is older than the dark chain on which she sits, I thought healthily, and she is famine, fire, destruction, and plague, she is the Dark Lady of the Sonnets, the snake-line bagatelle. She is a secret wrapped in an enigma inside a mystery, I thought, with a mental srun-to-run nod to Churchill. Her features were apocalyptic, they would topple empires down before her slightest whim. Indeed, her body was a miracle of construction and the work of an engineer of genius. It needed nothing except itself. It was true art, I thought, executed in terms of itself. It was unfettered by a vast passion. I used to think things like this, I was not long down from Oxford and Walter Pater was still talked of and I read the art reviews in the quality weeklies without much caring about the art itself, and it was a Sunday morning in Bel Air, and I was nervous, and there was the Scotch-on-the-rocks.

Like Madame Cherry I kept on drinking and, in the heady flow of the attention I was getting, told story after story in the afternoon heated directly on. I went in swimming once or twice. So did she, but, lamentably, always after I'd come out. She swam easily and gracefully in an Englishwomanly would and not with the masculine drive and kick of most American girls. She was unquestionably gorgeous. I can think of no other word to describe a combination of plenitude, fragility, abundance, tightness. She was lavish. She was a dark unyielding lazyeous. She was, in short, too bloody much, and not only that, she was totally ignoring me. I became fractured about to screaming when I had finished a well-received and humorous story about the death of my grandfather and found that she was turned away in deep conversation with another woman. I think I tried to sidestep but was stayed by words like—Tony and Janet and Marlon and Sammy. She was not, obviously, talking about me.

Eventually, with half-sniped cunning and with all the nonchalance of a traffic jam, I worked my way to her side of the pool. She was describing—in words not normally within—what the thought of a producer at M.G.M. This was my first encounter with freedom of speech in the U.S.A., and I took my breath away. My brain throbbed; I almost sobered up. I was profoundly shocked. It was ripe stuff. I checked her again. There was no question about it. She was female. In America the women apparently had not only got the vote—they'd put the words to go with it.

I was also somewhat puzzled and disturbed by the half-look she gave me as she uttered the enormities. Was she deliberately trying to shock me? Those huge violet-blue eyes (the biggest I've ever seen, outside those who have glandular trouble—thyroid, et cetera) had an odd glint in them. You couldn't describe it as a twinkle. ... Searchlights can not twinkle, they turn on and off and probe the heavens and so on.

And say something. I didn't reckon on the Scotch though. I didn't reckon that it had warped my judgment and my sense of timing, my choice of occasion. With all the studied tones of Dutch courage I waded into the depths of those perilous eyes.

and there was the Scotch-on-the-rocks.

(Continued on page 132)

131

The notorious relationship between Richard Burton and Elizabeth Taylor was immortalized in the pages of *Vogue*. This shoot took place during the filming of Vincente Minnelli's *The Sandpiper*.

131

Cool and young, and pretty in the contrary unprettied way of the Generation; a Breakaway's Breakaway—that's Mia Farrow, you might say in the first thirty seconds. And you wouldn't quite be getting the message. As one woman of wide experience and no mean intelligence put it, "She has the wonderful looks of the modern girl but not all the tiresome talk of youth...she listens a great deal and talks quite little. She's incredibly sensible, and with all her gentleness and sweetness, she has a normal worldliness."

*T*o interviewers she prefers to talk even less—"I'm a very private person." She puts it straight, almost without rancour, and without losing the charm of her easy, bred-in-the-bone good manners. But after two years as a Name on tv's *Peyton Place*, with four big movies slated to start this summer, she's feeling the sweet pull of stardust: "I always wanted to act, but I didn't want to say so. I wanted to do something that counted, that meant something. Now I can't even refuse an autograph, because I think by God! I can finally do something that means something to other people. That's a nice feeling."

*T*he breaks began three years ago when her mother, Maureen O'Sullivan, was appearing in the play, *Never Too Late*, and the girl who understudied her stage daughter took Mia with her to an audition for an off-Broadway production of *The Importance of Being Earnest*. The upshot—in no-business-like-show-business tradition—was that Mia Farrow read a few lines, then did Cecily in the tea party scene, and got the part. ("It was literally the first time I ever set foot on a stage.") Enter, a few nights later, Man from Twentieth-Century Fox—incognito. Heard soon after: ringing of pay telephone backstage. If she could do an American accent as well as she was doing high-comedy British....

*S*he could. And that's how Mia Farrow came to *Peyton Place*. "I'm sort of a believer in fates," she explained recently on the set of P.P. "I'd thought about a stage career, but I decided if the pilot show of *Peyton Place* was meant to sell, I was meant to do the show."...There it was: the canvas-backed Hollywood chair marked MIA FARROW. There it was again: her secretary and her cat, a sleepy white mop named Malcolm with his own leopard-spotted chair. And a melee of more than sixty actors, technicians, production people, all dominated by the ponderous mechanism of the camera. The essence of the scene in progress stacked up as four nice kids being miserable at the corner table of a discothèque—Allison Mackenzie (that's Mia), her beau Rodney, and their friends Norman and Rita who are teen-aged though married. Natalie Wood's sister, Lana, playing a baby vamp, was giving Rodney the one-two-three play for romance, and, well, as somebody explained, "It's one of your usual Peyton-Place-type scenes."

*O*ne take lasted for perhaps twelve bars of frug and monkey, six lines of dialogue; then break and repeat, break and repeat, a tedious ritual that goes on from eight A.M. to after six, five days a week. There's an easy give-and-take among the hard-core regulars at which Mia Farrow is so good you might say she exploits the technique. After a particularly complex set of instructions from the director, she played back in small, dewily *intime* tones, "And then we walk out of the shot like a dream...float out. Okay, Maestro?" They floated out, and she talked about what it was like to be Allison Mackenzie: "I have no real technique. I rely mainly on instinct, and when I believe in things I do them better. There have been moments *I'm proud of....*I created a whole being for Allison and I can feel things for her without knowing why. I know how she reacts. The other day we had a new director who wanted me to take my date's arm—well, *me*, I'd take anybody's arm, but I knew Allison couldn't do that in front of her mother."

*W*alter Doniger, who was not the director in question but has been a *Peyton Place* director since he reshot the original pilot, confessed later that she's quite often right about these nuances. "She knows how to use herself to an exquisite degree," he said with conviction. "You know, the most important thing you do is what you do when you're not doing anything. When she has a silent thing, she still transmits emotion. And another thing, she's a representative of her time; all the good ones are—they represent either the fantasies or the realities of their era." Carried away to greater heights, he plunged all the way: "She's almost a female Billy Budd."... Leland Hayward, a man who has mastered the art of fast telephone repartee with such economy that three syllables are an extravaganza, raps it out this way: "Nice girl. I think she'll be a star."

MIA FARROW *wears* breakaway fashion
ON THE NEXT PAGES

72

X marks the bodice where marigold knit stripped away at the armhole. Rudi Gernreich for Harmon Knitwear. Acetate. About $60. Bonwit Teller; Daytonia; Neiman-Marcus. Orange and plum band the rib cage, right: halter-clinging of Arnel and nylon. Stanley Herman for Mr. Mort. Stohl Arnel and nylon. Junior sizes. About $30. Altman's; Julius Garfinckel; Joseph's.

Mia Farrow—breakaway

Split of chiffon, left: half shock-pink, half apple green—a little bit of a thing dancing away from cutaway shoulders. Dress and stole by Joel Schumacher for Mam'selle; Onondaga silk. Junior sizes. About $75. Henri Bendel; Bramson; Hovland-Swanson; Sakowitz; Joseph Magnin. Mia through the looking glass, right, in a storybook dress of white lace ruffles and piqué embroidery hung up on tiny string straps. By Anthony L. Muto for Devonshire, of cotton lace and cotton piqué. About $65. At Lord & Taylor; Woodward & Lothrop; Marshall Field; Joske's, Houston.

Mia Farrow—
breakaway

APRIL 15, 1966
PHOTOGRAPHED BY RICHARD AVEDON

Avedon joined Vreeland in 1966 at *Vogue*, where he immediately started photographing models and personalities. Vreeland recalled, "He was on such a scale that my dear, I mean, munitions manufacturers could learn from him, and there is no one like Dick... I said 'Don't you think we should have Avedon, because after all we are the best magazine in the world and we have every other best photographer—why leave old Avedon stranded over at the Hearst place with no one to judge him or do anything for him?'"

MARIA CALLAS

Passion and talent arm her. She has the power of genius. In Maria Callas the fire of her presence and the ice of her control meet with almost frightening force. "There is no one like her," said Rudolf Bing, of New York's Metropolitan Opera, arena of some of her most crashing battles with management. "She is an artistic personality of unique fascination and power." Recently, at the Royal Opera House at Covent Garden, Maria Callas, after a year-and-a-half off-stage, shattered her own superlatives as Tosca in Franco Zeffirelli's emblazed new production. (*Tosca* became the toughest ticket in London.) "A radiant personality steeped in music," Sir David Webster of the Royal Opera called her: "She has the ability to make an audience part of her own experience...she can raise a Tosca to the level of classical tragedy." She was photographed for Vogue, right, in her new white first-act costume for *Tosca*—gone the traditional sweeping hat and cane—and, on this page, in a dress by Biki-Milan, as her own triumphantly beautiful self. This month in Paris she will sing Norma, and later, record *Carmen*—an event needled with anticipation. Of Maria Callas, the director of Milan's La Scala where her fame sprang, said, "Her voice—her vocal technique—has been easily compared to the nineteenth-century singers, Pasta and Malibran. But I think these very great singers were not up to her in psychological penetration of rôles. She is extraordinary in being a real actress. She is also so extraordinary that you have to go back to these nineteenth-century examples in the interest she has been able to create...to bring new audiences to opera, and bring back audiences that had drifted away. Maria Callas," Antonio Ghiringhelli went on, "is one of the greatest and most complete personalities of the theatre in all time."

HENRY CLARKE

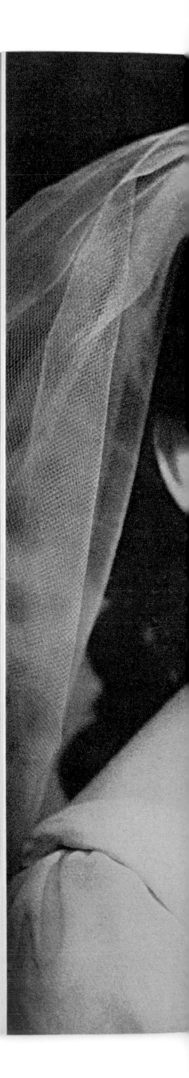

MAY 1964
PHOTOGRAPHED BY HENRY CLARKE

Vreeland loved Maria Callas: "For years, I couldn't get over Callas... she was the most extraordinary performer I have ever seen in my life—ever. She *just* opened her throat. But I want to tell you that a tenth of a second later I was *totally* drenched, I mean totally—it had nothing to do with crying or weeping. It was shock. It was total electricity. I had prepared to hear the most dramatic singer in the world, but *this*... and by God, when she died, was she *dead*. I've never seen such a death scene. On stage she didn't have a gauche thing about her. She was unique. That's a word I use sparingly."

CHANEL

...RIGOROUS DISCIPLINE TO THE VERY END

LEFT: ON THE FAMOUS MIRRORED STAIRCASE IN THE RUE CAMBON.
ABOVE: IN THE SALON OF HER APARTMENT FILLED WITH BOOKS,
BRONZES, FRIENDS, AND FLOWERS.

CECIL BEATON   79

FEBRUARY 1971
PHOTOGRAPHED BY CECIL BEATON

"She was extraordinary. The *alertness* of the woman! The *charm*! You would have fallen in love with her. She was mesmerizing, strange, alarming, witty... you can't compare anyone with Chanel. They haven't got the *chien*! Or the chic. She was French, don't forget—totally French!"

CHANEL
1883-1971

... HER INDOMITABLE SPIRIT, LOGIC, AND
FORESIGHT SWEPT THE WOMEN OF THE WORLD
OUT OF THE EIGHTEENTH CENTURY...
STRAIGHT INTO THE TWENTIETH

THREE EXTRAORDINARY PHOTOGRAPHS BY CECIL BEATON.
RIGHT: COCO CHANEL IN LONDON—ABOUT 1935.

VOGUE

60¢
APRIL 1

ACCESSORIES
PLOTTED FOR CHIC

WHITE:
WHAT MAKES IT NEW
AND EXCITING

THE CLOTHES
TO BUY
RIGHT NOW

"Women and Money"
by Albert E. Schwabacher, Jr.

"The Snobs of Paris"
by Pierre Daninos

Articles by
Walter Kerr
Gilbert Highet

VOGUE FASHION 1962–1971

AS RULES WERE BEING BROKEN IN THE STREETS DURING THE SIXTIES, VREELAND HAD A DISTINCT VISION FOR THE FASHION PAGES OF THE MAGAZINE. "IN FASHION, YOU HAVE TO BE ONE STEP AHEAD OF THE PUBLIC. THIS WAS NEVER MORE TRUE THAN IN THE SIXTIES."

PARIS WHITE:
WRAPPED
OVERBLOUSE;
CARVED OTTOMAN

From Simonetta and Fabiani, a long white overblouse, left, wrapped and tied—a signature of this collection. Of silk shantung; black shantung skirt and gilet. Worn with white kidskin gloves, octagonal pearls, and—not shown here—a narrow black cape. The costume of silk by Moreau. The hat by Barthet.

Capucci's carved white sliver, right. Of marvellous, thick, ribbed ottoman—embossed in a pattern of Roman stripes, densely fringed. With a black sailor hat; black kidskin gloves. Dress of Orlon and cotton (Horel fabric). On both pages: Kislav gloves.

OPPOSITE PAGE
APRIL 1963
PHOTOGRAPHED BY WILLIAM KLEIN

APRIL 1963
PHOTOGRAPHED BY WILLIAM KLEIN

William Klein did not have a typical fashion approach when he took pictures; he was a filmmaker who made some of the most innovative fashion movies around. *Who Are You, Polly Magoo?* was a parody of the world of fashion, with the fashion editor based on Diana Vreeland.

VERY FEW PEOPLE HAD EVER BREATHED THE PANTRY
AIR OF A HOUSE OF A WOMAN WHO WORE THE KIND OF DRESS
VOGUE USED TO SHOW WHEN I WAS YOUNG. BUT I LIVED IN
THAT WORLD, NOT ONLY DURING MY YEARS IN THE MAGAZINE
BUSINESS BUT FOR YEARS BEFORE, BECAUSE I WAS ALWAYS OF THAT
WORLD—AT LEAST IN MY IMAGINATION.

APRIL 1963
PHOTOGRAPHED BY BERT STERN

Hubert de Givenchy and Audrey Hepburn's friendship was
legendary. Vreeland was close to both of them and included
them frequently in her pages.

Vivid silk evening dress, left, narrowly
curved to the body, with a décolletage
like a night-blooming flower. (Made of
gauzy dotted shantung. At I. Magnin.)

"Very teahouse," said Miss Hepburn.
*"It's like a tiger lily—a wonderful colour
at night, radiant and life-giving.
And it's tremendous when a dress can
make you take on a different personality."*

Cloqué silk déshabillé, right, printed
in shades of china blue. At the front,
a slightly lifted waist; at the back,
loose folds falling to a miniature train.

*"I love that long, narrow
string-bean-with-a-bow look designed
completely around the body with so
much line it's almost as if you had
nothing on. Very feminine. Very natural."*

DRESSING AT GIVENCHY

Cloqué silk evening dress of candy-pink,
left, with a fascinating serpentine wrap
that shows a stretch of leg in front, dips to
a tiny-fishtail train. Moderately bare back,
falling, bombé, from a fat drawstring.
Chunks of bogus rubies and brilliants clasp
the double strand of pearls at the neck.

"All line," was Audrey Hepburn's
instant evaluation. *"Extremely simple, with
a little ankle and foot—
very seductive in a pretty sense without
necessarily being designed for that....It
stayed with me after I'd left the showing."*

A delectable evening dress—all shape
and glitter: daisy-medallions of mauve,
pink, yellow, and blue silk are appliquéd
inside a shell of white lace, embroidered
with gilt thread, minute sequins. Worn with
Miss Hepburn's own pink silk slippers.

"If I were going to splurge," she said,
"this is the dress I'd have."
For real life she bought instead a dress
in the same genre—white tulle, with
white embroidered dots, dot-sized brilliants,
and a sash of bright pink silk.

DRESSING AT GIVENCHY
70

141

If it's true that as ...
the flattery of his ...
the human figure—...
ways, he elongates ...
short printed silks ...
in back, real fit on ...
at the hem. Wonde...
piece dress with a ...
in a fresh spinach-...
longer-jacket suit ...
stretched-out, very ...
really wide throug...
an astonishingly fl...
felt beret, and his ...
charming, delicate ...
coat in camel and ...
tiny pillbox. As al...
est, most practical, ...
ciré, with layers of ...
navy tights, silver ...
and belted organza...
swinging from tiny ...
soft, very moving ...
ample: strapless, sl...
sweeping Doge co...

Mrs. Yul Brynne...
Flemish eyes vei...
—a delicious eve...
black, cape-sleev...

BERT STERN

APRIL 15, 1964
PHOTOGRAPHED BY BERT STERN

142

ga goes, so goes fashion, well then: cheers—we could live forever on
ection. Nobody is more sensitive to what is most subtly beautiful in
th and curve of the back, the grace of it in motion. And in a thousand
es is supple—drawstring tops gathered and very full at the back of
d tunic dresses with blousing and oval yokes dropped below the waist
—particularly pretty in black crêpe with a sharp sliver of white piqué
avy linens throughout, always with fascinating backs—a biased two-
l overblouse lowered in back and a straight back-dipped yoke; this
ith—a surprise for Balenciaga—a fake rose in palest pink . . . his
linen, seamed behind the easiest shoulders in the world, making a
profile. A marvellous new soft-tailored coat: dolman-sleeved and
p, narrowing to the hem, with S-seams forming a deep yoke across
s. He showed it in camel wool, with a navy shantung dress, white
te day shoes—laced beige-blond leather with stacked heels and a
the foot. Same shoes for an adventure in sport-deluxe—double-faced
Spanish-pink, pod-green linen dress, beige chiffon scarf tied over a
alenciaga is inspired by weather—his rainy-day ideas are the gay-
h. We loved his sou'wester and over-the-knee coat in white cloqué
underneath—navy poplin rainsuit, marigold jersey blouse, red-and-
shoes. Navy blue was a Balenciaga delight for evening too—flounced
to the floor; a cocoon-of-ruffles cape . . . a floaty little navy-blue lace,
His evening looks have never seemed more alluring—a stream of very
. . strapless tops again, and curved slits to the knee. A ravishing ex-
sheath worn under the most spectacular wrap in Paris—an enormous
e entirely of appliquéd sweetpeas in white, pinks, and leaf-greens.

B

ALENCIAGA

redhead's fair, faintly freckled skin and fascinating pale
petal lids. Here, she wears Balenciaga's new matador hat
antasy made of nine cut-tulle pompons. This, and the short,
oman coat: I. Magain. The hat, also at Bergdorf Goodman.

MAY 1964
PHOTOGRAPHED BY BERT STERN

Vreeland reached out to writers all over the world to cover different aspects of the magazine. Here, French novelist Violette Leduc muses on the untouchable Balenciaga: "Balenciaga sculpts, paints, writes in the act of making dresses. That is why he is above the others. To create dresses, beginning endlessly over and over again with the same model, the body, is to choose incessantly, without respite. As we breathe in order to live. To choose, is to help the formless to breathe, to give life to what is unborn. In this, Balenciega is supreme."

DAVID BAILEY

f ASHION WHERE THE FUN IS…SAMMY DAVIS

Sammy Davis, *Golden Boy*, is the entertainers' entertainer: actor, impersonator, stand-up comic, singer, dancer. (Once, for the benefit of a wowed interviewer, he explained his versatility in perfect deadpan: "Well, as you know, we're all born with this fantastic sense of rhythm…")….Shimmering at his side, a two-piece dress in **willowy white crêpe with a fringe of crystal beads** shedding light on hips and ankles. By Harvey Berin, of Celanese acetate and rayon (Chardon-Marché fabric). Bonwit Teller; Wanamaker's, Phila.; Gidding-Jenny; Wm. H. Block. Robert Originals ring: Lord & Taylor. Coiffure: Ara Gallant, Garrison-Ramon.

BERT STERN

…vid Bailey is the busman-on-… below—a small, dark, scowl-… ly handsome man with a … Cockney wit and a pen-… nt for dressing in odd bits … pieces, he is England's … ght young fashion photog-… her — the one every model … gs to pose for. Possibly … ause, through the eye of his … era, all women turn out to … prettier than even their … thers had dreamed…. … ough the eye of all cameras, … , a pretty girl growing pret-… by the second in a **river of** … **ite crêpe, high-waisted** … **slim** with a swish of pleats … ading out in back like a … cock's tail. By Estévez, of … nchini silk; about $160. … Gilbert jewellery. Both … Miss Bergdorf of Bergdorf … dman. Dress also at Julius … finckel; Halle Bros.; Joseph … gnin. Kenneth coiffure.

MARCH 1, 1965
PHOTOGRAPHED BY BERT STERN

This very familiar image was inspirational to Michelangelo Antonioni when he directed *Blow-Up*. Bert Stern recalls taking this photo: "I had just met David Bailey at Alex Liberman's because this was his first trip to New York. I was to do a series of personalities and I thought that I'd like to photograph him. And I got this idea that he could… be *me*, so I had him pose in a way that I shot pictures, which was to be over or under a girl. And I used Veruschka. So that picture was very much self-portrait, even though I wasn't in it. But he seemed so much like me."

I WAS ALWAYS <u>MAD</u> ABOUT CLOTHES. YOU DON'T GET BORN

IN PARIS TO FORGET <u>ABOUT CLOTHES</u> FOR FIVE MINUTES.

Molyneux: the
Guardsman's coat.
Shaped...double-
breasted...full-
skirted. Of tangerine
Nattier wool.
At Bonwit Teller;
I. Magnin.
Roger Faré gloves.
Alexandre coiffure.

PARIS is swinging this spring with oranges and tangerines and floating skirts and blowing chiffon ponchos....Action is at the hemline. *Volant*. All kick and bounce and flounce. Puffed dirndls of tweed, pleats, ruffle and ripple....Most prophetic thing in Paris: the outline of the body—held, and thrown over it, a bias of lace, organza, or chiffon, with the figure always clearly defined beneath it....

Bias: a bright yellow chiffon poncho to the ground, worn over white shantung pants....Tangerine wool: a Guardsman's coat, double-breasted, fitted at the top, full-skirted. Next winter's most important coat....Monkey-jacket suits with the prettiest, smallest sleeves and high, tight tight armholes. Perfectly fitted like little Persian coats...very snug, very flat across the shoulders....

All the colours of the sun: mimosa and lemon through tangerine to bright pumpkin and red orange ...clear Chinese colours, Chinese greens, japonica pink...perfect pale blue....For wools, café crème to cheese: camel tones paling to baby camel to white...pure pure white.

Textures for day: springy dry wools...matte matte matte....At night it's a floating world, the lightest airiest chiffons, lace, and organza, diaphanous and flou....

"Zamors": miniature, deftly wrapped turbans of Indian silks, striped silks, clear jade greens, japonicas, and cleanest white...which we called "Zamors" in honour of the tiny boy-Moor who carried the train of Madame du Barry....

A marvellous white crêpe dress—two-piece, bare, with a single diagonal strap, beautifully draped, cut on the bias; this covered with its own delicate white ermine topcoat, very slim, very white....

A new gypsy length for evening, just above the ankle....*Volants* at night: short dresses wrapped to the back with double puffed and rippling ruffles of lace and organza moving deliciously....For a spring wedding: a suit of thick rich Swiss embroidery on the finest muslin banded in snowy white mink....

Who are these rarefied exquisite floating creatures who project and animate the amazing and gay new shapes of Paris?...Every mannequin has the smallest calves, straightest legs, knees like little peaches, tiny narrow supple feet, rounded arms and beautiful wrists and throats....

With this spring's fashion we are entering a new world of dressmaking...great dressmaking that touches the senses...asymmetric sarongs and a great big muu-muu to the ground—Paisley organza with the figure showing through...a mystique that's all bias and movement breathing fashion...feminine and beautiful....

DV.

...tangerine...
a Guardsman's coat...

105

MARCH 1, 1965
PHOTOGRAPHED BY WILLIAM KLEIN

The bi-annual fashion reports from Paris would allow Vreeland to set up shop at the Hôtel de Crillon for a month while she attended shows and focused on different aspects of the magazine. She signed these stories with her distinct red initials

Courrèges—the new suit-proportions. Far left: Short-sleeved jacket, double-breasted... double-breasted skirt in white wool. Bergdorf Goodman; Neiman-Marcus. Left: Tattersall zipped over white wool dress...low belt, low pockets. Five-gallon hats with both. Right: Best new dress—white wool... neck square, wide, low...waistline low on the hips, belted. Bonwit Teller; Frederick & Nelson. Courrèges white with everything— little kidskin gloves ...slit-toe boots. All hats at Bergdorf Goodman.

PARIS
...the gayest young suits...
best little dresses...

110

WILLIAM KLEIN

MARCH 1, 1965
PHOTOGRAPHED BY WILLIAM KLEIN

André Courrèges's futuristic designs most clearly showed the attitude of the 1960s was. Vreeland said, "Courrèges's clothes weren't just little dinky things. They were beautifully made clothes."

IN THE SNOW COUNTRY

Verushka at Yuzawa—hot springs, geisha to play the samisen, and forty-foot snow drifts locked in by dormant volcanoes....
Right: A sumo wrestler with ritual topknot—one of the rare giants who pursue this sport of gods—prays for a good harvest before a young tree tied with rice cakes....*Left:* Pale-honey mink burnoose spread to the ankle. Of "Tourmaline," Emba natural pale-beige mink. Made to order at Maximilian. The giant's hair was dressed with camellia oil; Verushka, coiffed by Ara Gallant.

IN THE JAPAN ALPS: HIGH, COLD
At Yuzawa: facing the snow-laden wind that sweeps across from Manchuria... *Opposite,* Veruschka in silver fox—deep black, pure silver against the snow. Knee-length cape, muffler, mittens, all by Fredrica, in Fromm natural bright silver fox. At Halle Bros.; Hudson's; I. Magnin. Adolfo natural silver fox baby cap. Capezio grey suede boots. *This page,* the same cape with a natural honey-lynx cap by Adolfo. *On both pages,* the giant wears a superb full-length greatcoat of alpaca sheepskin. This is Georges Kaplan, of natural Argentine alpaca.

WINTER LANDSCAPE WITH FIGURES
In the deep snows of Hokkaido, Veruschka, left, carrying a huge Japanese *kasa,* wearing a long-slashed smock of ermine; ermine boots; white mink cap and a mink muffler knotted like a shrine rope. Smock and boots of natural white Russian ermine. Boots: Roger Vivier for Revillon. The *kasa,* a ceremonial umbrella, is by John Reynolds. *Opposite:* A young admirer, serene as a pine, the children's wayside guardian. Her hooded cape, of white Canadian ermine, by Georges Kaplan.

OCTOBER 1966
PHOTOGRAPHED BY RICHARD AVEDON

Polly Mellen recalls meeting with Vreeland in preparation for this iconic shoot: "'It's going to be a fur caravan... we'll have to have furs made for Veruschka.' And so Mrs. Vreeland and I went everywhere." This epic love affair between a Caucasian woman and a Japanese man brought the talented team of Mellen, Avedon, Veruschka, and hair stylist Ara Gallant together.

Veruschka remembers, "Dick had the idea to find for me, as a partner in the pictures, a man taller than me. He was a sumo wrestler who was thin and much taller than me—I mean he was so tall that he couldn't fit in the car... he had hands and feet so big that we couldn't find shoes for him—they had to be draped. Polly had to drape his feet."

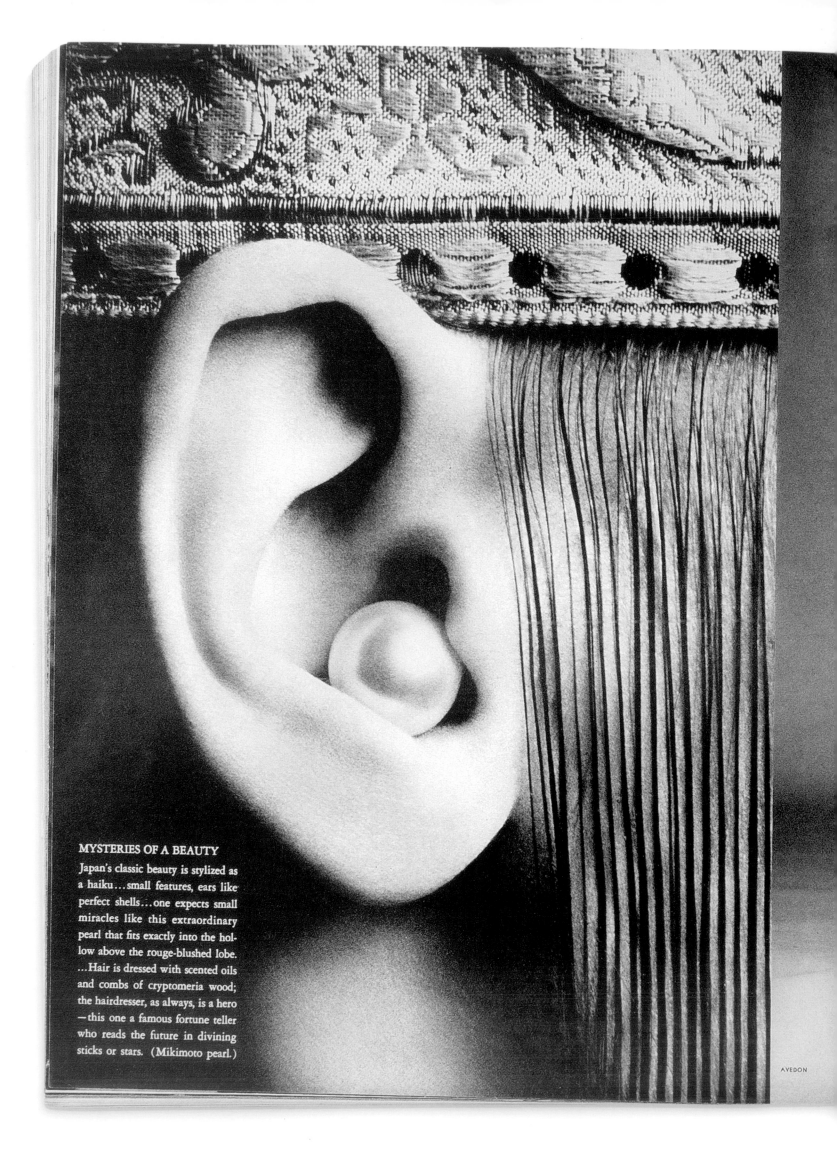

MYSTERIES OF A BEAUTY

Japan's classic beauty is stylized as a haiku…small features, ears like perfect shells…one expects small miracles like this extraordinary pearl that fits exactly into the hollow above the rouge-blushed lobe. …Hair is dressed with scented oils and combs of cryptomeria wood; the hairdresser, as always, is a hero —this one a famous fortune teller who reads the future in divining sticks or stars. (Mikimoto pearl.)

AVEDON

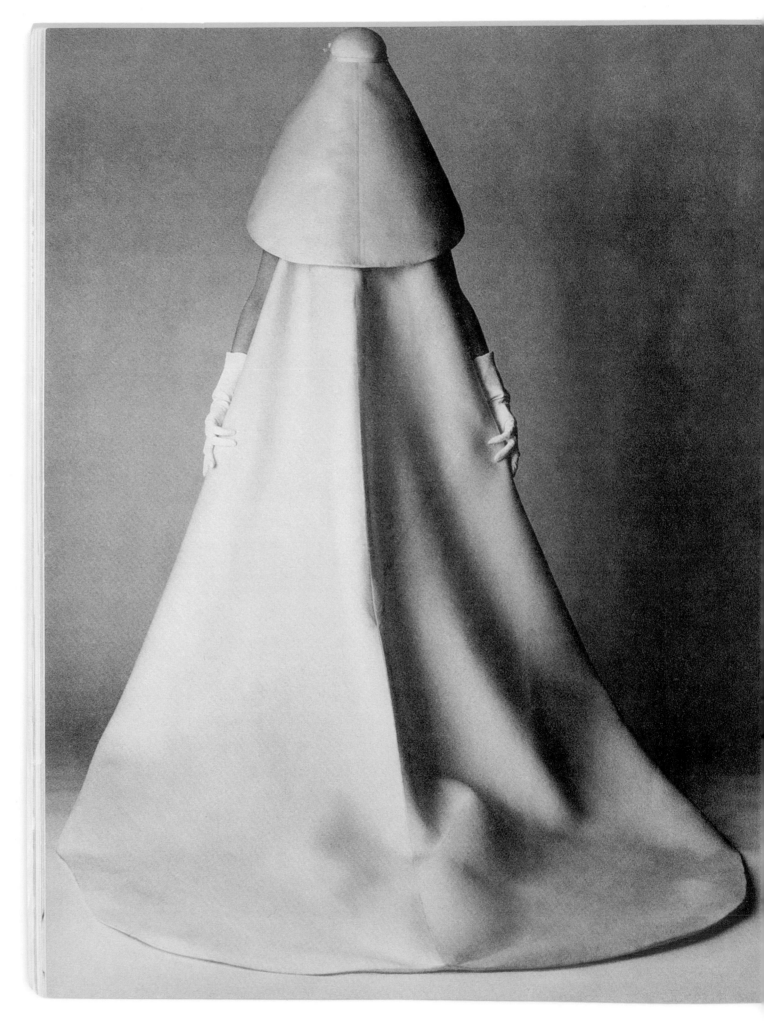

BALEN CIAGA'S

*MARVELS OF FORM—
THE BRIDE'S DRESS.
THE CAPE DRESS:
ALL BIAS OVALS*

Balenciaga gives cloth a purity and calm nothing can disturb—the bias oval curves of gazar spread taut the length of a bridal headdress and train, a dinner cape and dress. *Left:* There is no wedding dress on earth as young and beautiful as this—Balenciaga carves ivory gazar in a shoulder-circling headdress, a taut long oval train; in front, the dress falls straight from tiny sleeves. Both: Marshall Field. *Right:* Balenciaga's flag-blue gazar cape repeats the bias oval curve of the dinner dress beneath—both hems rise in front, dip low in back. Cape and dress, both at I. Magnin.

**JULY 1967
PHOTOGRAPHED BY
DAVID BAILEY**

"Balenciaga was incredible...
I was madly infatuated with
his clothes. His clothes were
devastating. One fainted. One
simply blew up and died."

DAVID BAILEY

...LIGHT

Cool sun, bluish light— filtering down on a braided wig like Hatshepsut's, right. Chill-silver lamé feather, above, harnessing a long printed linen skirt of night-cold blue—a kalasiris, in Irish Looms fabric. To order: Saks Fifth Avenue.

FRANCO RUBARTELLI

APRIL 1967
PHOTOGRAPHED BY FRANCO RUBARTELLI

"I was frustrated very fast about being a model, I think that Vreeland must have sensed it. She said, 'I want you to meet Franco Rubartelli in Rome.' So when I went to Rome for collections, I called him up and we met and then I understood because I was looking already in my mind. I had the idea that to get out of this, the only way would be to work with a photographer, to have your own ideas and visions about how you wanted to transform yourself."

158

JOURNEY TO
THE LIGHT

Sun-disc hair, right; like the source of light worshipped in the desert past. Sun-stripes, above, reflecting the gold of burnished desert light—gilt circled on transparent organza. Djellaba, in Gladstone fabric. To order: Saks Fifth Avenue.

MIRAGE IN
AIR-DANCING
COLOURS
DETAILS ON PAGE 222

MIRAGE IN
REGENCY COLOURS,
JEWEL-BOLD
EMBROIDERY

**LEFT AND
FOLLOWING SPREAD
JULY 1, 1968
PHOTOGRAPHED BY
FRANCO RUBARTELLI**

THE MAGNIFICENT MIRAGE

A Vogue preview
of the new fabrics for fall and winter—
made up out of whole cloth

Wrapping, furling, whirling about Veruschka for extraordinary yard upon yard—visions of tomorrow's textures and colours that draw on the cloth, the whole cloth, and nothing but the cloth for each wonderful mirage: thong-swirled folds of supple jersey swaddling piles of fur...shimmering ornamentation shimmered further with raw uncut stones...fluid moiré-embossed velvet...lofty shades of blue or sun-drenched grassy greens, sultry Oriental cerise or serene Regency fawn...marvellous surfaces touching off marvellous movement across this eight-page and eighty-mile span of Arizona's Painted Desert reaching out to vermilion-tinged cliffs....This magnificent wind-up of cloth, accessories, makeup—all from the nomadic workshop of Giorgio di Sant'Angelo's imagination. Details on page 122.

JUNE 1967
PHOTOGRAPHED BY HORST P. HORST

Veruschka says of Vreeland, "She was very opinionated, opinionated about certain things. Like, she didn't like nonsymmetric things, she didn't like hair parted on one side, it had to be parted in the middle, and clothes too. The other thing was the melancholic look on the face of mine. She always had to remark, 'Veruschka, don't look into space, be now and happy.'"

BEAUTY
bulletin
TRENDS TO COUNT ON THIS SUMMER

"All right," said a longtime acquaintance, presenting herself to our startled eyes at the hairdresser's one recent midday, "Look, I'm In—and I'm ugly as sin." . . . Hair shorn smartly as a newborn baby's; thick, chic sideburns pointing out a pair of somewhat widish jowls; chalkwhite stockings making unmissable a pair of legs never meant for stardom—she was, in truth, a sight. Not only a sight; a sound. A-glint and a-clank at shoe, waist, and handbag were yards of chain. . . . In reply to the flash of fury that shot its way down hair-dryer row where we sat entrapped, we could only murmur to this essentially pretty woman: "Baby, you kept the faith too well." . . .

She had. Nobody ever said anyone was meant to be a *mass* of trends. Nobody said trends were to be swallowed whole. With that tremulous forewarning, we list some summer beauty trends coming on—some of which, you'll notice, are in obvious conflict with each other. (Meaning: There's More Than One Look.) We hope you'll also notice *beauty in general is going far from freaky*. Which is the way to go, when clothes make power plays. . . .

There's a move toward warmer, tanner makeup. Naturally. To gold in makeup (see next page). To bodies gleamed with care (newest polish in sight is Germaine Monteil's *pearled* arm and leg lotion). To more transparent ways to get colour on cheekbones and face-edges (Eve of Rome's new Tiber Touch does this; so does the clear-as-water blusher in Helena Rubinstein's Lightworks). Trend to much more luminosity (if you haven't met Revlon's Blushing Silk, do; see how silky luminosity can be). To toenails lacquered in fluorescence (Cutex doing). . . .

There's a trend to highly organized makeup sequences. Some involve next to no makeup at all (the Erno Laszlo preparations, in which face powder is the makeup, period). Some have every makeup move figured out for you (Estée Lauder does this, look by look). And some sequences have more brushes than Fuller (Mary Quant's for example. Even her freckles go on by brush—golden-brown cake shadow, stippled over nose-bridge, under eyes). . . .

If the trend-list at right leaves you hanging as to who makes what, know this: Shiseido, Max Factor, and Helen Rubinstein have shiny eyeliners. Tourneur's new Frivolash is built on an easy-to-apply base. Evelyn Marshall's quick-sticking fake-eyelash glue does everything but take you by the hand to Saks Fifth Avenue to buy it. Kenneth has one of the best short wigs in wigdom all ready in his wig-room (base is so light you can't believe you have the thing on). Setsation is the magic word in a mini-permanent; body built in minutes, not hours. . . .

If you're hung up about whether to have your hair cut short or not, think of it this way. If short, has to be very short, no compromise; have a thick nape-fringe cut like transplanted bangs. But if you're not ready for shortness, there's this: the great head of hair pieced out at back and sides, tied or seamed somewhere with more hair. Flawless. Romantic. Feminine. And, in certain circles, so boring the eyes glaze over whenever another of these magnificences enters the room. If you've had enough of the look but love it anyway, de-conventionalize it. Try sleekery (see pages 122 to 125). Or do the newest thing: at each side, have a chin-length sidepiece cut. Puts long hair—and your face—in a whole new framework. . . .

We are a camera. Girl on the facing page is a poster. The trend to accent-lipsticks is what she's here to announce. The *odd* colour that illuminates whatever you're wearing. With a Chinese green dress, a grape-iris lipstick. With pink, a peach-gold mouth. With yellow, a lipstick that might combine marigold and rosy pink. From DuBarry's newest collection of Glissando lipsticks (the lipstick devised to mix a swirl of shades *within* the stick itself), these effects emerge. Creamier in formula, newly gleamed, the lot. Iris #57 is grapiest. Apricot #53, pure sun.

126

Trend: go | beiger bo | all skin t

Trend: sm | haircuts | with bang

Trend: go | silver hig | in makeup

Trend: ac | lilac, apri

Trend: ha | with fine | of tiger st

Trend: "D | lacquers f

Trend: mo | of more fr | nose-bridg

Trend: ye | sunned sk | transparen | face bare

Trend: Jap | for long h | long hairp

Trend: shi

Trend: bo | two forms- | or quite co

Trend: hai | on more w

Trend: fak | in more w

Trend: bod | for hair wi | mini-perma

Anti-trend | "refined" | coating of

faces,

l and enriched

winsome
ered
the nape

eplacing
ters

lipsticks,
gold

reaked
s instead

"Glo"
oenails

powderings
es—
under eyes

eyelids,

ushers—
rwise

se sleekery

eye liners

makeups in
ear
ng

es, wigs,
able bases

elashes
able ways

uilding
ast
t waves

d: faces
thick
powder

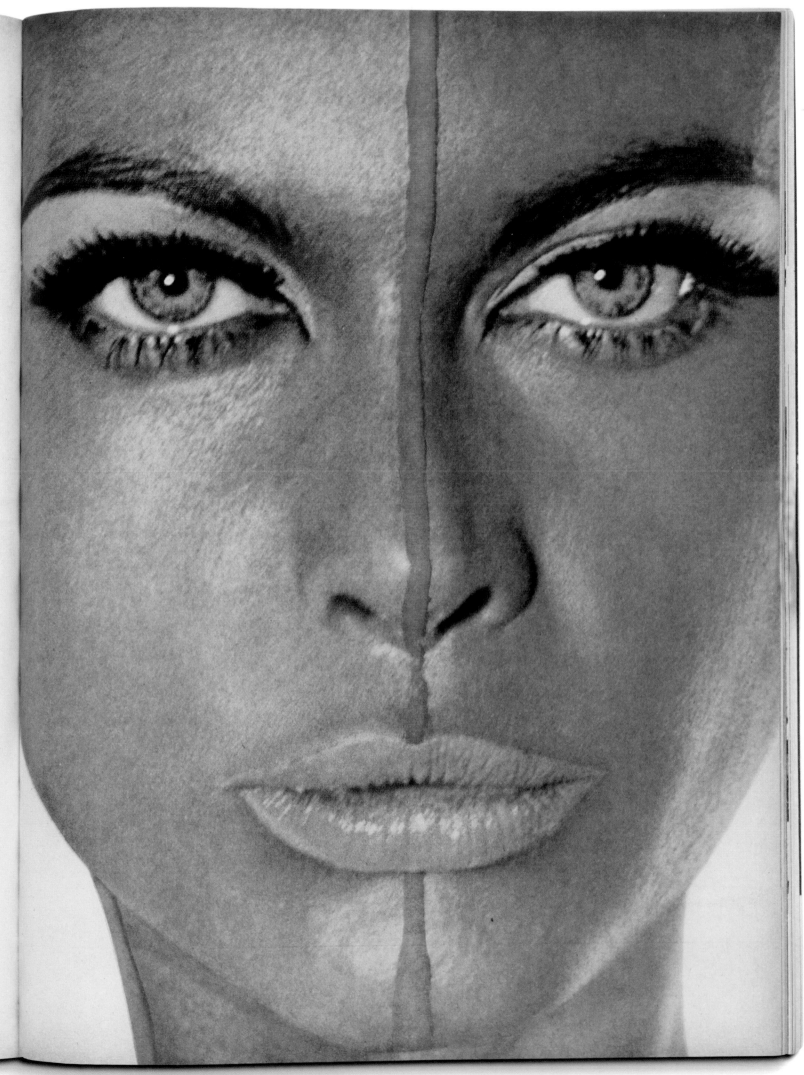

HORST

the Tree...

UNGARO:
an impression of
pleasure—love,
health, youth,
experiment—and
intoxicating from
start to finish.
From masks to mink
weskit to ribboned
organdie pyjamas

A natural: Twiggy and Penelope Tree, two pretty chickadees with a joyous appetite for fashion, just longing to act out the dreams of the great designers. So, packed them off to Paris we did—simply turned them loose to amuse themselves in the most amusing clothes we saw there. They played it by ear and played it to the hilt; even through masks you see it—all the excitement, gaiety, and seductiveness that comes naturally to Paris...naturally to the Twig and the Tree. Butterfly in mink and organdie, opposite; a shaped rounds-of-white-mink weskit beaded with red ribbon over divine pyjamas—tunic and pants of open-work white organdie with Saint Gall embroidery and intervals of ribbon beading. I. Magnin. The masks—the brass-and-copper one shown on Twiggy a page ago; the silver butterfly and silver African mask here on Penelope—Ungaro fantasies sculptured by Gustin. Ungaro masks, Ungaro speaks: "When you see people for the first time you tend to label them without knowing what they really are. These masks represent the 'inner face' of a person —once you know her, know what is going on in her mind. It's the whole problem of human communication— the masks force people to understand that one must learn really to look; they incite the search for what is beyond the first impression."

paris

MRS. VREELAND HAD A DIFFERENT SENSE OF WHAT THE SIXTIES WERE AND SHE REALLY STUCK TO HER OWN VISION... SHE WANTED HER SORT OF OVERVIEW AND HER LOOK TO PRESIDE AND SHE WAS VERY MUCH IN CONTROL OF THE WAY THINGS WERE LAID OUT.

JANUARY 15, 1968
PHOTOGRAPHED BY RICHARD AVEDON

OPPOSITE PAGE
MARCH 15, 1968
PHOTOGRAPHED BY RICHARD AVEDON

Penelope Tree recalls this time in her life fondly: "We all had a sense of what the sixties were, but Mrs. Vreeland had a different sense of what the sixties were, and she really stuck to her own vision. And even though she brought the best out of people—she could see what they were up to and stimulated their creativity and ideas—nonetheless, she wanted her sort of overview and her look to preside, and she was very much in control of the way things were laid out."

BEAUTY *bulletin*

The Nat
Marsha

How does the London
keep this body? She
really. It just happens.
up to no diet or beau
"Except bad ones. Li
masses of candy and t
on crash diets."...She
does no exercises. But
in *Hair*. That's an ex
Speaking of *Hair*, how
keep her spectacular da
mop? That just happen
wash-and-dry, no ro
hairdressers, no cut
year now. Shampoo ev
days. Conditioner af
Then a brush with a s
natural bristle. To keep
ural, the Afro, soaring
on the up-and-up....

PATRICK LICHFIELD

166

JANUARY 1969
PHOTOGRAPHED BY PATRICK LICHFIELD

"The young black girls I see in New York today are the most attractive girls—from top to toe! Their hands are the most beautiful things on *earth*—they always have been. But these girls' *legs* are so extraordinary! They used to stand with their behinds out. You know the walk—they'd sort of sink into their stomachs and then stick out their behinds. But these girls today haven't got a *trace* of it. They stand *tall*, and when they *stride*... they're like a race of gazelles! They're strong. They've got the *strength*."

APRIL 15, 1969
PHOTOGRAPHED BY BERT STERN

"I was definitely sure of what I was doing, and I always would run the risk of being wrong. Of course, I would take correction if a better idea came along, but I wouldn't just be criticized if there was no better thing to do, do you see what I mean."

Tiger, tiger, burning bright...
RED HAI[R]
as a way of
The privileges.
The responsibiliti[es]
The ground rules

There are more red-headed girls around than there used to be, say, six months ago. One sees them glowing [?] raking their rosy manes with permissive fingers, basking, with a healthily narcissistic delight, in the way pe[ople] them. Most to the point, in the way men look at them. Even plain redheads get looked at quite a lot. A really g[ood] one comes through every door like a thunderclap. Born redheads are rare; the figure is something absurd, [?] cent. But the lure of red hair is far more primitive than the prosy mathematics of supply and demand. Red is t[he] heat, of wine, of fever, of blood. Red is the signal of danger. It is both a welcome and a warning, and eve[n] civilized man feels a curiously atavistic quickening of the senses at the sight of a red-haired woman. Never m[ind] may be a notorious mouse. *He* knows that, deep inside, she is a quivering mass of passion and fireworks—a[nd?] paperweights when displeased. That's pretty challenging stuff, and therein lies the heart (also red) of his co[?] a man. He is warmed, fed, sustained, electrified by passion. He loves a challenge. That is, he loves a challenge [?] time. If he's feeling up to it. On the other hand, a man can't spend all his time tilting at passion and dodging pa[?] What about his work? What about his golf? What about eight hours of sleep? . . . It's not easy for a girl wit[h?] to hang on to her blistering temperament, while simultaneously transmitting waves of comfort, understanding[?] bility. We know one notable success in her seventies, who has, with the cooperation of a gifted colourist, kept up t[he] hair and disposition, but has drenched it all with a helplessness that would embarrass a new-born kitten. Her hus[band?] . . . Red hair can be any colour from marmalade to strong tea. Usually it is accompanied by sun-shunning skin[?] and fragility of onionskin paper, with a charming frequency of freckles. The hair can be tenderly and creatively [?] to deepen from marmalade to bronze, or soften from orange to autumn leaf. However, the skin must be ch[?] protected more than any other. Recent research by Dr. Peter Flesch of the University of Pennsylvania Medical S[chool?] that the pigment that makes a redhead is predominantly an iron-containing substance. Her pigmentary syste[m?] somewhat differently from brunettes and blondes, whose pigment is predominantly melanin. The redhead's [?] fore, has more susceptibility to sun, wind, cold, heat, and careless handling. Cosmetically, it's a time bomb.[?] man of Elizabeth Arden, told us that he abhors clichés in makeup for the red-haired. He almost never us[es] shadow, or even green, but does intriguing subtleties with grey, from smoke-wisp to pewter. He admires f[?] prefers a translucent foundation that lets them twinkle. Eyebrows are kept light and un-fakey, but he rather [?] darkish brown lashes (accomplished easily enough with mascara, false lashes, or even dye, which lasts for mo[re?] important, a redhead's lips must be bright . . . bright pink, geranium, sizzling orange. . . . One of the minor but [?] gratifying triumphs of those romantic types in the chemistry labs is that any woman can become a believable [?] twenty minutes. That's if her own hair is blond, grey, or light brown. A brunette needs a little more time. The[?] nificantly, many more red-haired Beautiful People this year. There are more red-haired photographic mode[ls?] French farmer can predict, with stunning accuracy, the season ahead, by spotting on which side of the tree[?] building their nests. . . . If you're a woman, there's a lot to be learned by observing the avant-red-garde.

BALL O[F?]
Ear, ear, gentlemen. Eternal femme coquetry: just the little ear exposed on a rou[nd?]
small burnished head calculated to strike sparks in the stonie[st?]
A man, looking at it with his inner eye, would have the whole glorious smoulder of hair fa[lling?]
bare shoulders like a single suffusing blush. Carita, in Paris, is [?]
She wrapped the silken skein as if it were a chiffon scarf in a 1920 Lagonda[?]
and tucked the ends into a throat-embracing fantasy of turquoise and diamonds fr[om?]

44

R

ife

s.

orches,
look at
looking
ive per
lour of
e most
hat she
ower of
t. He is
e of the
weights.
er hair
d dura-
ackling
d dotes.
colour
uraged
ed and
l shows
perates
, there-
o, wise
lue eye
es, and
oves of
). Most
edingly
head in
are, sig-
. . The
pies are

IRE

smooth,
hearts.
around
subtle.
ing car,
Cartier.

BERT STERN

Anjelica Huston

Anjelica Huston, this page, John Huston's tall, narrow daughter, spectacular in a sable coat with a wonderful *Borsalino* look—shawl-collared, long and wrapped and stocked with white crêpe over cuffed black pants …perfect with a slightly sinister trilby of black felt. Coat by Ben Kahn, of natural Russian Crown sable. At Ben Kahn; Gidding-Jenny; I. Magnin; Creed's of Toronto. Hat from Rakes Boutique. Pants by Victor Joris for Cuddlecoat. Scarf by Echo. Espadrilles at Bonwit Teller. **The rose and the cape,** right: Anjelica plays the Tolstoy heroine in the most romantic sable cape, luxuriously wrapped, falling to the floor, a nimbus of sable against her face. Cape by Pauline Trigère for Oliver Gintel, of tip-dyed Russian sable. At Thomas E. McElroy, Chicago; Davidson's, Indianapolis; I. Magnin. Mr. John hat of natural Russian sable.…To warm romantic winter looks like this one, the new Rubaiyat Collection from Germaine Monteil— Superglow Pressed Powder and a dozen fruit-and-flower shades of Super-Creme Lipstick.

S ABLE AND YOU… IN THE WRAP OF LUXURY

AVEDON

170

NOVEMBER 1, 1970
PHOTOGRAPHED BY RICHARD AVEDON

Anjelica Huston met Vreeland in 1959 and immediately started working with Avedon. She recalls, "Nobody did pure female glamour like Dick Avedon. And no one knew it like Diana Vreeland. She had this taste for the extraordinary and for the extreme and for the royal and the rich and the tasty. And she was a *croqueuse de diamant*, you know? She made it extraordinary, she took the mundane and the mediocre and she made it ravishing, and she made it okay for women to be ambitious, for women to be outlandish and extraordinary and for women to garner attention."

WHAT'S NEW—
YOU. RAVISHING IN PAISLEY AT NIGHT

Nights and nights of
marvellous looks unfolding
on these pages—everything
fresh, feminine, madly
attractive . . . furs, brocades,
and jewel cascades . . .
prints, patterns, pants.
The choice is yours.
You know who you are.
**The peasant dress strikes
gold,** right. It's a gleam of
golden Paisley after dark—
lighting up Lauren Hutton,
here—with a deep,
scalloped décolletage and
a little shawl to catch
wisping tendrils of hair.
Mididress by Donald
Brooks, of acetate and
polyester (Kandelatt
fabric). Saks Fifth Avenue;
Gus Mayer; Swanson's;
Neusteters; Neiman-Marcus.
Coiffures, these twenty
pages, all by Ara Gallant.

124

AVEDON

**NOVEMBER 1, 1970
PHOTOGRAPHED BY RICHARD AVEDON**

Vreeland's choice of Lauren Hutton as a new face in the
pages of *Vogue* indicated a shift to the natural. "She must
have been starting to see these few young girls, who were
showing up, with very little make-up, and their hair right out
of the shower, with T-shirts, no bras, and jeans and sneakers. I think she saw that I was one of these new things, I
wasn't this *swan*, these European put-together '50s swans. I
was sort of this new American idea."

GLIMMER OF PALE FUR AT NIGHT...RAVISHING

Like drifting snow night-shadowed in a wood...the subtle, glimmering off-whiteness of pale mink, done here in three totally opulent ways— all worn with fling and panache by Lauren Hutton. For left: Sleeveless surtout that plunges from shoulders to floor; deep-collared, wrapped; the skins used in long, straight vertical sweeps, like the narrow panels. To order from Reiss & Fabrizio, of "Azurene," Emba natural blue-grey mink. Neck scarf by Emily Wetherby. Bracelets and belt by Thomas Robbins. Scarf at waist by Echo. Left: Wrapped midicoat with an uneven hemline that falls in points, the skins used horizontally, sleeves luxuriously round, full. An Emeric Partos design made to order at Bergdorf Goodman, of "Morning Light," Emba natural pale blue-beige mink. Silver cuff by Frances Whitney. Leg sash by Thomas Robbins. Boots, to order at Battani Boutique. Right: Pale fur swirled in circular tiers in an extravagant full-length coat...the silvery skins lightly shadowed with delicate greys, mauves. Of "Apollo," Emba rare quality extra-pale mink. Made to order at Ritter Brothers, New York, also at Goldwaters. Dora scarf. Gloves by Crescendoe-Superb. Coiffures on both pages, by Ara Gaillant.

AVEDON

Lauren Hutton

DESIGNS ON YOUR EVENING—SPRIGGED BROCADE AND CRÊPE WITH TINY BOUND WAISTS

Sprigged and trellised with tiny roses, left: Lauren wears a delicious marriage deep of green striped brocade, the décolletage crossed deep and visible, key waist girdled in orange poison...plus a Niagara fling of cascade silk shawl. Made to order at Arnold Scaasi, of Onondi brocade. Earrings by Flemming for Judith McCann. Right: Oran lamé, October streaked slippery, Trapagolla. Gilded restrained crêpe, right: Orange-blossomed input crêpe stitched with golden spots, peaks at the subtlety wrapt and the close-wrapped wrist-bound with a smile slit with gilt-edged in leather. Dress by Triplex, at Garfinckel's, Washington, D.C. Jewelled columns, Garfinckel's. Bracelet, Cartier rings. Shoe lotsaways sandals by Latinas.

jane birkin Serge gainsbourg

MORE DASH THAN CASH —THE LONG LEGGY MIDIS AT MINI PRICES

Jane Birkin—the girl with the cat-green eyes and swishing hair. Young and happy . . . this year's girl. Laughing it up here with her best beau, Serge Gainsbourg. Both of them white-hot stars, hitting first in Europe, blazing now on college campuses across the country with their super first album, *Je T'Aime*, written by Serge, and their movies—*Slogan, Cannabis*. Jane's next picture, sans Serge, *The Movement*. . . . On these six pages, she's moving and grooving the kind of free and easy fashion that all modern girls adore—all at adorable little prices. . . .

$89 wraps it up, left, and just look at Jane and Serge rapping together, tied up in a tug-of-war—Jane's midi skirt is forest-green matte jersey slit open to show her long legs. With a deep-red jersey wraparound top and red jersey wrapping Serge. All: Maxime de La Falaise for Blousecraft. Of rayon (Style Trends fabric). Bloomingdale's; Miss Magnin. Cross by Bruce Rudow. Capezio boots.

$40 buys an Empire for Jane B. below: a soft black jersey midi, all décolletage with a little tie on the bosom. Of acrylic jersey. 499-Division of Kloss-Pruzan. At Henri Bendel; Sakowitz; Miss Magnin. Necklace by Danecraft. Battani patent boots. All of Jane's coiffures, these six pages, by Franklyn Welsh.

JUNE 1970
PHOTOGRAPHED BY
BERT STERN
The French "It" couple Jane Birkin and Serge Gainsbourg had fun with Bert Stern.

VOGUE INTERIORS 1962–1971

VREELAND'S ERA AT VOGUE REVITALIZED THE PHOTOGRAPHY OF INTERIORS AND SET A CERTAIN STANDARD OF ELEGANCE. SHE WAS ABLE TO ACCESS HER VAST ASSORTMENT OF FRIENDS TO PLAY ALONG AND BE PHOTOGRAPHED WITHIN THE PAGES OF THE MAGAZINE.

PUCCI THE MAGNIFICENT

A PROFILE OF THE BLAZING FLORENTINE DESIGNER AND OF HIS PALAZZO HEADQUARTERS

BY VALENTINE LAWFORD WITH PHOTOGRAPHS BY HORST

Emilio Pucci of Florence is one of the greatest fashion forces at work today. He is a visionary whose vision of women is the essence of modernity. Pucci's vision has become reality. He has largely invented the look of the woman of the moment—one might almost say he has invented the woman herself: narrow, athletic, strong, brilliantly at home in the sun, and still brilliant in the evening. She is the most beautiful and luxurious woman in the world. On a ski slope, she wears the most practical and amusing and correct clothes; at dinner in some palazzo, she appears in the most beautifully coloured pyjamas cut in the most perfect way; at a bistro beside the Mediterranean, she turns up in some ravishing absurdity. Pucci is an artist with an architect's sense of proportion. His vision is wholly personal, his effects wholly contemporary. But he has ten centuries of Italian past on which to draw.

Pucci's feeling for Italian tradition is passionately serious, inherent, and unforced. The Pucci family have been well known in Florence for about a thousand years. Within a stone's throw of Florence's cathedral, the Duomo, their palazzo still stands in the heart of the city, on a street bearing their name. Austerely impressive, stained and worn, its walls echo today, as they have echoed for centuries, to Florentine traffic and Florentine bells.

"Dark, narrow, and elegant"—Pasternak's adjectives for Florence might just as well have been applied to this present-day Pucci. And there is more than a fanciful resemblance between his unusually character-revealing profile and Pontormo's portrait of Cosimo the Elder, with its sad but undefeatable eye, and its reminder of an age when it was a matter of course for an outstanding man to have an outstandingly manly nose. He hardly ever laughs and rather seldom smiles; but mostly goes, rapt and preoccupied, head down and chin in hand, about his business. Like some figure from Cellini's memoirs, he seems always to be striding briskly away around a corner or (Continued on page 162)

MARCHESE EMILIO PUCCI DI BARSENTO

The greatest colourist in the field of fashion design, a unique practical power in fashion, and a member of the Italian Parliament, Emilio Pucci was photographed here in one of his fantastic, frescoed workrooms in the Palazzo Pucci in Florence. In his sombre clothes, which are individual but never frivolous (his jacket may be of some discreet but unexpected pattern or weave), he moves like a dark flame among the glorious colours he thinks women everywhere should wear—the yachting pants, ski pants, dresses, jewellery, all designed with the Pucci perfection of cut. In fact, the only luxury Pucci recognizes is perfection.

MARCH 15, 1964
PHOTOGRAPHED BY HORST P. HORST

Vreeland's role as a mentor and confidante to many designers was an integral part of her career. Emilio Pucci and Vreeland communicated frequently, and in a letter to the Marchese, Vreeland said, "Well, Emilio, you do make such amazingly modern and perfect things—and what we would have done without your shirts, pants, looks, divine color, and designed fabrics, I cannot imagine—you are a full renaissance in yourself and we must all be so very grateful for your wonderful work."

banners of the Palio horse race in Siena. On this page: The Pucci look as it runs today. An evening tunic, the print snowed under with sequins; an after-dinner skirt with a Balinese-prompted design; and, worn with white pants, one of Pucci's famous shirts which some women collect as if they were an armful of wildflowers. In the foreground: A scattering of present Pucci prints.

ROMAN CLASSIC SURPRISE

AMERICAN MAN TRANSPLANTED: THE PAINTER CY TWOMBLY
LIVES WITH HIS ITALIAN WIFE IN A BORGIA PALAZZO.
PHOTOGRAPHS BY HORST

BY VALENTINE LAWFORD

Exactly a decade ago, an eccentrically handsome, moderately uncertain young American named Cy Twombly, who had begun to achieve a measure of recognition as an avant-garde painter of promise, left New York to spend the spring and summer in Italy. Except for rare, brief visits to America, he has lived and worked almost ever since in Rome. In Europe, Twombly's work led to an introduction to Baron Giorgio Franchetti, a patron and collector of modern art who has an interest in the La Tartaruga gallery in Rome. Before long, Twombly was a regular exhibitor there and something of a leader among its youthful contributors. He met Franchetti's sister, Tatiana, and they were married in 1958.

The Roman apartment where the Twomblys now live, with their one-year-old son, Alexander, happens to be in a palazzo. In certain quarters, where it is assumed that avant-garde American artists should live in avant-garde American discomfort, this relatively insignificant fact has led to Twombly's being suspected of having fallen for "gracidnie," and somehow betrayed the cause. His own explanation is simpler and less parochial. Many of his canvases are immense. He needs vast wall space to hang them on, and vast doors, if he is to move them from room to room. *(Continued on page 193)*

In their serenely pale Roman palazzo, Mr. and Mrs. Cy Twombly, *left,* with, on the wall, a bust of the Emperor Hadrian, a Rauschenberg painting, and, above it, one of Cy Twombly's calligraphic paintings. *Above,* under a great sunshade, a bust of the Emperor Septimus Severus.

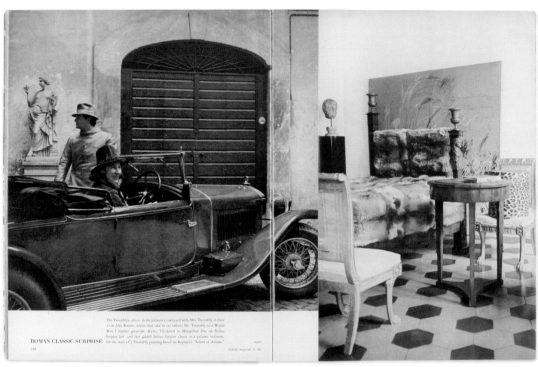

ROMAN CLASSIC SURPRISE

The Twomblys, *above,* in the palazzo's courtyard with Mrs. Twombly in their 1928 Alfa Romeo, which they take to car rallies. Mr. Twombly in a World War I leather greatcoat. *Right:* Thickened in Mongolian fur, an Italian Empire bed and two gilded Italian Empire chairs in a palazzo bedroom. On the wall a Cy Twombly painting based on Raphael's "School of Athens."

NOVEMBER 15, 1966
PHOTOGRAPHED BY HORST P. HORST
Horst P. Horst and Valentine Lawford traveled throughout
the world capturing the elegance and spirit of the era.

ROMAN CLASSIC SURPRISE Alessandro Twombly, aged six, *left*, in a Bersagliere hat (and sneakers), mounted on an eighteenth-century terra-cotta bust. *Above*, in front of his father's vast painting, "Triumph of Galatea," Alessandro, wearing a Knight of Malta's hat, with the Twomblys' silver-grey Neapolitan mastiff couchant on an Aubusson rug. The sum, a definition of Twombly magic.

FOLLOWING SPREAD
NOVEMBER 1967
PHOTOGRAPHED BY PATRICK LICHFIELD

Wallis Simpson had become a close friend of Vreeland's prior to marrying the Duke of Windsor. Frederick Vreeland recalls, "When Wallis Warfield Simpson, twice-divorced American, was invited to spend the weekend at the Prince of Wales's small country house, she went to Mom's lingerie shop and equipped herself appropriately, and of course, the rest is history. It was one of the most successful seductions in contemporary history, and it led to the abdication of a king, which, at the time, was a major political event."

A WEEKEND WITH
H.R.H. THE DUKE AND THE
DUCHESS OF WINDSOR

At the Moulin de la Tuilerie, their captivating country house near Paris where the royal touch is on everything except the atmosphere. *Above:* The Duke and Duchess with one of their five pugs in the garden the Duke created. *Right:* In the evening, the Duchess with the Duke, who is in Royal Stewart tartan with dark-green velvet evening jacket, dark-green bow tie, and buckled shoes. It is only at the Moulin that the Duke wears kilts.

JUNE 1969
PHOTOGRAPHED BY HORST P. HORST

Pauline de Rothschild and Diana Vreeland were very close throughout their lives. *The Irrational Journey*, a tale of the baroness's voyage to Russia in the dead of winter, was dedicated to Vreeland. Pauline felt her friend had two important characteristics: "You held two keys, discipline and wisdom. They gave you a vision. Of the real, of the unreal, of the unreality waiting somewhere in the wings to be made real. In your work as well as in yourself, you were the proof that noble things can be recognized and prosper."

OPPOSITE PAGE
FEBRUARY 1, 1970
PHOTOGRAPHED BY HORST P. HORST

Gloria Vanderbilt first posed for Vreeland in *Bazaar*, and continued to appear in the pages of *Vogue* throughout Vreeland's career

Mrs. Wyatt Emory Cooper

"It is partly Japonaiserie by Whistler,
an Oriental dream of Vuillard,
Boris Godunov interpreted by Sarah Bernhardt,
and Catherine the Great's idea of a dacha,
a hideaway in mediaeval Russia."
Horst

GLORIA THE GREAT'S PATCHWORK BEDROOM

PATCHWORK BEDROOM

The room dances. . . . The floor glints and gleams like terrazzo, its parts quarried from a through-the-looking-glass land where anything that can be imaged becomes real. . . . The walls and ceiling vibrate like the candle-lit, mosaic-covered chapels of Ravenna's Romanesque churches, and its furnishings and fixtures are a curious conglomeration of diverse elements in as richly-complicated crossbreeding, as exotic variation, as the empire of Catherine the Great.

This is the bedroom of Mrs. Wyatt Emory Cooper, who is also, (Continued on page 220)

Opposite far left: Close-up, the patchwork floor covering of highly varnished, square and rectangular pieces of brightly patterned fabric, has the feeling of old-fashioned linoleum in a Mondrian-gone-mad pattern. *Opposite above:* The enamel-white mantelpiece displays one of Mrs. Cooper's favourite pieces—a Victorian wedding memento with bride and groom figures in a garden whose flowers and trees are made of tiny shells. The English Chinese-style desk, left, is an old family heirloom as is the Queen Anne chest which conceals a television set. In the foreground are a petit-point-covered 17th-century French bench and Elizabethan jewellery chest, embroidered with seed pearls. *Opposite below:* The room is entered through its own little closet-lined foyer covered with red and white gingham fabric. Above the sofa is one of Mrs. Cooper's collages of the Virgin and Child. The ivory figure of the Virgin and Child is French 14th century. *Above:* The draperies were originally supposed to be lined but were not to retain their translucent, stained-glass effect. *Left:* A collage of a cavalier by Mrs. Cooper.

185

YOUTH QUAKE

There is a marvellous moment that starts at thirteen and wastes no time. No longer waits to grow up, but makes its own way, its own look by the end of the week. Gone is the once-upon-a-daydream world. The dreams, still there, break into action: writing, singing, acting, designing. Youth, warm and gay as a kitten yet self-sufficient as James Bond, is surprising countries east and west with a sense of assurance serene beyond all years.

First hit by the surprise-wave, England and France already accept the new jump-off age as one of the exhilarating realities of life today. The same exuberant tremor is now coursing through America—which practically invented this century's youth in the first place.

The year's in its youth, the youth in its year. Under 24 and over 90,000,000 strong in the U. S. alone. More dreamers. More doers. Here. Now. Youthquake 1965.

HEIDI MURRAY VANDERBILT. Brown hair, level brown-eyed gaze, a brow of candour. At sixteen, she is what she wants to be: an acting actress—TV, movies, a featured rôle in the national company of *Take Her, She's Mine*, another in a summer stock tour of *Sound of Music*. Trains on ballet, modern dance, opera lessons. Writes poetry for pleasure, plays the guitar—has given concerts around New York. For Heidi Vanderbilt, nothing could be more fun than life, here and now. She is the daughter of Mrs. Murray Vanderbilt and Mr. Alfred Gwynne Vanderbilt.

112

JANUARY 1, 1965
PHOTOGRAPHED BY GIANNI PENATI

"Youthquake" and "the beautiful people" were terms coined during Vreeland's years at *Vogue*. Here, Gianni Penati, whose photographs frequently appeared in the pages of *Vogue*, focused on what he loved best: portraiture and beautiful young women.

VOGUE CULTURE 1962–1971

UNDER VREELAND, VOGUE BECAME A COMBINATION OF CULTURE, ART, HAPPENINGS, AND VIBRANT FASHION. "I THINK PART OF MY SUCCESS AS AN EDITOR CAME FROM NEVER WORRYING ABOUT A FACT, A CAUSE, AN ATMOSPHERE. IT WAS ME — PROJECTING TO THE PUBLIC. THAT WAS MY JOB. I THINK I ALWAYS HAD A PERFECTLY CLEAR VIEW OF WHAT WAS POSSIBLE FOR THE PUBLIC. GIVE 'EM WHAT THEY NEVER KNEW THEY WANTED."

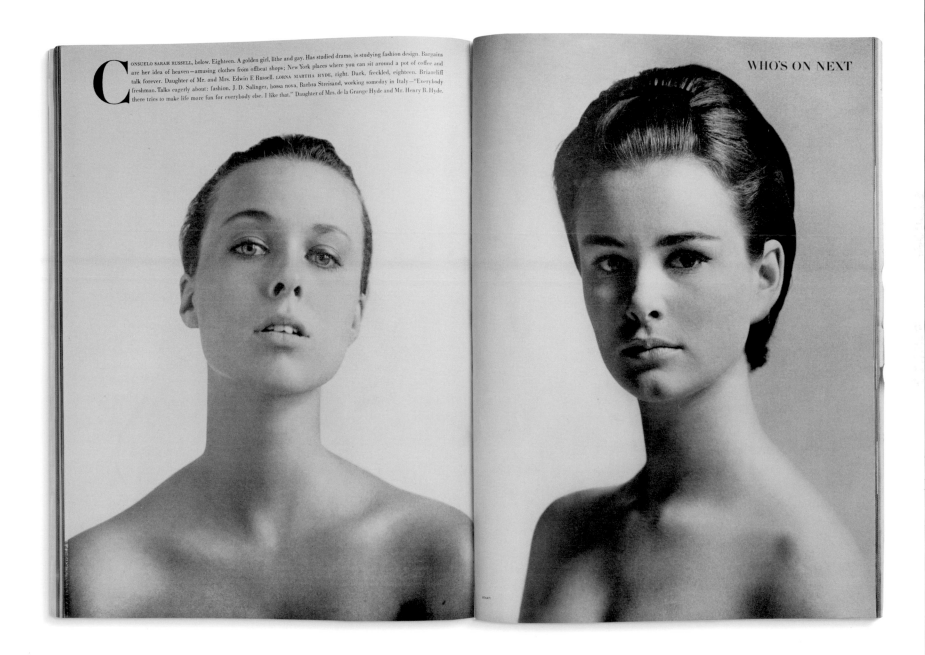

CONSUELO SARAH RUSSELL, below. Eighteen. A golden girl, lithe and gay. Has studied drama, is studying fashion design. Bargains are her idea of heaven—amusing clothes from offbeat shops; New York places where you can sit around a pot of coffee and talk forever. Daughter of Mr. and Mrs. Edwin F. Russell. LORNA MARTHA HYDE, right. Dark, freckled, eighteen. Briarcliff freshman. Talks eagerly about: fashion, J. D. Salinger, bossa nova, Barbra Streisand, working someday in Italy—"Everybody there tries to make life more fun for everybody else. I like that." Daughter of Mrs. de la Grange Hyde and Mr. Henry B. Hyde.

WHO'S ON NEXT

For Lady Godiva, left, fame, virtue, and courage flowed from a veil of abundant tresses—their shining hue curvaceously registered here in a version of the painting, "Lady Godiva's Ride," by Emanuel Leutze, who documented, in a similar, if less flamboyant, manner, "Washington Crossing the Delaware." ... This year in British Godiva's show-stopping ride—an eleventh-century protest against high tax rates—was eulogized by a Ministry of Transport poster showing a long-haired girl in a crash helmet whipping through Coventry on a motorbike.

JANUARY 15, 1964
PHOTOGRAPHED BY KAREN RADKAI

JANUARY 15, 1964
PHOTOGRAPHED BY BERT STERN

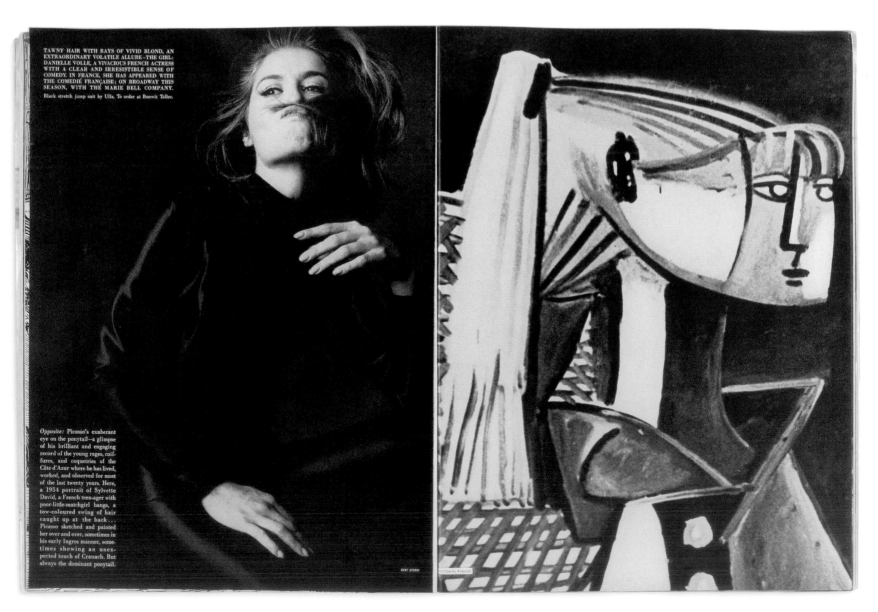

TAWNY HAIR WITH RAYS OF VIVID BLOND, AN EXTRAORDINARY VOLATILE ALLURE—THE GIRL: DANIELLE VOLLE, A VIVACIOUS FRENCH ACTRESS WITH A CLEAR AND IRRESISTIBLE SENSE OF COMEDY. IN FRANCE, SHE HAS APPEARED WITH THE COMEDIE FRANÇAISE; ON BROADWAY THIS SEASON, WITH THE MARIE BELL COMPANY.

Black-stretch jump suit by Ulla. To order at Bonwit Teller.

Opposite: Picasso's exuberant eye on the ponytail—a glimpse of his brilliant and engaging record of the young rages, coiffures, and coquetries of the Côte d'Azur where he has lived, worked, and observed for most of the last twenty years. Here, a 1954 portrait of Sylvette David, a French teen-ager with poor-little-matchgirl bangs, a tow-coloured swing of hair caught up at the back... Picasso sketched and painted her over and over, sometimes in his early Ingres manner, sometimes showing an unexpected touch of Cranach. But always the dominant ponytail.

188

Cléo
de Mérode
today

as seen by Cecil Beaton

The spring sun misted through the avenues of tender-budded trees, creating a Pissarro-like scene as my taxi swept along the lofty grey streets.

I imagined Paris as it was in the heyday of the woman I was about to see. Perhaps the Japanese fruit trees in the Parc Monceau, now in their first tender moment of pointillist blossoming, have grown taller, and the large apartment houses, built in a Victorian eighteenth-century style, have fallen a rung in the social scale, but the hand-painted lettering over small restaurants, and the announcements for opera and music halls, are unchanged since the turn of the century.

On arrival at number 15 Rue de Teheran, a gaunt and still imposing stone building in a vague "Louis" style, the tall wrought-iron-and-glass door opened to the touch of a button, but inside there was no response to the bell of the concierge's lodge. Nothing to do but work one's way up. I rang at the first floor: no reply. Then to the second. What if Mlle. de Mérode lived at the very top of the building? Someone high above could be heard opening a door. I shouted, "Hullo?", and a gruff voice replied, "Oui." "Mlle. de Mérode?" "Ici—montez au soleil! Je vous attend—le concierge est sorti. Tout le monde est parti pour la campagne. Les dimanches je reste seule à Paris, et j'aime ça. J'aime la solitude."

At the first sight of the solitary figure who greeted me over the wrought-iron balcony of her landing, preconceived images of a somewhat cold-hearted-looking face disappeared. Although this little woman, smiling her welcome, must be nearly ninety, her eyes sparkled, her complexion was pink and white and fine, her cheeks smooth and rouged, with only a spider web of wrinkles near the deep-set eyes. Her delicately chiselled nose and pointed lips were the valid features of beauty.

She apologized jovially that, having lately caught a cold, she had muffled up her throat and put this absurd stocking-cap on her head. Indeed the brown woven cap, worn low to her eyebrows, did appear somewhat eccentric, and it all but covered the hair, now slightly tinted, which was worn as it always had been, in the manner of Leonardo's "Belle Ferronnière," parted in the centre and drawn so low at the sides that her rivals had said she possessed no ears.

"How was it you maintained your classical hairstyle when every other woman was coiffed à la brioche?" I asked.

"It wasn't thought out at all; it just happened. As a child

I wore a square fringe. This would fall in my eyes when I was a coryphée at the Opéra ballet, and I kept pushing it back from the centre; gradually the hair grew and, in order to keep it from falling forward, I knotted it in a bun. When big hats came in it was difficult to fix them on without padding, but I invented a little hidden crown."

We had passed through a circular hallway with grey panelled walls and Boulle furniture and were now sitting by a window overlooking the roofs of Paris in a room with plaster decorations in the style of Louis XVI, with rococo wall brackets, biscuit-de-Sèvres figures in loving attitudes on ormolu-mounted ebony tables. Everywhere there seemed to be a collection of glitter-frosted Christmas cards.

My offering of an enormous bunch of May-Day lilies of the valley delighted Mlle. de Mérode. They must be put in water at once. I followed her. The vase chosen was huge, of Edwardian dark blue mounted with ormolu, and very much out of fashion. In days past it must have been constantly refilled with red roses sent by the King of the Belgians. As she walked with it held in her outstretched hands, I noticed that her figure had retained its youthful proportions and, although her legs and feet were lacking in the svelte grace of line, she moved like a girl. Her essential dignity dominated her whole being.

In a deep voice she told me that she was part of the Austrian branch of the French De Mérode family. She had come to Paris as a young girl and, fond of music, had become a dancer at the Opéra. For years she had studied, and when, regretfully, she left the Opéra, she had enormous success as a dancer on her own. She performed in every country, not only in the capital cities, but in every small town. She had never travelled with her own troupe: it was so much less trouble to do one's own act, to be entirely responsible. At the beginning she had a choreographer from the Opéra to work out her dances, but gradually she realized she was quite capable of doing them herself.

Her whole life, she said, had been one of dedication to her art. Even now, when she posed, to illustrate a point, with her head turned away and her hands (Continued on page 134)

CLÉO DE MÉRODE AT NINETY, PHOTOGRAPHED IN PARIS BY CECIL BEATON

92

FEBRUARY 15, 1964
PHOTOGRAPHED BY CECIL BEATON

Cecil Beaton and Vreeland had forged an important friendship from her time in London in the 1930s.

"Now Cecil may have been from the middle class, but he didn't have a middle-class bone in his body... Cecil used the camera. He had something that went farther than doctor's privilege, which I've always thought as almost ideal because there's nothing of the getting-to-know-you department. Cecil really could call up anyone in the world. He couldn't call up royalty—they don't take telephone calls—but *they'd* call *him. Everyone* wanted to meet this extraordinary character and be photographed by him."

FOLLOWING SPREAD
JANUARY 15, 1965
PHOTOGRAPHED BY IRVING PENN

Irving Penn's fashion coverage at *Vogue* is well documented, but his ethnographic pictures left an indelible mark on the magazine's pages. Vreeland worked with Penn on the fashion pages, but it was Alexander Liberman who gave him the liberty to create these unforgettable images.

THE MOUNTAIN MEN OF CRETE

PROUD, SIMPLE PEOPLE, MANY WERE PARTISANS WHO FLED TO THE HIGH PASSES WHERE THE NAZIS FEARED TO HUNT THEM DOWN DURING WORLD WAR II. "THE OLD FUGITIVES ARE ABOVE ALL UNAFRAID OF LIFE OR DEATH. LIFE IS HARD AND DEATH IS AN OCCURRENCE, AND THAT'S THAT."

PENN

Right: Their Majesties driving in a 1949 Delahaye through the park of Chitraladda Palace. *Left:* In a marbled pavilion of the Grand Palace, Queen Sirikit's gold-handled ceremonial umbrellas, made for her in Paris.

THE GOLDEN COURT OF THAILAND

H. M. KING BHUMIBOL ADULYADEJ AND H. M. QUEEN SIRIKIT

TEN PAGES PHOTOGRAPHED BY HENRY CLARKE

FEBRUARY 15, 1965
PHOTOGRAPHED BY HENRY CLARKE

Vreeland's fascination with royalty started when, at a young age, she was present at the coronation ceremony of King George V. In a letter to Henry Clarke regarding this shoot, she wrote, "About the Queen of Thailand: I do think she is the most beautiful thing in the world—like a little flower, with the most exquisite clothes, and as you know Alexandre does all her parukes and coiffures."

I'M MAD ABOUT HER NOSE. A NOSE WITHOUT

STRENGTH IS A PRETTY POOR PERFORMANCE. IT'S THE ONE

THING YOU HOLD AGAINST SOMEONE TODAY. IF

YOU'RE BORN WITH TOO SMALL A NOSE, THE ONE THING

YOU WANT TO DO IS BUILD IT UP.

The exquisite, learned Princess of Berar, wearing, *left*, ropes of pearls, emeralds, and uncut rubies, and, *right*, a torrent of carved emeralds.

FEBRUARY 15, 1966
PHOTOGRAPHED BY CECIL BEATON

Vreeland was enchanted by this portrait of the Princess of Berar, and wrote to Cecil Beaton, "I do want to tell you that I think they are among the most beautiful photographs you have ever taken in your life."

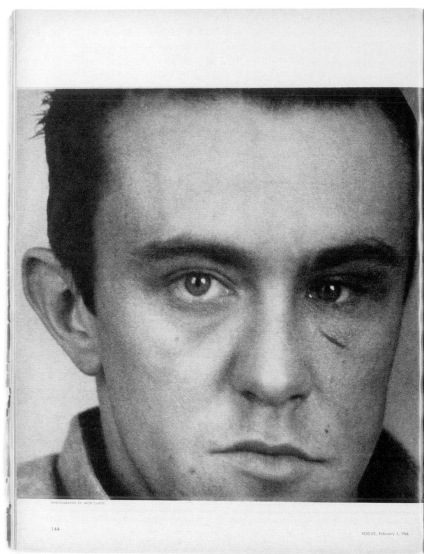

TWO FACES AND...

FEBRUARY 1, 1966
PHOTOGRAPHED BY JACK CURTIS

OPPOSITE PAGE
PHOTOGRAPHED BY TRUMAN CAPOTE

Fashion magazines rarely covered material like the murder of the Clutter family, vividly depicted in the pages of Truman Capote's *In Cold Blood*. Vreeland wrote to Cecil Beaton, "Truman was deeply shaken by the two men in Kansas being hung, even though it means the release of his book at last..."

The two faces belong to Perry Edward Smith and Richard Eugene Hickock. Smith, half Cherokee, half Irish, is the man with black hair, bangs, and a misty, brooding gaze. The other, the one with eyes of uneven size, he's Hickock. Together, they committed a quadruple murder on a lonely ranch in western Kansas; ended the lives, soon after midnight on a moonlit night in November, 1959, of a prosperous rancher, H. W. Clutter, his wife, and two of their children, a son and a daughter, aged fifteen and sixteen. Six weeks later, following a nationwide search, the pair was captured in Las Vegas and returned to the scene of the crime, a small prairie town named Garden City. These portraits, the work of a local photographer more accustomed to taking high school graduation pictures, were made in the Garden City jailhouse the morning after their return and incarceration—a snowy morning in January, 1960.

The landscape, a desolate sand road winding across the western Kansas prairies, was photographed by me one afternoon last October, almost exactly six months after the two murderers were hanged for their crime in a cold warehouse at Kansas State Penitentiary in Lansing, Kansas.

During the more than five years separating those two dates, I wrote my book *In Cold Blood*, a true account of the case (and its manifold consequences), which attempts to explain the men behind these faces, and the breed of Americans who inhabit it.

The first time I spoke to either Perry Smith or Richard Hickock was the day they posed for these pictures; the last was the night of their execution. In the half-decade interval, there developed between us an exceptional relationship, certainly the most intense I've ever had with anyone unrelated or with whom I was not in love. But the beginnings were difficult, the development a very gradual matter.

Well, no—not with Hickock. The basis of our relationship (mutual gain; he required certain kinds of assistance, I required his confidence) was quickly arrived at and, though it extended itself to an easy rapport, it never really altered, for Hickock, who had a mind that skated across surfaces with a cutting, chilling precision, could not adjust to any friendship with anyone of any depth or duration; he just liked to gab and entertain—amuse, as it were, a fellow passenger on a long train ride.

Perry Smith was another matter. At first nothing could win him; he wanted no part of me—or anyone else. He was like a broken-legged, ensnared animal. Yet, while he was awaiting trial, he over and again consented to my interviewing him—why not? He was bored and rather curious. He just didn't want me getting too close, that's all, and so was always suspicious, surly, and often asked, in a superior manner, my reason for wanting to write about him: "What is your *moral* justification?" My answer ("The only moral justification is the work itself") seemed to him, perhaps correctly, glib and evasive. More frequently than not our conversations ended with both of us feeling a high degree of frustration, even anger.

I don't know what caused him to change his mind and admit me to the lair where he had so long lain wounded and with rebuffing eyes. But I think it happened when one day he said, in tones of begrudging wonderment: "Maybe it's so. Maybe you don't think I'm just some monster. Maybe you even do like me a little." I told him I did, which was true, and he laughed and said then in that case I must be crazy. But from that moment, and though we were to have many disagreements, we became good friends and collaborators—I could not have written the book without his faithful cooperation. "The important thing is, it's got to be accurate," he never tired of reminding me. "You can write anything about me you want to. Provided it's the truth. But if you lie about me I'll kill you. I mean it. I will. I'll kill you."

He had every opportunity to enforce this threat, for I spent a lot of time alone with him in an unguarded visitor's room at the Kansas State Penitentiary. After he and Hickock had been sentenced to hang, and had begun their five-year stay on Death Row while appealing their convictions through the Federal courts, I visited them every few months, and we exchanged letters twice a week, which was the maximum amount of correspondence the prison allowed. Dick's letters were like himself: brisk, factual, organized, peppered with dubious jokes, self-pitying in a tough style. Perry, on the other hand, wrote like a primitive poet: all was dreams and searchings, emotions remembered, illusions gone wrong.

He once wrote: "I live for your visits."

But in reality we both felt these visits were sad occasions, I remember, at the end of one visit, watching Perry as he was led by two guards across the prison yard toward the dark hostile little building that contained Death Row. It was winter, and it was raining, and I watched from a window as Perry and his companions receded into the rain, Perry, a small, handcuffed, child-man in drenched prison denims walking with bowed head. Then I returned to New York by train, and when I arrived, there was a letter for me: "I knew you were watching me from the window, I could feel it, and what I felt wasn't good. I don't want to be pitied. When you pity me I feel cheated. The one thing I know about life is that nobody can hurt you unless you expect more from them than they can give. And I want more than you can give. More than pity. That hurts. If I have to die, I guess it's better that I have nothing to look forward to or live for. So all in all I think it would be best if you never came here anymore, I say this for your sake also. Out of affection, if you want to call it that."

And the next time I saw him, six months later, was the last: 14 April 1965, the night Smith and Hickock were hanged. I said goodbye to them in the shadow of the gallows, first to Hickock, who grinned and shook hands as though we were standing on a station platform at the end of our long train ride, then to Perry, who kissed me and said: "Adiós, amigo."

And so, like their victims, they perished. As for the landscape, the stark earth upon which this tragic design was inscribed, that endures.

...BY TRUMAN CAPOTE

PHOTOGRAPH BY TRUMAN CAPOTE

VOGUE, February 1, 1966. VOGUE, February 1, 1966.

A LANDSCAPE...

THE SYLVIA Odyssey

Photographs with (handwritten) Comment by TRUMAN CAPOTE

Carlo, a crew-member, looking like a stone head among the stone ruins along lonely Turkish shores.

The "Sylvia", a white sailing yacht of grace and speed (seen here anchored in the bay at MYRA, TURKEY), manned by an all-Italian crew of courage and charm. Last summer, when the "Sylvia" spent a month sliding among the Greek islands and along the stark coast of Southern Turkey, most of the passengers were Italian as well, including the hosts of this Elysian adventure, Gianni and Marella Agnelli, and their young son, Eduardo; also Prince Adolfo CARACCIOLO, who was chaperoning his beautiful daughter, Allegra. The other guests were: a gentleman from Copenhagen, Mr. Eric Nielsen; and two Americans: this scribe, and a charming Tycoon from Washington, D.C.: Mrs. Philip Graham.

Marella, directing a speed-boat into safe-harbor at a Turkish cove where we want to bathe. But, lovely as it was, it turned out not to be too damned safe— a flock of wild bees swarmed out to meet us.

JANUARY 15, 1966
PHOTOGRAPHED BY TRUMAN CAPOTE

Truman Capote and Diana Vreeland carried on a prolific correspondence. Capote remarked that "[Vreeland] has contributed more than anyone else I can think of to the level of taste of American women in the sense of the way they move, what they wear, and how they think. She's a genius but she's the kind of genius that very few people will ever recognize because you have to have genius yourself to recognize it. Otherwise you think she's a rather foolish woman."

196

A STOP AT SPETSOPOULA

Suddenly, while swimming in the green, ice-clear waters of a Turkish bay near Myra, Kay Graham shouted: "My God! Look! That animal! That octopus!"

Everybody rushed shoreward — except little Eduardo and crew-member Giorgio, who captured the writhing beast, slew him, and, later, sliced, fried, and ate him

— the Greek island privately owned by Stavros Niarchos. Above, Eugenia Niarchos in one of a fleet of little al fresco Fiats used to jaunt about the island's mountainous, pheasant-infested roads, what a place! — for example, there are two yachts in the harbor: the "Creole", that famous black pearl of the Aegean, and the comely "Eros", which is known as "the guests' yacht." Other items: a helicopter-port, from where you can helihop to Athens in 50 minutes; a Hansel-and-Gretel hunting-lodge hidden high in cool pine-strewn hills; a classic white Greek-island church with windows of pure colored red glass and green glass; a white-sand beach, immaculate as a Japanese rock garden, and a beach-house complete with sauna-bath and a jukebox stocked with everything from Bach to The Supremes.

All in all, the Niarchos self-made paradise (the island was an uninhabitable rock when they bought it eight years ago) is quite an illustration of what you can do with money and a romantic imagination.

On the beach at remote and serene Olympus: a happy Kay Graham, an uninterested camel, and a congregation of friendly and very interested Turkish mountaineers — hard, weathered fellows who fed us delicate cakes, hot mint tea, and, through an interpreter, amused themselves by shyly flirting with the ladies

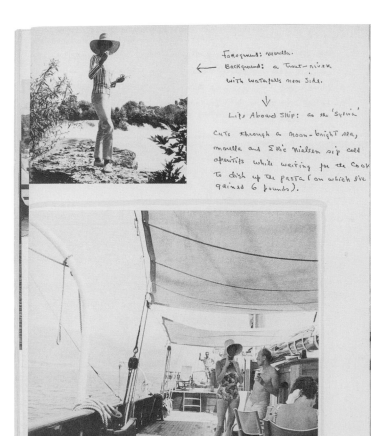

Foreground: Marella. Background: a trout-river with waterfalls near Sidi.

Life Aboard Ship: as the 'Sylvia' cuts through a moon-bright sea, Marella and Eric Nielsen sip cold aperitifs while waiting for the cook to dish up the pasta (on which I've gained 6 pounds).

Three generations of a finely-made Italian family. Right to left: Marella, son Eduardo, and Marella's elongated, languid, witty Uncle, Prince Adolfo Caracciolo. Someone once said of Marella: "It took two thousand years to produce that face." Yet the interesting thing is: her mother was not Italian, nor even Latin, but American — a famous American beauty born & bred in Pass Christian, Mississippi (of all places).

73

**APRIL 1, 1967
PHOTOGRAPHED BY
HANS NAMUTH**

Alexander Liberman once said, "Vreeland was an extraordinary impresario. She was a bit like Diaghilev, or at any rate she wanted to be. She had a feeling for the grand gesture, and there was something very regal in her generosity. She would give sixteen or twenty pages to something she liked."

POLLOCK,

GREAT PAINTER WHO WRESTED "AESTHETIC ORDER FROM THE LOOK OF ACCIDENT"

JACKSON POLLOCK, RIGHT, IN FULL ACTION AT EAST HAMPTON, LONG ISLAND, 1950. LEFT, A SUPERB POLLOCK OF THE GREAT PERIOD: "NO. 15," 1949, IS NOW IN THE MAGNIFICENT POLLOCK EXHIBITION, OPENING THIS MONTH AT THE MUSEUM OF MODERN ART IN NEW YORK. COLL. PRISCILLA PECK

HANS NAMUTH

O'KEEFFE

grace. She is almost totally unsentimental and barely tolerates sentimentality in others. Her much-touted rock collection is really only a collection of hard forms which satisfy the eye and the hand. The only pictures she hangs in her ultramodern interiors are her own, for testing . . . and an occasional Arthur Dove, perhaps the only painter of her own generation and after whom she sincerely admires.

Of course, O'Keeffe has helped to create her public images. She displays the stamina and country qualities associated with those born in the nineteenth-century Midwest. For her huge fiftieth-year retrospective exhibition at the Amon Carter Museum in Fort Worth and, later, in Houston last spring, she painted the largest picture of her career, possibly larger than any produced in New York that year . . . a massive canvas twenty-four feet long and eight feet high. With one inexperienced helper she stretched this canvas herself. Any but the youngest and poorest New York artist would have turned the job over to the pros.

Despite the fact that all these characteristic images of O'Keeffe are true to a degree, they only adumbrate, but do not really illuminate her painting.

In the Metropolitan Museum there is a watercolour titled "Blue Lines, No. 10," painted in 1916 by a young schoolteacher. This picture con- (Continued on page 221)

Right: Georgia O'Keeffe at the entrance of her Abiquiu house with an enormous elk horn on one wall; stones, bones, a wood pile, a bleached and polished wooden door, a working of textures, mushroom colours and browns. Above: In her patio at the ranch house with one of her two silver-grey chows. She grows in her small wild garden sage, chamisa, lace vines. The ladder takes her to the flat roof to see the sunsets, the gentian-blue mountains. Left: Like a Harnett still life, exact rows of empty wine bottles, kept for their labels, Mexican baskets ordered into proper confusion.

CECIL BEATON

MARCH 1, 1967
PHOTOGRAPHED BY CECIL BEATON

Georgia O'Keeffe's retreat in New Mexico, Ghost Ranch, was a source of inspiration for countless artists. Alexander Liberman, an artist himself, worked alongside Vreeland in securing the artists for the issue. She embraced his world, as it added more diversity to the pages of the magazine.

O'KEEFFE

GEORGIA O'KEEFFE, GREAT PAINTER,
PHENOMENON, NOW EIGHTY—
PHOTOGRAPHED ONLY FOR VOGUE
AT HER NEW MEXICO HOUSES.
HERE AND ON THE NEXT FIVE PAGES

174

CECIL BEATON

FOLLOWING SPREAD
JULY 1970
PHOTOGRAPHED BY IRVING PENN

Vreeland often compared her make-up ritual to that of a
geisha. She was fascinated by geishas and mimicked them,
especially when applying her rouge. In *Allure*, she commented on this image: "Look at the *texture* of this hair, look
at the pores on that geisha's skin… I don't think an arty
photographer can do close-ups. Only the paparazzi can
do close-ups—and Irving Penn."

T HE
GEISHA
1970

Four new
photographic
studies by
Irving Penn. The
geisha—except
for her false eyelashes
and her TV—is still
an enigmatic symbol of old
rituals in a country sparkling
with the future. Meticulously
contrived, she entertains the
men of Japan as she did a century
ago—and guards all secrets.

VOGUE DECEMBER ISSUES 1962–1971

THE DECEMBER ISSUES OF VOGUE WERE DEVOTED ENTIRELY TO FANTASY. VREELAND SAID, "I THINK I AM MORE PROUD OF THE DECEMBER ISSUES THAN ANYTHING ELSE BECAUSE I WORKED ON THEM SOMETIMES FOR AS MUCH AS TWO YEARS. 'NOW, THIS WOULD BE GOOD FOR DECEMBER '65, IT IS '63 AT THE MOMENT'—DO YOU SEE WHAT I MEAN? WE WILL PUT THIS OUTSIDE, AND THAT, AND THEN THAT, THEN WE WILL LEAD THIS INTO THAT BECAUSE I DID SAY THAT ONE OF THE DELIGHTS OF MY LIFE HAD BEEN THE LONDON ILLUSTRATED NEWS—ISN'T THAT WHAT IT'S CALLED, THAT FAT MAGAZINE?—AND I THINK THAT IS WHAT OUR DECEMBER ISSUE SHOULD BE. AND WE WENT AHEAD AND DID IT. I DO REMEMBER EVERYTHING ATTRACTIVE THAT I COULD THINK OF IN THE WORLD WE WOULD PUT INTO THAT MAGAZINE FOR DECEMBER."

"I don't want to be 'Liza…"

The delicious dilemma we have here is simply this: When Audrey Hepburn, on the brink of the plummiest part of the decade, cast those great enrapturing eyes on the clothes Cecil Beaton designed for everyone else in the cast, she suddenly knew that 'Liza is one of those heroines with almost Nothing to Wear. . . . Shaw invented her long before he wrote *Pygmalion*, as a "rapscalliony flower girl in an apron and three orange and red ostrich feathers." Tatters and violets, that's what Eliza starts with. But Audrey Hepburn, before taking to those real garn rags, had one glorious whirl with the gilded-lily dazzle clothes designed for the swells and chiquerinos of the Ascot chorus and Covent Garden. It was a play within a play photographed here and on the next six pages by Cecil Beaton, who did the costumes for the Broadway musical and will do both sets and costumes for the Warner Bros.-Lerner and Loewe movie of *My Fair Lady*. "The costumes must step ahead of the past to have influence," said Beaton. "But the ghost of my Aunt Jessie is present in all of them. . . . I remember her now as she returned from Paris with enormous five-foot-square boxes filled with hats and glittering finery." Said Audrey Hepburn: "He makes you look the way you have always wanted to look. . . . I adore the hats; they seem to be always in motion . . . the dress becomes a stem to the hat. Cecil Beaton's dresses are the sculpted statue—like Pygmalion's. With his hats he 'blows life into the statue.'" With that our heroine was off for the next scene.

For Ascot's Opening Day: white broderie anglaise…a hat ebullient with organdie, lined in black velvet.

"One of my most favourite hats". . .black velvet bows, white coq feathers.

DESIGNED, DEVISED, AND PHOTOGRAPHED BY **CECIL BEATON** ON THE SET FOR 'MY FAIR LADY'

AN AUDREY HEPBURN FANTASY

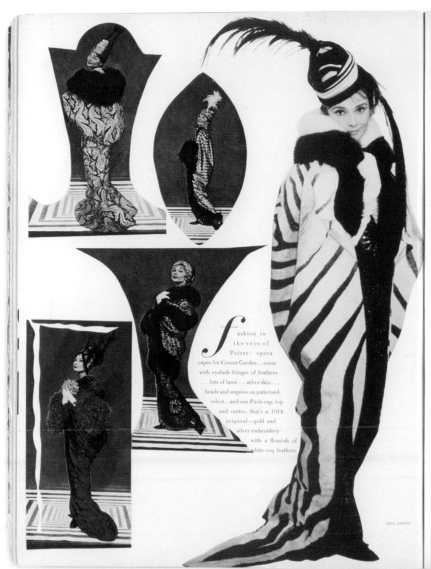

fashion in the vein of Poiret: opera capes for Covent Garden...some with eyelash fringes of feathers ...lots of lamé...zebra skin... beads and sequins on patterned velvet...and one Paris cap, top and centre, that's a 1914 original—gold and silver embroidery with a flourish of white coq feathers.

CECIL BEATON

When it's Ascot, there's nothing like a hat...black hatter's plush, a slanted bow of white piqué.

CECIL BEATON

DECEMBER 1963
PHOTOGRAPHED BY CECIL BEATON

While Beaton was in Los Angeles to begin work on *My Fair Lady*, he wrote to her, "I have been deep in back numbers of *Vogue* and *Harper's Bazaar* of 1913, and wonderful unknown French magazines. I have come on to a marvelous trick, which is to convert the back view of some of the dresses into the front. It really works. Already we are sending out magnets in every direction, hoping to attract lace-inserted stockings, huge blister pearl hat pins, kiss-curls on a wire, crystal necklaces, and disks of parma violets. It is a monumental job and I only wish it had not been necessary to take so much time. We shall be very much older when, and if, we come through it."

205

EASTWARD TO EDEN

PARADISE FOUND IN THE SUNNY SECRET REACHES OF TURKEY.... 26 PAGES OF NEW RESORT FASHIONS PHOTOGRAPHED BY HENRY CLARKE

Adventure: eastward through Turkey. To the edge of the Euphrates. To the very rim of the Fertile Crescent where civilization began. . . . A voyage of fulfillment for the imagination, already drawn to the Near East by fashions garnered from Asia Minor—the chalwars, spahis, and babouches which have brought a thousand and one nights of Turquerie to America and Europe and touched off a desire to see the wonders of Turkey itself. . . . The land of Troy and Byzantium where the empires of Hittites, Phrygians, Lydians, Persians, Macedonians, Romans, and Mongols waxed and waned before the enduring rule of the Ottoman Turks; the country where St. Paul preached the Gospel; where Saladin fought Richard Coeur de Lion and then served him sherbet cooled with mountain snow; the European promontory of Asia where armies and cultures clashed and mingled century after century, and where once stood two of the Seven Wonders of the Ancient World: the Temple of Artemis at Ephesus and the Tomb of King Mausolus at Halicarnassus. . . . Today, archaeological spadework is bringing to light an unsuspected wealth of treasures from the Anatolian past; only last year, the earliest paintings ever discovered on buildings were unearthed at Çatal Huyuk—giant hunting scenes of bulls and panthers covering the unbaked clay walls of shrines in the first known settlement on the plains of central Anatolia and dating back to 6000 B.C. Other treasures appear in a remarkable art collection now touring the United States and including in its 7,000-year range fertility idols of the earliest tribes, gold Trojan jewellery, riches from Midas and Croesus, a bronze of Emperor Trajan, a portrait of Süleyman the Magnificent. Across miles and millennia, the remote country as well as the art of Turkey is coming within reach as the interior begins to open up with roads and air routes to places hitherto inaccessible. Even places as removed as those we reached after three stalwart weeks of Jeeps, mule-trains, and sleeping bags—for the photographs on these twenty-six pages and the accompanying article on page 162: the Valley of Göreme's towering rocky spires hollowed into eyrie dwellings by mediaeval Anchorites; Pamukkale's lime-frozen fountains, terracing white and still down travertine ledges from the sacred Roman spa of Hierapolis to the plains of Çürüksu far below; Nemrud Dagh's formidable tumulus guarded by colossal limestone deities sky-high in the Anti-Taurus mountains—Tomb Sanctuary of Antiochus I of Commagene, a kingdom which flourished 2,000 years ago and commanded the upper Euphrates along Anatolia's eastern border . . . the western border of Eden.

Beeline to the sun

Great buzz of colour: chrome-yellow-and-black-striped djellaba dresses tucked high on the thigh—and on the first sunny leg of a Turkish adventure. Both silk dresses by Donald Brooks were photographed in the wind-carved Valley of Göreme. Coiffures, on these twenty-six pages, by Alexandre, Paris. Fashion details, page 262.

THE IVORY GODDESSES...
IN CHIFFON...IN JERSEY

Nike in a flight of chiffon, above: flowing
blowing, all biased and draped...layers of
ivory chiffon in a ravishing blur of motion,
with bare shoulders showing through a
transparent bodice. By Sarmi opposite.
A thousand yards of ivory jersey, opposite,
unfurled from a small curved bodice,
cutaway at the sides...nothing but
moonlight at the back. By Malcolm Starr.
Desert background in Syria: the ancient
city of Palmyra, where Queen Zenobia
once reigned....Fashion details, page 254

OPPOSITE PAGE AND ABOVE
DECEMBER 1965
PHOTOGRAPHED BY HENRY CLARKE

Henry Clarke, Ara Gallant, and the *Vogue* team would
travel to faraway lands to create these fantastical images. These trips were shot months ahead, and the preparation was endless. Vreeland commented in a memo to her
staff, "We usually do not have the most remarkable things
and we should have the most remarkable things, remembering that the December issue is dedicated to 'Wonders
of the World.' It is not a commercial issue, it is an issue for
which we only think of the reader and her delight in which
we can show her something remarkable to wear north or
south for the holiday."

A passion, a business, an exacting game of fortune, the raising of Arabian horses in this country has splurged from a trifling few after World War I to more than thirty-five thousand of these staunch, spirited creatures. In stables so immaculate and ingeniously equipped they seem at times more like spas than farms, these horses are clustered in Virginia and Maryland, the Southwest and California, the Midwest and New England. With far and away more Arabian horses in the United States than in any other country in the world, American breeders boil with perfectionism and partisanship. Is the larger Polish Arabian more desirable than the English Arabian with its elegance of line, or the wiry Egyptian Arabian with its enormous eyes? Or is the highest achievement a peculiarly American animal bred to take advantage of the best traits all around?

Give or take intentionally bred-in variations, the Arabian horse remains the only breed of horse to be preserved through history, its blood lines known and protected for five thousand years. Spectacular in endurance, too small to win in short races against larger horses, Arabian horses clean up in distance races. Strong, unafraid, and affectionate, they can serve in almost any capacity. But that is not the point. No statistics of efficiency explain the passion for the Arabian horse. Their beauty is part of it: In 1840 James Christie Whyte wrote in *History of the British Turf* about the Arabian horse, ". . . he possesses the rare union of strength with lightness, so essential to the endurance of fatigue in all quick motions; . . . to these qualifications are added the peculiar and deer-like elegance of his form, the broad squareness of forehead, the short fine muzzle, the prominent and brilliant eye. . . ." There is, as well, a quality of character, of devotion, of gaiety, of understanding not foolishly to be called human (possibly preferable to human): a quality too easily sentimentalized, and too imprecise for definition, but *there*. The owner of an Arabian horse attaches himself, not just to an animal, but to a spirit. (Shown on these pages and page 201, *Emaus, a champion Arabian stallion; and on page 200, Al-Marah Countess Eleanor Tee; both horses photographed at Al-Marah Arabians.)

A RABIAN HORSES, A NEW SURGE IN AMERICA

PHOTOGRAPHED IN MARYLAND BY LORD SNOWDON

210

DECEMBER 1967
PHOTOGRAPHED BY LORD SNOWDON

At *Vogue*, Lord Snowdon primarily photographed artists, but did work with Vreeland on the December issues. She was enchanted with the series on which they worked together. Here, an Arabian horse is enveloped in a surreal white light. A horsewoman during her younger years, she loved the elegance of the animal: "I mean, look at the way he carries his head; look at the size of his chest. You know, Arabs are so beautiful, if you have examined them narrowly. I've seen them in the sand, and they've got these beautiful faces with the eyes of a Madonna. Little faces, tender faces, and then these big chests."

A DANCER'S LIFE MUST BE THE MOST EXALTING THING IN THE WORLD—AND THE MOST EXCRUCIATING. BUT, TO HAVE PERFORMED ONE ARC OF THE ARM, ONE MOMENT OF BEAUTY, ONE SOMETHING...

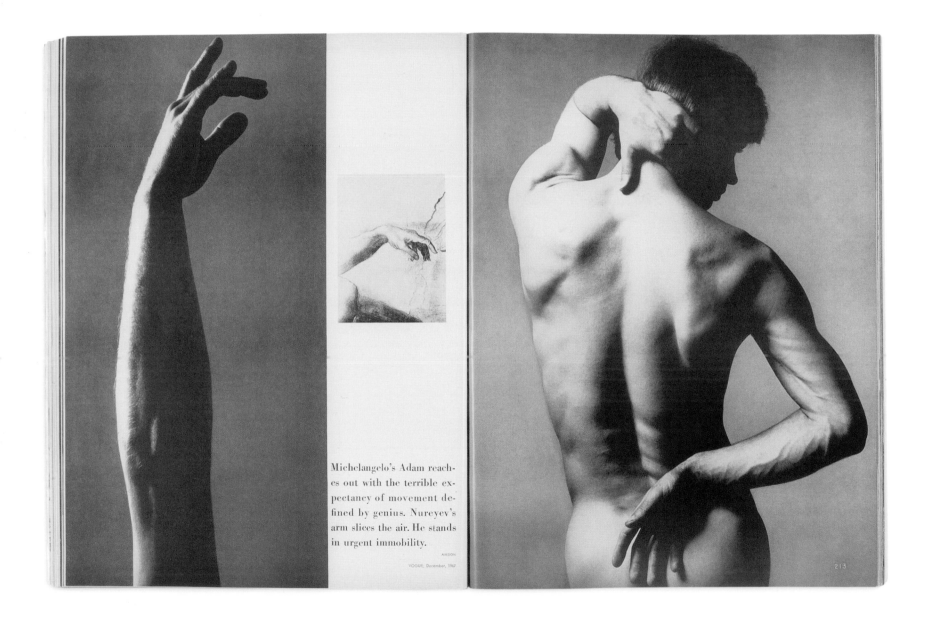

Michelangelo's Adam reaches out with the terrible expectancy of movement defined by genius. Nureyev's arm slices the air. He stands in urgent immobility.

AVEDON

VOGUE, December, 1967

DECEMBER 1967
PHOTOGRAPHED BY RICHARD AVEDON

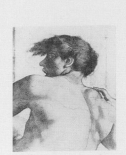

The everyday miracle of man, made suddenly memorable and rare by the exultant stretch of Nureyev's body. Those arms reaching desperately to conquer space, body and legs defying the constraint of the air, reiterate the perpetual yearning magnificence of man. Nureyev, here in an agony of action, could have been the source and inspiration for many of Michelangelo's sublime realizations of the human form. The taut, young muscled shoulders, *above*, of one of the Genii of the Anima Razionale in the Sistine Chapel have a prophetic similarity and express a total desire for movement that seems in Nureyev, to have reached fulfillment. In their perfection these bodies span the centuries.

NUREYEV
A PHOTOGRAPHIC STUDY OF THE HUMAN FORM IN ACTION BY AVEDON

210

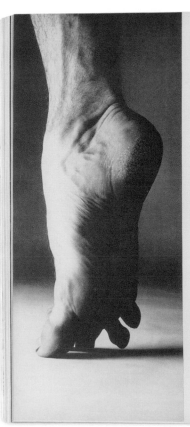

The fearful ecstasy of Michelangelo's Jonah, caught halfway between heaven and the abyss. The face of Nureyev, *right*, transfigured by the effort and energy needed to power his grace. *Left*, the tough, tensile strength of Nureyev's foot.

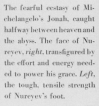

214

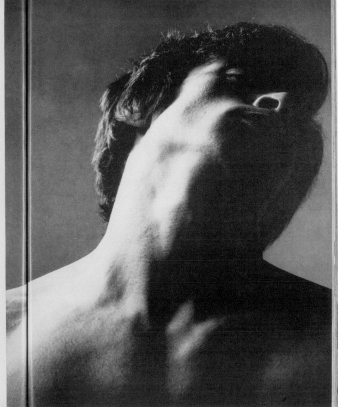

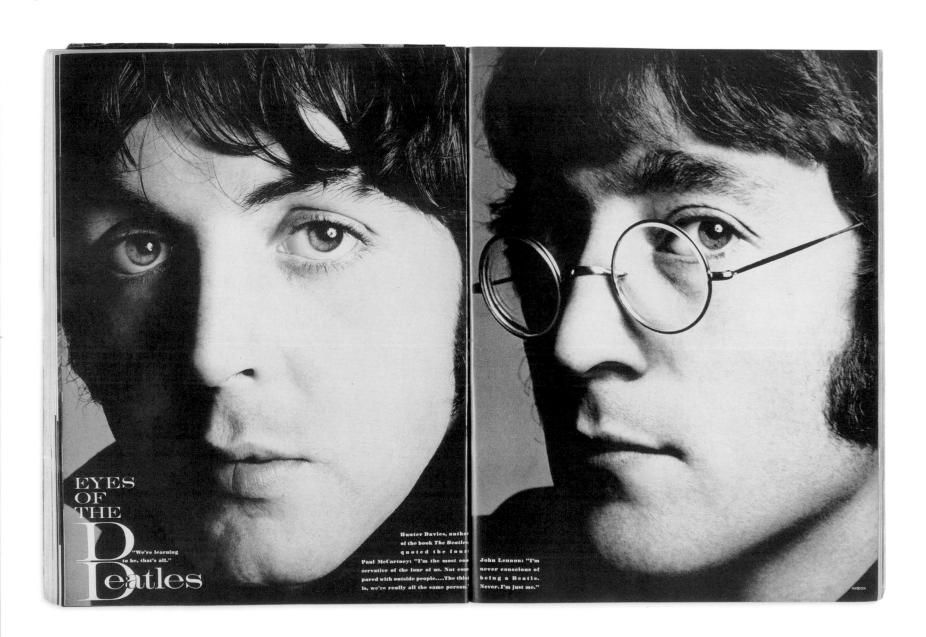

EYES OF THE Beatles

"We're learning to be, that's all."

Hunter Davies, author of the book *The Beatles*, quoted the four: Paul McCartney: "I'm the most conservative of the four of us. Not compared with outside people....The thing is, we're really all the same person."

John Lennon: "I'm never conscious of being a Beatle. Never. I'm just me."

AVEDON

DECEMBER 1968
PHOTOGRAPHED BY RICHARD AVEDON

Among the marvels of the 1968 December issue was a section devoted to eyes. Here, Avedon captures the Beatles' eyes, as their fame was spreading throughout the world. Vreeland was equally captured by them: "My point is the music, and also—I have to say it in flat language—the refinement of all four of them, out of Liverpool... there is nothing tougher on God's green earth than Liverpool."

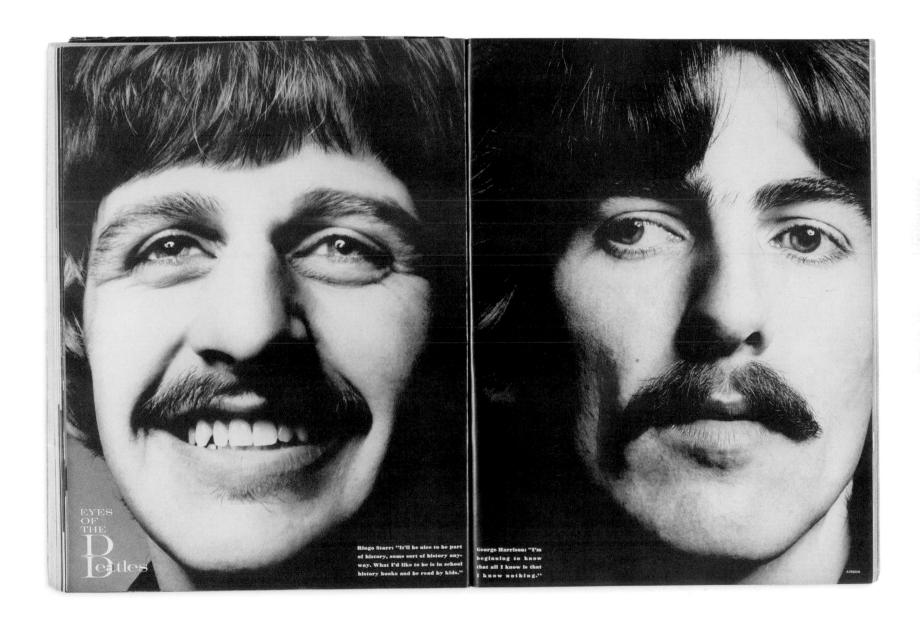

EYES
OF
THE
Beatles

Ringo Starr: "It'll be nice to be part of history, some sort of history anyway. What I'd like to be is in school history books and be read by kids."

George Harrison: "I'm beginning to know that all I know is that I know nothing."

AVEDON

192

AVEDON

EYES

The conquering, direct, and brilliant eyes of Catherine Deneuve, the star of the new film *The April Fools*: "I read that I am the most beautiful girl in the world, but I do not believe it."

eneuve

DECEMBER 1968
PHOTOGRAPHED BY RICHARD AVEDON

Vreeland loved filling the pages of *Vogue* with personalities. "Today only personalities count, with very few exceptions unless it is a 'new' beauty. Ravishing personalities are the most riveting things in the world—conversation, people's interests, the atmosphere that they create around them—these are the things that I feel are the only things worth putting in any issue."

FOLLOWING PAGE
DECEMBER 1969
PHOTOGRAPHED BY IRVING PENN

Penn always made a significant contribution to the December issues. He used his lens to transform his subjects into a painting, as he did with these poppies, giving them a visual rhythm and depth that only he could create.

'Arab Chief'

Kore-sculpture in cloth: mrs. wyatt emory cooper in her fabled fortuny dresses

PHOTOGRAPHED BY AVEDON

Of all the outdoor and indoor gowns that Mme. de Guermantes wore, those which seemed to respond to a definite intention, to be endowed with a special significance, were the garments made by Fortuny from old Venetian models. Is it their historical character, is it rather the fact that each one of them is unique that gives them so special significance that the pose of the woman who is wearing one while she waits for you to appear or while she talks to you assumes an exceptional importance as though the costume had been the fruit of a long deliberation. . . . MARCEL PROUST—"THE CAPTIVE"

In Gloria Vanderbilt Cooper, as in the Duchesse de Guermantes, the towering social figure of Proust's *Remembrance of Things Past*, personal style exists ultimately as a natural appanage of character, personality, and station.

"The purest function of fashion is to make a woman feel her best self," says Mrs. Cooper. "Immaturity in anything shows itself in self-consciousness.

"The choice of what one wears or does not wear is profoundly individual," she adds, "so the development of true personal style comes through a natural process of selection, and fashion success from satisfying one's own special instincts and imagination."

Recently, Mrs. Cooper's fastidious fashion instinct and imagination were fired by her rediscovery of her own collection of Fortuny dresses.

Each is a full-length volute (Continued on page 243)

183

DECEMBER 1969
PHOTOGRAPHED BY RICHARD AVEDON

Mariano Fortuny dresses ranked among Vreeland's passions. His aesthetic was deeply entrenched in the tradition of Grecian gowns. Here, her friend Gloria Vanderbilt models Fortuny gowns from her private collection.

FOLLOWING SPREAD
DECEMBER 1970
PHOTOGRAPHED BY IRVING PENN

(Continued) age group. In traditional European society, a kindred convention exists. This evolution is reinforced by the evolution of design in response to the influence of fashion, so that the clothing of elderly people in some countries can be at once symbolically old and morphologically archaic. Depending on the societies and the individuals, one or the other nuance prevails.

To the symbols of sex and age are added the symbols of social situation. These are first of all related to the major stages of life — for example, initiation costumes, wedding clothes, the signs of widowhood — found among primitive peoples as well as among those living at all other stages of civilization. They are then related to the techno-economic situation, and from group to group offer the endless variety of costume and decoration worn by soldiers of varying rank, executives, tradespeople, workers — in a word, by all representatives of the mosaic of functions on which the material life of the group depends.

In the conditions in which European societies lived a century ago, and more recently for other agricultural-pastoral societies, the individual, male or female, bore on his person all the tokens which adequately insured his identification for the purposes of making initial contact and of adopting the attitudes and language that were appropriate to connections among the different categories of the group. Industrial techno-economic development has considerably altered this traditional symbolic apparatus. To the extent that social mobility has increased because of an ideological evolution wrought by worldwide means of communication, the number of social models has decreased, the symbolic European model tending everywhere to replace regional styles of dress. The loss of national costumes and of professional uniforms is the most striking sign of ethnic disintegration. It is not a minor accident such as would occur in the course of a major process of adaptation to new conditions: It is one of the principal conditions of the adaptation, and one which often precedes the real adaptation by (Continued)

NEW GUINEA HIGHLANDERS

Chimbu women mourning a dead warrior

Death exacts a drastic change in
appearance from these lamenting women of Wandi
who trade the splendour of bright paint
for sombre clay and dress in jute string and
withered leaves. Dried grass replaces
nose ornaments and shell necklaces are discarded
for mourning beads, called Job's Tears.

DIANA VREELAND'S ARRIVAL AT THE COSTUME
INSTITUTE AT THE METROPOLITAN MUSEUM OF
ART TRANSFORMED MUSEOLOGY WORLDWIDE.
HER MULTITEXTURED SHOWS ENGAGED A NEW
AUDIENCE BASE AND INTEREST IN THE WORLD
OF DRESS AND COSTUME.

THE COSTUME INSTITUTE 1972–1989

"I FELL IN LOVE WITH THE DIVINE FULL-LENGTH PORTRAIT
OF THE EMPRESS ELISABETH WITH HER MAGNIFICENT HAIR
FILLED WITH DIAMOND STARS, WHICH IS OUT OF THE
HOFBURG FOR THE FIRST TIME IN ITS HISTORY WITH US
HERE. I RARELY BELIEVE ANYTHING THAT I SEE IN A PAINT-
ING, BUT I MAKE AN EXCEPTION FOR WINTERHALTER'S
PORTRAIT OF ELISABETH. HE SHOWS HER AS SHE WAS,
A FANTASY, A DREAM."

BOTH THE PORTRAIT OF ELISABETH AND THE QUOTE TAKEN
FROM VREELAND'S BRIEF INTRODUCTORY TEXT IN THE
HAPSBURG EXHIBITION'S ACCOMPANYING CATALOGUE
REVEAL HER PASSIONATE RESPONSE TO OBJECTS AS
WELL AS HER PRIORITIES: THAT OF AN OBJECT'S ENDUR-
ING ABILITY TO COMMUNICATE A DREAM, AND THE
PROFOUND LINK BETWEEN DRESS AND ESCAPISM THAT
PERMEATES HER WORK.

RE–STYLING HISTORY: D.V. AT THE COSTUME INSTITUTE

BY JUDITH CLARK

Diana Vreeland's years at the Metropolitan Museum of Art were bookended with exhibitions of fashion, the world with which she had been so intimately involved for thirty-five years as editor of *Harper's Bazaar* and *Vogue*. Regardless of historical period, she continued to rework the ideas about beauty, decadence, and drama that had informed her personal and professional life.

Over seventeen years, Vreeland brought to the Metropolitan Museum for the first time examples of the magic of court dress from Russia, unknown Balenciaga gowns from private European aristocratic collections, the blouse Empress Elisabeth was wearing when she was stabbed, Peter the Great's boots. It was also the first time film costume had been studied, as she recognized its exquisite couture qualities and semiotic power. She brought together original costumes from the Ballets Russes; she themed (and therefore redefined) iconic modernist couture from Paris; she showed off the strengths of the Met's own rich collections through the show *Vanity Fair*; and introduced New Yorkers to the extremes of the *Eighteenth-Century Woman*.

In contrast to her years as a magazine editor confined to the two-dimensional double-page spread, Vreeland knew that exhibitions existed as three-dimensional worlds—and needed to be totally immersive. She knew that despite being a largely visual experience (the visitor was of course denied touch), she could play with sound and smell; that exhibitions also needed to be capable of reflecting the complex nature of fashion; and that she importantly could use the whole exhibition experience (and not just the individual objects) to reveal those complexities. She asked us to imagine what ideas the gowns were standing in for; she asked us to suspend disbelief and be transported to other times and places, and to be irreverent of historical fact.

To take her exhibitions prescriptively would be a mistake, as—like fashion—her work is underwritten by the movement of time and taste, of historical flirtation, and of personal desires and passions. Her catalog introductions were often written in the first person; criticized as egocentric, she placed herself at the center of any history. They read more like a magazine editor writing to every woman, as if always to say, "If I can do it, you can as well. If I am fascinated by this, then so might you be." She knew that in the same way she could have sold any American housewife a dress through *Vogue*, she could inspire them with a glamorous historical tale through an exhibition. Hers was work of absolute astuteness—she understood contemporary life and its imagination; that exhibitions had to be as convincing to the visitor as the progressive (and protagonist-driven) narrative of a fairy tale. She knew that fashion within the context of exhibitions of historic dress could add glamour, and more important that fashion could represent the contemporary; that it is the standard from or by which all historic dress is inevitably judged.

Diana Vreeland was employed as special consultant to the Metropolitan Museum of Art's Costume Institute from 1972 up until her death in 1989. The Costume Institute had been established in 1946, though the collection had existed since 1937, when the Museum of Costume Art merged with the Metropolitan Museum. In 1959 it established its own curatorial department within the museum. The Met was of course always aware of the potential for fashion's glamour to be an important fund-raising pull, and indeed the idea for the lavish Party of the Year, a ticketed extravaganza, was introduced in 1948—the brainchild of Eleanor Lambert—and continues to successfully fund the department today.

Vreeland's agreement with the museum was made official on July 19, 1972. Negotiated by the museum's lawyer, Ashton Hawkins, her responsibilities as special consultant were clearly laid out as "generating ideas for exhibitions and ideas for the final form such exhibitions would take"; "suggesting sources for additions to the Museum's costume collection"; and "initiating and supervising the contacts made between the Museum and the fashion industry with regard to financial support for the Costume Institute."

In her first year she was to receive $25,000 a year, added to which she could incur expenses in connection with her responsibilities, including the travel abroad which was so fundamental to her research—as long as these did not exceed $10,000. (It is believed that her first year was underwritten by her friends who were concerned that her transition into new employment after her dismissal from Vogue be a smooth one.)

When Vreeland joined the department, it was run by the hugely respected dress historian and curator Stella Blum, who had been at the Metropolitan Museum since 1953. Blum continued as senior curator during Vreeland's time there so there was a clear division of labor: Blum would care for the vast collection of dress in the more traditional curatorial role, overseeing both its conservation and documentation; Vreeland would work on exhibitions as well as nurture the Metropolitan Museum's relationship to (and with) the fashion industry. It was acknowledged that Vreeland was neither a dress historian nor a curator, and it has often been the different approaches of these two women that have polarized the opinion and practice of dress historians ever since: caricatured as Vreeland being whimsical and reckless with historical fact at the service of glamour, and Blum as the modest protector of best practice.

Philippe de Montebello, director of the museum between 1977 and 2008, recalls:

The hiring of Diana Vreeland was part of the Hoving plan to give new life and completely change the programming, the way in which the Met did things, by doing great big, what he called "Blockbuster," exhibitions.

Tom [Hoving] wanted somebody flashy, [who] would really make an impact. And he chose well, so Diana came in, not to be so much curator of the Costume Institute, [but] as curator of the exhibitions of the Costume Institute, and there were other members of the staff who did the routine work of curatorial study of the collection.

The director at the time of Vreeland's appointment, Tom Hoving, was planning both the physical expansion of the museum and the extending of its visitor demographic. The Costume Institute had no permanent chronological display and so relied entirely on temporary exhibitions for the visibility of its huge collection. It was through these exhibitions that Vreeland fulfilled her promise to Hoving, presenting displays such as The Glory of Russian Costume, which attracted 835,862 visitors, and Romantic and Glamorous Hollywood Design, which attracted 798,665, figures that had been unheard of before this time. In one exhibition a year, her work occupied a window of opportunity that allowed dress to be exhibited for nine months, thereby ensuring greater access, but which has subsequently been seen to be too strenuous on the textile fibers (and so loans now, and therefore exhibitions, are often restricted to a maximum of three months).

The Costume Institute's allocated space at the time was made up of six galleries, where the staff cafeteria is now situated. Underground and with low ceilings, they did not have the status of the fine art and artifacts galleries aboveground. As with all sequential galleries, they imposed their own architectural rhythm on the exhibitions: They formed a simple counterclockwise circular route characterized by one long vista and one possibility for real three-dimensional drama (gallery 5 was a square room with a raised central area), as well as good wall lengths for sequences, multiples, and chronologies. These galleries would provide the backdrop for the twelve exhibitions staged during Vreeland's tenure at the Metropolitan Museum of Art which opened up the language of exhibiting dress to radical changes that are now seen as representing the beginnings of what is described as contemporary fashion curating.

During her time at the Costume Institute, Vreeland staged: The World of Balenciaga (March–September 1973); The '10s, the '20s, the '30s: Inventive Clothes, 1909–39 (December 1973–March 1974); Romantic and Glamorous Hollywood Design (November 1974–August 1975); American Women of Style (December 1975–August 1976); The Glory of Russian Costume (December 1976–September 1977); Vanity Fair: A Treasure Trove of the Costume Institute (December 1977–September 1978); Diaghilev: Costumes and Designs of the Ballets Russes (November 1978–June 1979); Fashions of the Hapsburg Era: Austria-Hungary (December 1979–August 1980); The Manchu Dragon: Costumes of China, the Ch'ing Dynasty

HERE VREELAND DRESSES A
MANNEQUIN FOR THE
BALENCIAGA SHOW, THE FIRST
SHOW SHE PUT ON AT THE
COSTUME INSTITUTE.

(FROM TOP TO BOTTOM) *LA BELLE EPOQUE, ROMAN-TIC* AND *GLAMOROUS HOLLYWOOD.*

THE GALLERY PLAN DEPICTS THE SEQUENTIAL GALLERIES WHICH IMPOSED A DEFINED RHYTHM TO VREELAND'S SHOWS. ONE WOULD NEVER KNOW THAT THESE SHOWS WERE ALL IN THE BASE-MENT OF THE METROPOLITAN MUSEUM OF ART.

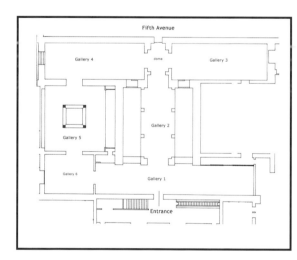

(December 1980–August 1981); *The Eighteenth-Century Woman* (December 1981–September 1982); *La Belle Epoque, 1890–1914* (December 1982–September 1983); *Yves Saint Laurent: 25 Years of Design* (December 1983–September 1984). For the later *Man and the Horse* (December 1984–September 1985) and *Costumes of Royal India* (December 1985–September 1986), she is still credited as the initiator of the project and indeed her notes for both exist, though she was not present and directly responsible for their implementation.

Though the list of exhibitions appears incredibly broad, if one reads it alongside her 1984 autobiography, *D.V.*, and her visual compendium of favorite photography, *Allure*, published in 1980, both written during her time at the Met, it becomes clear that she was working through a lifelong fascination with those periods and styles. The list of exhibitions unashamedly acknowledges (in a very contemporary way) the curator as author, and not as an invisible medium: Her work at the Met came late in her life, and so the repetitions become very significant; what she felt she needed to see again she re-presented: drama, the romance of the decadence and subsequent fall of empires (ancien régime and belle époque), Orientalism, and most of all her unashamed love of couture and luxury.

Tellingly, in her essay for *Allure* she describes working at the museum as delving into her past. If it were not Vreeland, one would assume this was a Freudian slip of the most interesting kind. The exhibitions allowed her to work through her passions: "You've got to make something out of it," she writes in *Allure*, an echo of her own pledge as a (plain) child to make something of herself and her preoccupations, and that was repeated as a chorus throughout her life.

You've got to make something out of it—the raw materials are not enough. A beautiful object was never enough; it always needed something to activate it, to make it interesting, to provide an exciting and compelling narrative. "I think" she once famously wrote, "laying out a beautiful picture in a beautiful way is a bloody bore."

Diana Vreeland transformed and extended a curatorial language that had been universally adopted. In the sixties and seventies, exhibitions of dress, or costume, were invariably made up of a simple equation: dressed mannequins styled meticulously for historical accuracy; a plinth raising the mannequin above the height of the visitor for both effect and to protect the gown from touch; a backdrop (painted or built with simple allusive architectural details) and gentle lighting (also aimed at reducing any deterioration of the textile).

Vreeland added props as centerpieces (carriages, sleighs, suits of seventeenth-century armor, even cast elephants), she piped in music and sprayed perfume through the galleries, installed dramatic directional lighting, and, most controversially of all, restyled historical silhouettes to her own taste, re-created the costumes she loved, and turned a blind eye to chronology. A dress became valuable insofar as it served the exhibition's narrative—her chosen narrative—and importantly the mise-en-scène's overall look and feel.

Mannequins represented a huge challenge— "the mannequin problem," as Vreeland memorably described it in a note to her staff. Inevitably, they lie at the heart of curating dress: They act as surrogates for the bodies we imagine wore the gowns and are also (through our inevitable identification with them) our way *into* the story. We may not know about a particular history, but Vreeland knew we do know about bodies.

When Vreeland arrived at the Met, it was customary that mannequins were dressed up to be continuous with the period in which the dress was created, so, as current curator in charge at the Costume Institute Harold Koda put it in a recent interview:

> A tennis player looked like a tennis player, the 1890s croquet player looked like an 1890s croquet player... the mannequins were styled to their period. It was about accuracy.

He continued:

> When Mrs. Vreeland did her first show... she painted all the walls these saturated glossy colors, green, red... She painted the mannequins because she felt that nothing suggested a time frame more than makeup. So she actually was getting rid of one of the details that help us understand the past because she was trying to make everything valid to a contemporary audience.

The cast mannequin bodies, like photography, were an opportunity for Vreeland to play with reality, to improve on it. "I adore artifice," she says over and over again. "I never took out fewer than two ribs," she claims of her doctored fashion photography within her many editorials.

VREELAND'S CATALOG COVERS WERE NOT OF STYLED GOWNS DRAMATICALLY LIT, NOR CLOSE-UP PHOTOGRAPHS OF INTRICATE DECORATIVE BEADING, BUT CAPTURED WHAT, FOR HER, REPRESENTED THE ESSENCE OF THE SHOW. IT WAS ABOUT THE IDEA THE DRESSES WITHIN THE EXHIBITION WERE CONSPIRING TO COMMUNICATE.

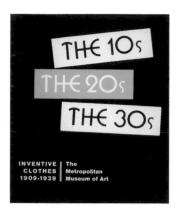

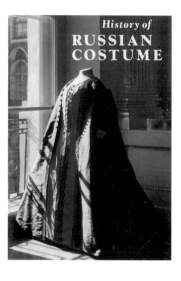

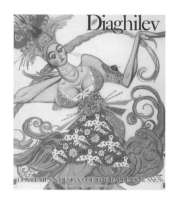

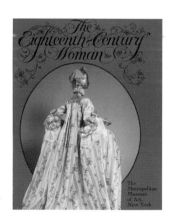

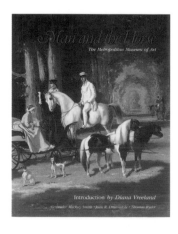

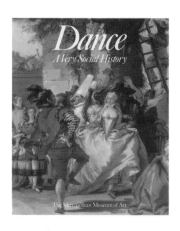

As a curator, she was always an editor and reused her magazine tactics. She worked unpredictably, in a solitary (and often single-minded) way: Everyone who was recently interviewed about her work noted there was never anyone who could anticipate her edits. She would find the thing that upset the rhythm, that threw a color off balance, and would edit fearlessly and irreverently, and that was her great gift.

Her exhibitions were haunted by fashion and conjured from its sophisticated language. If we look at the portraits by Steichen or Baron de Meyer that populate *Allure*, we find the origins of the stills of her exhibits. One only has to look at Beaton's portrait from the forties of Marjorie Wilson behind a framed gauze panel, in which he makes her features more abstract or blurred just as some of her other favorite pictures do. Why not put a stocking over the head of the mannequin as well? Disguise and blur its features? Her decisions were perceived as quite radical within the museum but were simply common practice in fashion, and had been for decades (with one exception, it was not the presentation of historical dress and therefore of historical fact).

Vreeland layered the visitor's experience, unafraid of excess. Perfume was hand-sprayed into the galleries every morning: She had Chanel's Cuir de Russie re-created for her Russian exhibition, she used YSL's Opium for *Manchu Dragon*—the present was always present even if in the form of a recognizable scent, letting its forceful branding work on the visitor's imagination. She was of course criticized for promoting fashion houses' interests, but had the perfumes not been recognizable, would they have worked? Exhibitions were suggestive for Vreeland or they were nothing.

(CLOCKWISE FROM LEFT) *BALENCIAGA, FASHION OF THE HAPSBURGS, THE MANCHU DRAGON.*

VREELAND DID NOT PLACE MANNEQUINS IN A ROW: SHE POPULATED GALLERIES WITH CHARACTERS, PROTAGONISTS IN HER EXHIBITION NARRATIVE. THE MANNEQUINS MAY NOT HAVE ARRIVED ON FOOT, BUT INSTEAD RIDING ON ELEPHANTS, ON A SLEIGH, IN A CARRIAGE DEPENDING ON HER PARTICULAR STORY, AND ADDED GRANDEUR. THEY OFTEN CONTAINED WITHIN THEM THE CLUE TO A ROMANTIC CONCEIT THAT HAD GENERATED THE EXHIBITION'S STORYLINE. PROPS OFTEN TOLD THE VISITOR MORE ABOUT THE CHARACTERS THAN A CAPTION EVER COULD.

JEFF DALY, CHIEF DESIGNER, RECALLS WORKING
FOR VREELAND ON A VAST TROMPE L'OEIL CHAN-
DELIER: "WHEN IT WAS DONE, IT LOOKED LIKE
THIS HUGE, CRYSTAL CHANDELIER WAS HANG-
ING THERE BUT THERE WAS NOTHING ABOVE IT,
SO IT WAS JUST SOMETHING YOU SAW FROM
A DISTANCE AND YOU COULD SEE THE PORTRAIT
FROM BEHIND IT. AND EVERYTHING ELSE, SO
IT WORKED."

(FROM TOP TO BOTTOM) *LA BELLE EPOQUE, VAN-ITY FAIR.* (OPPOSITE PAGE) *YVES SAINT LAURENT.*

VREELAND'S MANNEQUINS WERE ABSTRACTED, THOUGH NOT STRIPPED OF LIFE, AND EXPANSIVE; OFTEN, EXHILARATED GESTURE WAS USED TO ENSURE THEIR VITALITY. SHE PLACED "BODIES" ALWAYS IN RELATION TO ONE ANOTHER: SOME GROUPS IN HARMONY, SOME GROUPS IN DISCORD. THE GESTURES, OR RATHER POSES, SO IMPORTANT TO HER FROM HER LOVE OF DANCE AND THE FROZEN GESTURES OF FASHION PHOTOGRAPHY, WERE NOW ACHIEVED WITH MANNEQUINS' ARMS. THESE ELONGATED LIMBS OF HER IDEALIZED MUSEUM BODY BECAME THE DYNAMIC DIAGONAL LINES CREATING THE ALL-IMPORTANT ASYMMETRY WITHIN A ROOM.

To create a completely enveloping experience, speakers were also installed in the ceilings throughout the galleries. Ken Moore, who, along with Stephen Paley, collaborated with her by often composing music to accompany the exhibitions, said:

> I think music was an integral part of her exhibitions, that she thought of music as being the fluid through which people would see the show, sort of like a river, I guess. Be carried through the show... being reminded of the place and time by the musical hints that were being given because these were just short little examples of music.

Her exhibitions were also often driven—their narrative held together—by romantic conceits. Harold Koda, who worked for Vreeland, recounts a number of illustrative stories. Some are famously told in Eleanor Dwight's detailed biography of Vreeland. They are important because they illustrate something profound about her curatorial assumptions:

> Mrs. Vreeland corrected one of my projects and it infuriated me, but it suggests her strategy, in terms of museology. And, [this was] the reason why a lot of scholars really did not like her approach, because there was an aspect that was really ahistorical:
> It was during the Diaghilev preparations... and she asked me to do these headdresses for the Little Gods, which are these multi-headed

Gods. And... I was to replicate one of those, and she gave me the plum assignment of that show of creating the headdress of "Le Dieu Bleu," the Blue God, the Nijinsky role.

Koda recounts how he went to Kenny Lane and got the jewels and perfectly matched the headdress to the existing photograph of the headdress in black and white and the sketch with the color.

> Mrs. Vreeland comes in and... she says, "Harold, men don't wear pearls," and I said, "Mrs. Vreeland, this is the photograph... this is the drawing, these are pearls," and she said, "Harold, he's an Indian God! He's a Prince! He's thunder, and he's lightning! And he's the mountains! He does not wear pearls!" And then she walked away.... Once I had time to think about it, I realized, you know, it's a prop, it's not the real headdress. Who cares whether or not it looks like the real headdress; I mean, it's really about suggesting the character of this deity, and it made him look more like a warrior king.
> And so, there were these kinds of moments where perhaps in terms of the actual arid fact, she was not representing the historic truth but in a strange way she was capturing the real truth which is the sense of the integrity of the idea; that the idea is bigger than the actual facts. It just sort of breaks through the facts.

In 2010 the costumes have been once again exhibited by the V&A to celebrate the cente-

(CLOCKWISE FROM LEFT)
*10'S, 20'S, 30'S, YVES
SAINT LAURENT, AMERICAN
WOMEN OF STYLE.*

COLOR, IN ALL ITS INFINITE
SHADES, WAS VERY IMPOR-
TANT TO VREELAND: THE
POWER OF ONE COLOR TO
SHOW OFF ANOTHER. SHE
COLOR BLOCKED HER SHOWS
AS A GRAPHIC DESIGNER
MIGHT BLOCK DOUBLE-PAGE
SPREADS: GEOMETRIC, PAINT-
ED ISLANDS UPON WHICH
THE CLOTHES WOULD SIT TO
INCREASED DRAMATIC EF-
FECT. HER FAVORITES: SCARLET
RED, BILLIARD-TABLE GREEN,
TAXICAB YELLOW, AND VIOLET
ARE SEEN AGAIN AND AGAIN
WITHIN THE DESIGNS OF HER
EXHIBITIONS.

YVES SAINT LAURENT.

JUXTAPOSITIONS THAT HAD NOT, UNTIL THAT MOMENT, BEEN EXPLORED CREATED NEW CONNECTIONS WITHIN EXHIBITIONS. PAINTINGS EXISTED BOTH TO CONTEXTUALIZE COSTUME, THOUGH PORTRAITURE, BUT ALSO IMPORTANTLY ILLUSTRATED ITS COMPLEX RELATIONSHIP TO THE MORE CONCEPTUAL REALM OF ART. SHE NEVER STATED THAT FASHION WAS INDEED ART, BUT EXHIBITED THE LOVE AFFAIR BETWEEN THE TWO. SHE EXHIBITED YVES SAINT LAURENT'S "MONDRIAN DRESS" NEXT TO THE ORIGINAL MONDRIAN PAINTING. HER CLEVER HAND AS A CRITIC WAS TO EXHIBIT THE DRESS ON A FLATTENED BODY—HALFWAY BETWEEN 2-D AND 3-D—REVEALING A POSSIBLE AMBIGUOUS READING.

nary of Diaghilev's Ballets Russes, and there is the headdress, in gold, not a pearl to be found. The thunder of Diana Vreeland's own voice is palpable.

It was her eccentric attitude that has been criticized as creating unnecessary artifice, but her calculated distortion and corruption of history was perhaps her most profound statement within curatorial practice. She was asking something new of curating. She was asking how far a story could be delegated to the set, and how many characteristics can be invested in a silhouette. She made writing the story out on a caption (a more traditional approach) seem like a terrible defeat.

Having started her time at the Met by bringing in so many loans, in 1977 Vreeland decided to show off the museum's own rich collection with the exhibition *Vanity Fair*. Though it had "Treasure Trove of the Costume Institute" added to the title, it cannot but be associated with its original meaning, of empty ostentation in Thackeray's novel, a critique of mid-Victorian capitalism. With most curators the intention would be clear, a tongue-in-cheek reference to high fashion and to our ambivalence about it, but with Vreeland it was different. She was an arbiter of the audacity of glamour, and it was its resilience over time, over centuries, that she celebrated at her time at the museum.

"We are not presenting an anthology of the collection but a personal choice, Diana Vreeland's choice," said Philippe de Montebello, director at the time. Of course, all exhibitions are curators' choices, but usually they are mediated by a notion of scholarly objectivity. It is not clear whether de Montebello was celebrating the idiosyncratic nature of the exhibition or subtly distancing the museum from the exhibition's criteria. It is believed that this exhibition provoked the most internal tension in the department and clashes with Stella Blum. As she did not have external lenders to answer to, Vreeland had free rein, mixing elements of dress that were decades apart.

Her criteria was dress as aspiration to extreme beauty and decadence—the highest shoes, the biggest combs. She wanted people to be astonished, to look. Koda recalls listening to her audio guides to the show, and she would make statements like "'Now turn from the red gallery to the souk, as you know anything is possible in a souk,' and then she would say nothing else, and yet people would enter the souk, and they would see all these regional garments and then be thrilled by the masterful embroideries, the regional cuts. Her big contribution is she made people look."

The legacy that Diana Vreeland left behind at the Met Costume Institute is just as profound as

her mark on editorial flair, though it is much more contentious. Magazines have the intentionally short life of fashion itself. Her exhibitions of fashion were controversial, and she was criticized for them—the first being a memorial in celebration of a designer who had recently died, the second chartering new territory, celebrating a living designer, Yves Saint Laurent. The latter sparked a raging battle of the relationship between commerce and the museum, what dress historian Valerie Cumming refers to in her book *Understanding Fashion History* as the "hagiography of living designers." Her uncontained criticism of Vreeland is now infamous:

> Vreeland's success and monstrous ego overshadowed her talented but self-effacing colleague Stella Blum, the professional curator of the Costume Institute. Riding roughshod over curatorship and colleagues, Diana Vreeland reinvented costume exhibitions as glossy extravaganzas, fashionable social occasions and introduced the concept of hagiography of living designers. After her death in 1989 there were no more special consultants at the Costume Institute, but she had set a pattern that is still being followed: glamour, erratic scholarship and maximum celebrity appeal. It is a heady mix—fashion as spectacular theatre—and its impact has permeated well beyond America.

It is undeniable (and understandable) that it is problematic for dress historians when re-

search—so diligently and precisely collected—is trivialized in any way. But Vreeland's is not a cut-and-dry dumbing-down or cynical commercialism. Egocentric does not mean wrong or indeed uninteresting.

For Vreeland, looking was as good as reading, and exhibitions could contain narratives that were at once contradictory and provocative. If paper could stand in for hair, then exaggeration could stand in for exaggeration. Her recurring violet could be that of her sister's eyes, the beauty of which she was so proud to stand beside as a child in Central Park. Exhibitions can be eccentric and idiosyncratic in their allusions. Vreeland was relentlessly herself, so to judge her is to judge her whole body of work and to take her both more and less at her word.

EIGHTEENTH-CENTURY WOMAN.
(OPPOSITE PAGE) 10'S, 20'S, 30'S.

THE MANNEQUIN HEAD IS NOT ONLY THE MOST VISIBLE PART OF THE CLOTHED MANNEQUIN, BUT ALSO GIVES THE CURATOR THE CHANCE TO STYLE A SILHOUETTE. OFTEN AN IMPORTANT UNIFYING ELEMENT OF THE EXHIBITION, VREELAND USED THIS OPPORTUNITY TO GREAT EFFECT. IT WAS NOT ABOUT MAKING THE MANNEQUIN LOOK MORE LIKE A HISTORICAL FIGURE (WITH WIGS AND PAINTED-ON MAKEUP), IT WAS INSTEAD ABOUT BRINGING THE HISTORIC SILHOUETTE INTO THE PRESENT—DESIRABLE TO CONTEMPORARY EYES. PAINTING MINIMALIST HAIRLINES IN STRONG AND IMPORTANTLY UNNATURAL COLORS WAS ONE WAY OF ABSTRACTING THE MANNEQUINS' HEADS—BLURRING THEM BECOMINGLY BEHIND GAUZE WAS ANOTHER. WIGS WERE USED; NOT MADE FROM HAIR, BUT INSTEAD CURLED STRIPS OF PAPER, ONCE AGAIN GIVING THE IDEA OF A STYLE IN A MODERN WAY. OR SHE ALTERED THEIR PROPORTIONS, HARNESSING THE WIG AS A QUASI-PROP, AS IN THE CASE OF THE FAMOUS "EIGHTEENTH-CENTURY WIG" CREATED BY THEN-INTERN [NOW CHIEF CURATOR] HAROLD KODA, RECALLS VREELAND'S DIRECTIVE, "YOU KNOW THE 18TH CENTURY IS ALL ABOUT PROPORTION, IT'S THE HEEL OF THE SHOE TO THE ANKLE, IT'S THE WRIST TO THE ONGLE TO THE SLEEVE, ITS ALL ABOUT PROPORTION. NOW I NEED A WIG AND WANT IT TO BE HARD AS CONCRETE."

(FOLLOWING SPREAD)
IRVING PENN'S BEAUTIFUL BOOK, *INVENTIVE PARIS CLOTHES 1909–1939*, SERVED AS AN ACCOMPANY-ING CATALOG TO THE 10S, 20S, 30S: INVENTIVE CLOTHES EXHIBIT. PENN HAD FALLEN IN LOVE WITH VREELAND'S STYLING OF THE MANNEQUINS IN THE EXHIBITION AND PLAYFULLY SEEMS TO EXTEND HER DESIRE FOR AMBIGUITY BETWEEN ANIMATE AND INANIMATE BODIES.

CHANEL SEQUINED SUIT (1926), NEW YORK, 1974
VIONNET LONG ROBE, SIDE VIEW (1932–1935), NEW YORK, 1974

VREELAND SAID, "THE ENERGY OF IMAGINATION,
DELIBERATION, AND INVENTION, WHICH FALL INTO A
NATURAL RHYTHM TOTALLY ONE'S OWN, MAINTAINED
BY INNATE DISCIPLINE AND A KEEN SENSE OF PLEA-
SURE. THESE ARE THE INGREDIENTS OF STYLE." THIS
ICONIC IMAGE BY HARRY BENSON IMMORTALIZES
VREELAND AS THE HIGH PRIESTESS OF FASHION.

CONCLUSION

BY LISA IMMORDINO VREELAND

It is as difficult to sum up Diana Vreeland's career as it is to choose its apex. Her accomplishments and influence are extensive, and she has left her imprint on multiple decades. Her early inspirations evolved throughout her life as she was exposed to new surroundings, new experiences, and new people. Her gift was her openness, as she absorbed everything and applied it to whatever she was working on. She remained true to her vision, undeterred by anyone else's point of view, and was always ahead of the times. She invited the public to enter the world she created. She captured the zeitgeist and sealed it in the pages of *Bazaar* and *Vogue*, and in her exhibitions at the Costume Institute. Regardless of the medium, she dared us to look at things in a different manner and allowed us to let our imaginations run wild. In a profile on Vreeland, Jonathan Lieberson wrote: "She was perpetually scanning, monitoring, reaching for some idea, sensation, or tangible item—a fingernail, a color, an eye socket, a squashed banana, a jewel—that would, in her words, 'thrill me to madness.'"[20] Her talent lay in spreading her knowledge and passion for life, for people, and for diverse cultures to everyone. She did more than teach history; she gave us a template as she pushed us and allowed us to look at things with abandon. Vreeland's impact transcends generations. Throughout a career that spanned five decades, she remained acutely in tune with the times. Today her impact is just as relevant as when she was alive. She has an even larger group of admirers, who are fascinated with her personality, looks, and outlook on life. Vreeland gave her audience freedom of thought. She encouraged her followers to look at things from a different perspective, in the same way that Pablo Picasso and Andy Warhol did in the art world.

My own career began in the fashion industry, although art history has always been my true passion. Photography was a medium I came to appreciate quite early, especially the work of Richard Avedon and Irving Penn. Discovering Diana Vreeland's work at *Bazaar* and *Vogue* was the next step. Working through her archives, I realized I only knew the iconic images from the forties to the sixties and that there was so much more to see and discover. The photographs made me curious: They provoked questions on the "why and how" of achieving such strong and undiluted images. I was entranced with the sense of freedom and adventure the images evoked, leaving me with the desire to learn more about Vreeland's accomplishments. Thinking back, as I worked on various projects during my career, I now recognize the sense of freedom I was seeking within the constraints of my own daily work environment. I devised ways to get involved in interesting projects about which I was passionate. Perhaps this is the closest I got to Diana Vreeland's zeal for life. Passion, after all, was her driving force and the platform from which she leapt.

After marrying Alexander I began to live with some of her objects. A section of her bulletin board from her home is one of my favorites. It consists of a collage of her favorite images and has revealed the stories of the images she collected and why. The portrait that began to form in my mind was very different from the one I read about in the press. The media always focuses on her extravagant personality, her physical look, and her wit. I feel that they have overlooked her most important traits: her discipline, her vision, her curiosity, her passion, and her imagination.

Although her career was in fashion, it was clear that she was much more than "the empress of fashion," as she used this platform to firmly spread her philosophy of life. Her message was much greater than what she put forward visually: It was her perseverance and

THIS SITTING BY DEBORAH TURBERVILLE WAS PHOTOGRAPHED DURING VREELAND'S YEARS AT THE COSTUME INSTITUTE.

determination that showed us we could dare to think in a different way to transcend our lives. She was motivated by new experiences and new ideas and was able to transmit that to us. We should rejoice in this and thank her for allowing us to see the world through her eyes and mind. She inspired me to create this book. She has encouraged me to reach beyond what I perceived as my intellectual and mental limits to work on something that I will be proud of. She has given me the opportunity to do what I love the most: to research, and to enrich and broaden my mind. These qualities are what pushed her forward in life, helped her to create, and are responsible for what we see today. She imbued us not only with beautiful images to look at, but challenged us to think in a different way. As a woman, I think it is important to note the powerful role model that Diana Vreeland has been, helping people dream and live their lives regardless of gender. She did not believe in compromise and ushered in generations of working women who wanted it all.

Diana Vreeland's traits do not play a role in society today, and we should be reminded that these characteristics should be an essential ingredient to our daily lives. In today's world, where we rely on the Internet for everything, her vision is more essential. She has played a pivotal role not only in the fashion world but in the realm of creativity worldwide. She imbued life with a passion for beautiful and interesting individuals, objects, and places. She has inspired us to look at the world in a different fashion. This in itself is a rare quality that has not been carried forward in today's society. I am reminded of Cosimo Piovasco, the main

character in Italo Calvino's *The Baron in the Trees*, one of my favorite books. He chose to live in the trees because he felt that his vantage point on life would be more extraordinary up there, and it was. "Now it was a whole different world.... [H]e who spent his nights listening to the sap running through its cells; the circles marking the years inside the trunks... There is the moment when the silence of the countryside gathersin the ear and breaks into a myriad of sounds... the sounds follow one another, and the ear eventually discerns more and more of them... But at every rise or fall of the wind every sound changes and is renewed."[21] Diana Vreeland chose to live life in her own fashion and had her own perception of the world, like Cosimo. Their perspectives were different and unique, which singled them out as individuals who were strict, independent thinkers and wanted to live life in a different manner.

I was personally compelled to create this book to showcase her visual contributions to the world, unmarred by people's opinions and thoughts; I wanted her work and words to speak for themselves. The subtitle "The Eye Has to Travel" is a quotation from *Allure*. It is simple and yet reveals quite a lot about Vreeland's approach to the world. At a time when the world is changing so quickly, we need someone like Vreeland who celebrates original thought, beauty, and imagination. Through her work she has allowed us to live in other worlds and understand that life is malleable, just as beauty is. With her trained and diligent eye, she opened our minds and gave us the freedom to imagine. Her images and accomplishments are as fresh and relevant now as they were then. Her spirit is just as vibrant.

I HAD A <u>MARVELOUS</u> LIFE—I ALWAYS STUCK TO MY <u>DREAMS</u>.

DIANA VREELAND, NEW YORK, OCTOBER 1958
PHOTOGRAPH BY RICHARD AVEDON

247

NOTES

PAGE 8
Diana Vreeland and Christopher Hemphill, *Allure* (Bulfinch Press, 1980): 11.

PAGE 9, NOTE 1
John Duka, "Diana Vreeland—A Bravura Style," *New York Times*, late city edition (June 3, 1984): 63.

PAGE 10, NOTE 2
Jonathan Lieberson, "Empress of Fashion: Diana Vreeland," *Interview* (December 1980): 22.

PAGE 10, NOTE 3
Tim Vreeland's speech, Memorial Service for Diana Vreeland at the Metropolitan Museum of Art, New York (November 6, 1989).

PAGE 10, NOTE 4
Cecil Beaton, *The Glass of Fashion* (Doubleday & Company, Inc., 1954): 360.

PAGE 11, NOTE 5
Jonathan Lieberson, "Empress of Fashion: Diana Vreeland," *Interview* (December 1980): 25.

PAGE 11, NOTE 6
Diana Vreeland, recorded interview with George Plimpton, tape 3 side A, courtesy of the Diana Vreeland Estate, 1983.

PAGE 11, NOTE 7
Patricia Coffin, "*Vogue's* Diana Vreeland: She Sets the Fashion," *Look* (January 11, 1966): 59.

PAGE 11, NOTE 8
Richard Avedon's speech, Memorial Service for Diana Vreeland at the Metropolitan Museum of Art, New York (November 6, 1989).

PAGE 13, NOTE 9
Lillian Bassman, interview with Lisa Immordino Vreeland, July 2009.

PAGE 13, NOTE 10
Melvin Sokolsky, interview with Lisa Immordino Vreeland, September 2009.

PAGE 13, NOTE 11
Susan Train, interview with Lisa Immordino Vreeland, September 2009.

PAGE 13, NOTE 12
Manolo Blahnik, interview with Lisa Immordino Vreeland, February 2009.

PAGE 13, NOTE 13
Diana Vreeland, recorded interview with George Plimpton, tape 7 side A, courtesy of the Diana Vreeland Estate, 1983.

PAGE 14, NOTE 14
Bob Colacello, interview with Lisa Immordino Vreeland, April 2009.

PAGE 14, NOTE 15
Amy Fine Collins, "The Cult of Diana," *Vanity Fair* (November 1993).

PAGE 14, NOTE 16
Diana Vreeland and Christopher Hemphill, *Allure* (Bulfinch Press, 1980): 24.

PAGE 14, NOTE 17
Jonathan Lieberson, "Empress of Fashion: Diana Vreeland," *Interview* (December 1980): 28.

PAGE 15, NOTE 18
Diana Vreeland to Veruschka, September 9, 1970. Courtesy of the Diana Vreeland Papers, Manuscripts and Archives Division, The New York Public Library.

PAGE 16, NOTE 19
Francesca Stanfill, "A Vision of Style," *New York Times* (September 14, 1980).

PAGE 24
Pull quote: Diana Vreeland and Christopher Hemphill, *Allure* (Bulfinch Press, 1980): 134.

PAGES 24–39
Amy Fine Collins, "The Cult of Diana." *Vanity Fair* (November 1993): 174–190.

Eleanor Dwight, *Diana Vreeland* (Harper Collins, 2002).

Dodie Kazanjian and Calvin Tomkins, *Alex: The Life of Alexander Liberman* (Alfred A.Knopf, Inc, 1993).

Jonathan Lieberson, "Empress of Fashion: Diana Vreeland," *Interview* (December 1980): 24–29.

Thomas Maier, *Newhouse: All the Glitter, Power, and Glory of America's Richest Media Empire and the Secretive Man Behind It* (Johnson Books, 1997).

Penelope Rowlands, *A Dash of Daring: Carmel Snow and Her Life in Fashion, Art and Letters* (Atria Books, 2005).

Debora Silverman, *Selling Culture: Bloomingdale's, Diana Vreeland, and the New Aristocracy of Taste in Reagan's America* (Pantheon Books, 1986).

Carmel Snow with Mary Louise Aswell, *The World of Carmel Snow* (McGraw-Hill, 1962).

George W. S. Trow, "Haute, Haute Couture." *The New Yorker* (May 26, 1975): 81.

Diana Vreeland, *D.V.* (Alfred A. Knopf, Inc., 1984).

Diana Vreeland, "Why Don't You?" *Harper's Bazaar* (November 1936): 90.
   "Why Don't You?" *Harper's Bazaar* (January 1937): 88–89.

"Why Don't You?" *Harper's Bazaar* (February 1937): 82–83.
"Why Don't You?" *Harper's Bazaar* (March 1937): 121.
"Why Don't You?" *Harper's Bazaar* (April 1937): 82–83.
"Why Don't You?" *Harper's Bazaar* (August 1937): 90–91.
"Why Don't You?" *Harper's Bazaar* (November 1937): 111.
"Brides—Why Don't You?" *Harper's Bazaar* (April 1938): 102–103.

Lally Weymouth. "A Question of Style: A Conversation with Diana Vreeland." *Rolling Stone* (August 11, 1977): 38–55.

PAGE 29
Diana Vreeland, recorded interview with George Plimpton, tape 6 side A, courtesy of the Diana Vreeland Estate, 1983.

PAGE 31
Diana Vreeland, *D.V.* (Alfred A. Knopf, Inc., 1984): 149.

PAGE 32
Cecil Beaton, *The Glass of Fashion* (Doubleday & Company, Inc., 1954): 365.

PAGE 37
Diana Vreeland and Christopher Hemphill, *Allure* (Bulfinch Press, 1980): 203.

PAGE 39
Lally Weymouth. "A Question of Style: A Conversation with Diana Vreeland." *Rolling Stone* (August 11, 1977): 51.

PAGE 42:
Diana Vreeland, *D.V.* (Alfred A. Knopf, Inc., 1984): 106.

PAGE 43
Diana Vreeland, "WHY DON'T YOU," *Harper's Bazaar* (February 1937): 82–83.

PAGE 44
Harper's Bazaar (August 1937): 90–91.

PAGE 47
Pull quote: Diana Vreeland, *D.V.* (Alfred A. Knopf, Inc., 1984): 103.

PAGE 47
Diana Vreeland, "WHY DON'T YOU," *Harper's Bazaar* (November 1936): 138.

PAGE 48
Pull quote: Diana Vreeland and Christopher Hemphill, *Allure* (Bulfinch Press, 1980): 11.

PAGE 48
Diana Vreeland, *D.V.* (Alfred A. Knopf, Inc., 1984): 194.

PAGE 50
Diana Vreeland, *D.V.* (Alfred A. Knopf, Inc., 1984): 106.

PAGE 51
Lally Weymouth. "A Question of Style: A Conversation with Diana Vreeland." *Rolling Stone* (August 11, 1977): 45–46.

PAGE 53
Pull quote: Lally Weymouth. "A Question of Style: A Conversation with Diana Vreeland." *Rolling Stone* (August 11, 1977): 53.

PAGE 55
Bettina Ballard, *In My Fashion* (David McKay Company, Inc., 1960): 290.

PAGE 61
Vicki Goldberg and Nan Richardson, *Louise Dahl-Wolfe* (Abrams, 2000): 30.

PAGE 65
Diana Vreeland, "WHY DON'T YOU," *Harper's Bazaar* (February 1937): 82.

PAGE 67
Lauren Bacall, *Lauren Bacall: By Myself and Then Some* (Harper Collins, 2006): 72.

PAGE 67
Harper's Bazaar (January 1937): 132.

PAGE 67
Harper's Bazaar (January 1937): 132.

PAGE 71
Pull quote: Lally Weymouth. "A Question of Style: A Conversation with Diana Vreeland." *Rolling Stone* (August 11, 1977): 52.

PAGE 71
Louise Dahl-Wolfe, *A Photographer's Scrapbook* (St. Martin's Press, 1984): 26.

PAGE 73
Richard Avedon's speech, Memorial Service for Diana Vreeland at the Metropolitan Museum of Art, New York (November 6, 1989).

PAGE 77
Lally Weymouth. "A Question of Style: A Conversation with Diana Vreeland." *Rolling Stone* (August 11, 1977): 52.

PAGE 78
Diana Vreeland and Christopher Hemphill, *Allure* (Bulfinch Press, 1980): 50.

PAGE 79
Barbara Slifka, interview with Lisa Immordino Vreeland, September 2009.

PAGE 80
Pull quote: Diana Vreeland, recorded interview with George Plimpton, tape 9 side B, courtesy of the Diana Vreeland Estate, 1983.

PAGE 82
Lally Weymouth. "A Question of Style: A Conversation with Diana Vreeland." *Rolling Stone* (August 11, 1977): 53.

PAGE 84
Pull quote: Richard Avedon's speech, Memorial Service for Diana Vreeland at the Metropolitan Museum of Art, New York (November 6, 1989).

PAGE 87
Louise Dahl-Wolfe, *A Photographer's Scrapbook* (St. Martin's Press, 1984): 39.

PAGE 88
Lillian Bassman, interview with Lisa Immordino Vreeland, July 2009.

PAGE 89
Pull quote: Richard Martin and Harold Koda, *Diana Vreeland: Immoderate Style Catalog* (Metropolitan Museum of Art, 1993).

PAGE 91
Bettina Ballard, *In My Fashion* (David McKay Company, Inc., 1960): 290.

PAGE 93
Gleb Derujinksy, interview with Lisa Immordino Vreeland, September 2009.

PAGE 96
Diana Vreeland, *D.V.* (Alfred A. Knopf, Inc., 1984): 150.

PAGE 98
Comtesse de Ribes, telephone interview with Lisa Immordino Vreeland, November 4, 2010.

PAGE 100
C. Z. Guest speech, Memorial Service for Diana Vreeland at the Metropolitan Museum of Art, New York (November 6, 1989).

PAGE 101
Lillian Bassman, interview with Lisa Immordino Vreeland, July 2009.

PAGE 102
Diana Vreeland, *D.V.* (Alfred A. Knopf, Inc., 1984): 103.

PAGE 104
Diana Vreeland, *D.V.* (Alfred A. Knopf, Inc., 1984): 104.

PAGE 106
Bob Colacello, interview with Lisa Immordino Vreeland, April 2009.

PAGE 109
John Fairchild, interview with Lisa Immordino Vreeland, February 9, 2010.

PAGE 112
Pull quote: Lally Weymouth. "A Question of Style: A Conversation with Diana Vreeland." *Rolling Stone* (August 11, 1977): 53.

PAGE 112
Diana Vreeland and Christopher Hemphill, *Allure* (Bulfinch Press, 1980): 7.

PAGE 114
Melvin Sokolsky, interview with Lisa Immordino Vreeland, September 2009.

PAGE 116
Jackie Kennedy Onassis to Diana Vreeland, February 2, 1961. Courtesy of the Diana Vreeland Papers, Manuscripts and Archives Division, The New York Public Library; and Caroline Kennedy.

PAGE 122
Diana Vreeland, *D.V.* (Alfred A. Knopf, Inc., 1984): 147–148.

PAGE 124
Bert Stern, telephone interview with Lisa Immordino Vreeland, April 2009.

PAGE 125
Pull quote: Lally Weymouth. "A Question of Style: A Conversation with Diana Vreeland." *Rolling Stone* (August 11, 1977): 49.

PAGE 126
David Bailey, interview with Lisa Immordino Vreeland, February 2009.

PAGE 128–129
Diana Vreeland letter to Cecil Beaton, January 7, 1964. Courtesy of Condé Nast.

PAGE 130
Pull quote: Diana Vreeland, *D.V.* (Alfred A. Knopf, Inc., 1984): 148.

PAGE 132
Diana Vreeland, recorded interview with George Plimpton, tape 9 side B, courtesy of the Diana Vreeland Estate, 1983.

PAGE 135
Diana Vreeland and Christopher Hemphill, *Allure* (Bulfinch Press, 1980): 24–25.

INDEX

Editor: Rebecca Kaplan
Designer: Li, Inc. New York
Production Manager: Anet Sirna-Bruder

Library of Congress Cataloging-in-Publication Data:
Vreeland, Lisa Immordino.
Diana Vreeland : the eye has to travel / by Lisa
Immordino Vreeland ;
essays by Judith Clark, Judith Thurman,
and Lally Weymouth.
p. cm.

ISBN 978-0-8109-9743-1 (hardback)

1. Vreeland, Diana. 2. Fashion editors—United States—
Biography. I.
Title. II. Title: Eye has to travel.
TT505.V74V74 2011
746.9&2092—dc22

2011009735

Printed and bound in Hong Kong, China
10 9 8 7 6 5 4 3 2

Abrams books are available at special discounts when
purchased in quantity for premiums and promotions as
well as fundraising or educational use. Special editions
can also be created to specification. For details, contact
specialsales@abramsbooks.com or the address below.

115 West 18th Street
New York, NY 10011
www.abramsbooks.com

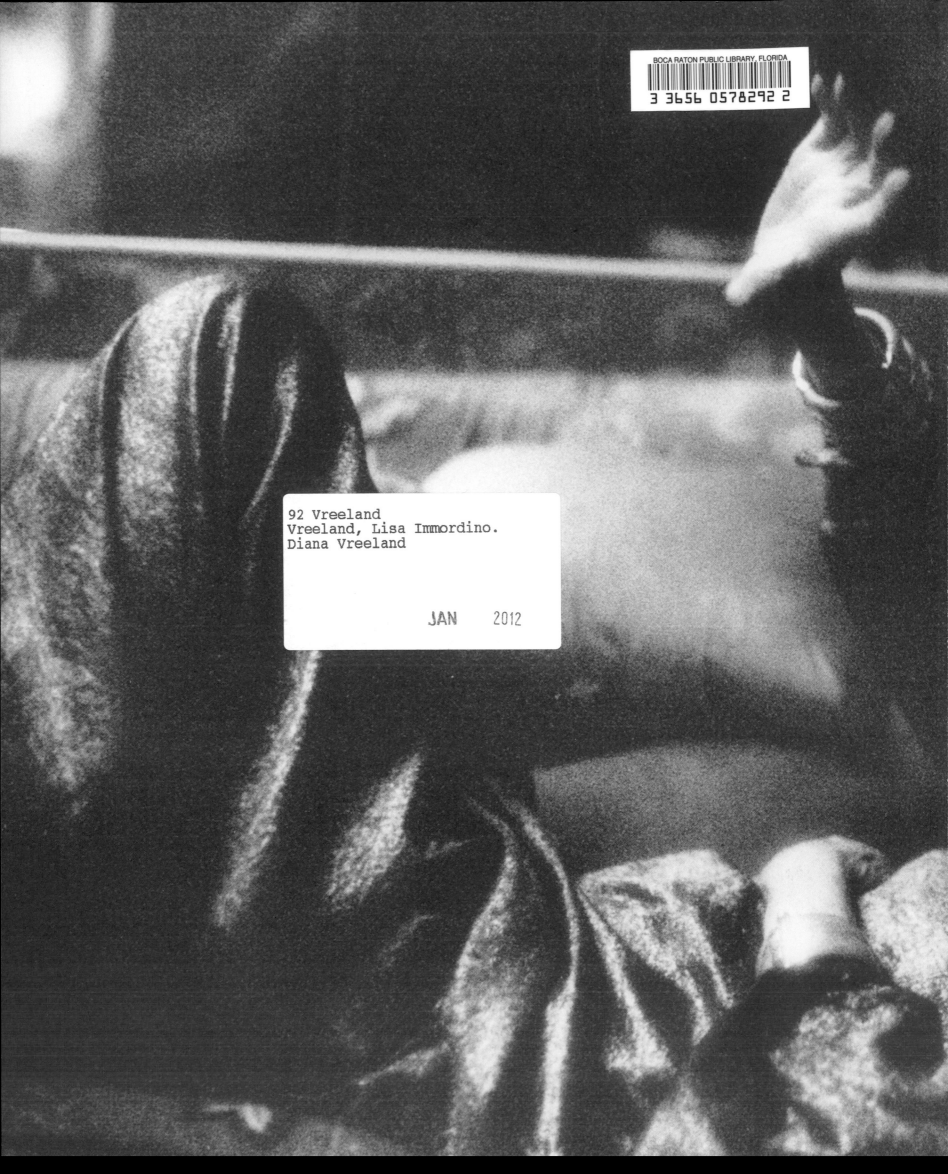